'English teachers are hardworking, cor
too often given too little time to grapp
questions of what it is to be an English
best of English literature. In *Making*
Didau explores the past of English teaching, the problematic
present, whilst offering an exploration of a better future. He
digs in the rich traditions of the discipline, whilst offering
teachers practical insights so that they can notice the artful
craft of English and turn it into compelling action.'

Alex Quigley, Author of *Closing the Reading Gap and*
Closing the Vocabulary Gap

'In this thoughtful and timely book, David Didau identifies
all the challenges involved with English curriculum design,
which many of us have wrestled with over the years. Through
disciplinary practice and substantive knowledge, which he
sees shaped by modes of thought such as metaphor, story and
pattern, Didau offers a practical means for English teachers
to structure their curricula and for students to learn and
appreciate the joys of the subject. I only wish this book had
been available when I was head of department!'

Phil Stock, Deputy Headteacher, Greenshaw
High School, Sutton

'This is a book that invites hyperbole and for good reason. Its
scope is spectacular, its details delightful and its provocations
powerful. The principles it proposes go beyond English
and make it an important read for anyone with curriculum
responsibilities who is concerned with creating a proper
curriculum. Written with considerable erudition and lightness
of touch *Making Meaning in English* is truly impressive.'

Mary Myatt, Education Adviser and Writer, Author of
The Curriculum: Gallimaufry to Coherence

'*Making Meaning in English* is a mature work, and this maturity can be detected in both its quietly meditative tone and the manner in which Didau, perhaps taking heed of Orwell's ideas about writing, has absented himself from centre stage in order to allow the material to sing. The voice in this text does not feel the need to make any dogmatic assertions of its rightness. It is more grown up than that. What it seeks to do is to quietly inform you of things that you might want to consider about the teaching of English. It is not the 'looking-for-the-quick-buck' of the series of implementable techniques but is more a compendium of interesting pieces of information about the subject that is more wistfully entertaining and informative than it is instrumental. It is punctuated with a host of literary quotations that, not only illustrate the points Didau is making but, of themselves, unlock a landscape of thought and image, and it's replete with interesting things that you had no idea that you needed to know and which caused this English teacher to consider quite deeply his own lack of knowledge in certain areas. It would be very good company indeed on a mazy, yet melancholy, Sunday afternoon sat on a verandah accompanied by wine, and I do not know a single teacher of English, be they NQT or classroom veteran, who would not benefit from reading this.'

Phil Beadle, Author of *The Facist Painting*

'David Didau has written the essential book for every English teacher. It is urgent and important; I've never read anything like it. But it's not a guide on how to teach English. It's a book about making meaning in English and, as David says, it's about reimagining English as a subject concerned primarily with significance. *Making Meaning in English* will challenge you, surprise you, niggle at you, and make you think really hard. As English teachers we're part of an ongoing conversation with our subject; David prompts us to consider how we can guide our children to pull up a chair and join in with the conversation, too.'

Claire Stoneman, English Teacher and Writer

'An antidote for a generation of teachers inducted into teaching English through technique-spotting and PEE, this book should be compulsory reading in English departments and ITE courses up and down the land.'

Lawrence Foley, Executive Principal, Harris Academy Tottenham

'David Didau is a singular force in education. It is well known that he writes, speaks, coaches and teaches from a position of restless curiosity and relishes capsizing a sacred school totem if it is an obstacle to young people's education. His publications help readers teach with excellence. With this wonderful, insightful and personal book, *Making Meaning in English*, you also learn how much he deeply loves literature too. You will already, but at the end you'll have fresh understanding of why you do.'

Jude Hunton, Principal, Skegness Grammar School

'David Didau's *Making Meaning in English* marks a significant, and timely, change in books related to the teaching of English. He looks at an area that has, all too often, been neglected. The knowledge. The ideas. The concepts. Rather than focus on how to teach English, Didau looks at what to teach and when to teach it. What should students learn about?

Refreshingly Didau doesn't polarise aspects in English to knowledge and creativity or traditional and progressive thinking; instead, he explores the key components of English and rationalises what should be taught and why. There are never easy answers in English. Like Van Helsing in Bram Stoker's *Dracula*, Didau is our moral compass in a confusing world where familiar and beloved things have been transformed out of shape and we can, easily, be seduced and bewitched by a powerful, domineering forces like exams. He boldly places a stake through the heart of "teaching to the exam" and reassuringly covers Years 7 through to 11 with garlic. Thankfully, he stops at chopping people's heads off.

The book is much more than a book on English ideas. It is an exploration of literature and its history from someone who loves it dearly. Crammed full of extracts and examples, Didau highlights the beauty and the subtlety of the English language in all its forms.

Making Meaning in English is the book I wished I had when I started teaching English. And, it is the book I want now as I revise our school's curriculum and decide what to teach and when to teach it. And, it will be the book I go back to when I start a new topic in English.

Making Meaning in English is paradigm shift in the teaching of English.'

Chris Curtis, Head of English

'Knowing things, in Saul Bellow's phrase, allows us to open the universe a little more. David's ambitious mission in this book is to explore what might be a body of knowledge for English, a subject that ironically has too often lacked a convincing narrative for its own existence. Through literature we all must attempt to come to terms with and "try on" a world lived differently, and as teachers, to help students as they start the lifelong process of defining how they see their world. The role of English is to change the way we understand the world around us as well as to unconsciously reinforce the power of Wittgenstein's assertion that, "The limits of my language are the limits of my world". In this insightful book, David does just that. This involves him approaching a wide variety of texts and dealing with their ambiguities and uncertainties, engaging with moral dilemmas and in turn illustrating the craft of writing. Richard Wright comments in *Black Boy* that he hungered for books, new ways of looking and seeing. In this book, David delivers this with scalpel like sharpness, skill and humour.'

Ian Warwick, Founder & Senior Director, London GTi

'This book is a remarkable achievement. It seeks to relocate the status of literature and English teaching as a vital engine of culture; a noble end in itself rather than a mere preparation for the workplace. It's simply the book I wish I had read when I started teaching English.'

Dr Carl Hendrick, Author of *How Learning Happens*

'This book is very special. It's about the beauty of English as an academic discipline whilst also offering a practical guide for teachers of the subject. *Making Meaning in English* addresses the subject with a nuance and faithfulness that warns against reductionism and instead celebrates and embraces the intricacies of English teaching. This book deserves a place on every English teacher's bookshelf.'

Claire Hill, English Teacher, Trust Vice Principal and Author of *Symbiosis: The Curriculum and the Classroom*

Making Meaning in English

What is English as a school subject for? What does knowledge look like in English and what should be taught? *Making Meaning in English* examines the broader purpose and reasons for teaching English and explores what knowledge looks like in a subject concerned with judgement, interpretation and value.

David Didau argues that the content of English is best explored through distinct disciplinary lenses – metaphor, story, argument, pattern, grammar and context – and considers the knowledge that needs to be explicitly taught so students can recognise, transfer, build and extend their knowledge of English. He discusses the principles and tools we can use to make decisions about what to teach and offers a curriculum framework that draws these strands together to allow students to make sense of the knowledge they encounter.

If students are going to enjoy English as a subject and do well in it, they not only need to be knowledgeable, but understand how to use their knowledge to create meaning. This insightful text offers a practical way for teachers to construct a curriculum in which the mastery of English can be planned, taught and assessed.

David Didau is an English teacher, education consultant and author. As well as having written a range of successful books for teachers, his blog learningspy.co.uk is widely recognised as one of the most influential education blogs in the UK.

Making Meaning in English

Exploring the Role of Knowledge in the English Curriculum

David Didau

Routledge
Taylor & Francis Group
LONDON AND NEW YORK

First published 2021
by Routledge
2 Park Square, Milton Park, Abingdon, Oxon OX14 4RN

and by Routledge
52 Vanderbilt Avenue, New York, NY 10017

Routledge is an imprint of the Taylor & Francis Group, an informa business

British Library Cataloguing-in-Publication Data
A catalogue record for this book is available from the British Library

Library of Congress Cataloging-in-Publication Data
Names: Didau, David, author.
Title: Making meaning in English : exploring the role of knowledge in the English curriculum / David Didau.
Description: Abingdon, Oxon ; New York, NY : Routledge, 2021. |
Includes bibliographical references and index.
Identifiers: LCCN 2020038922 | ISBN 9780367611101 (hardback) |
ISBN 9780367611118 (paperback) | ISBN 9781003104162 (ebook)
Subjects: LCSH: English language–Study and teaching (Middle school) |
English language–Study and teaching (Secondary) |
Language arts–Correlation with content subjects.
Classification: LCC LB1576 .D4642 2021 | DDC 428.0071/2–dc23
LC record available at https://lccn.loc.gov/2020038922

ISBN: 978-0-367-61110-1 (hbk)
ISBN: 978-0-367-61111-8 (pbk)
ISBN: 978-1-003-10416-2 (ebk)

Typeset in Optima
by Newgen Publishing UK

To two English teachers who are no longer with us: Roy Birch, who shaped and gave direction to my love of language and literature, and Derek Adams, who showed me the joy to be had in teaching this, the best of subjects.

Contents

Contents

Acknowledgements

As always, there are more people to thank for the existence of this book than I can either remember or find space for here. Foremost of those who deserve acknowledgement is Molly Janz, who, over a cup of coffee at Waterloo railway station, helped shape what has become the defining conceptual framework I now use to think about English.

I should also thank Phil Stock and his colleagues in the English department at Greenshaw School. Phil is very much a fellow traveller and many of the ideas and approaches herein owe themselves to his insight and energy.

While a vast array of dramatis personae has contributed indirectly, those who offered direct help, challenge and support include some of my favourite English teachers: David Williams, Sarah Barker, Claire Stoneman, Alex Quigley, Lyndsay Bawden, Patrick Cragg, Jude Hunton, Phil Beadle and the incomparably erudite Ian Warwick, and the eagle-eyed Roz Burrows. And special thanks too to Christine Counsell, probably the world's foremost expert of school curricula, on whom I confer the rank of honorary English teacher.

Thanks must also go to Annamarie Kino, Molly Selby, Emily Boyd and all at Routledge who have made the book a reality.

Finally, and always, Rosie.

Foreword

Over the last fifteen years, little in education has brought me so near to despair as the strange corrosion of English in England's state secondary schools. The corrosion has been far-reaching and has felt, at times, inexorable.

It has been dispiriting to observe three invariably well-meaning but ultimately damaging processes. Like three grinding wheels, each seems to bear in and do fresh damage, grinding the subject into a strange set of proxies that now pass for 'English', removing its pleasure, obscuring its beauty and diminishing its educational role and value.

The first process has been underway for decades. Ian Warwick and Ray Speakman recently called it 'the tyranny of relevance'. This has both a curricular dimension – the supplanting of traditional, foundational or challenging texts with those deemed to provide most immediate appeal – and a pedagogic one – the fashion for seeking 'engagement' through ever more tantalising activities, rather than through the subject itself. The second process, arising in the last two decades, has been a trend towards drilling in the surface skills defined by assessment criteria, retrofitting everything to a GCSE markscheme. Far from achieving GCSE's avowed goals of wide reading, personal response and clear communication, this results in rehearsal of pointless formulae, the wearyingly familiar writing you'll find in Figure 2.1 of this book. At worst, with every lesson a mini-exam, Year 11 English becomes a joyless place. This second problem is all the more pernicious for having been pursued in the name of 'raising achievement' and 'standards'. Sometimes, the entire secondary school English experience becomes a set of practice exercises for English GCSE. Denying pupils the really secure progress that would come from a fuller encounter, from authentic experience of reading, and from really systematic training in rich, broad literature and language, is an attack on standards, not an improvement in them.

The third and most recent process is perhaps the most revealing. New attention to the cognitive science of memory and new calls for knowledge-rich curricula ought to be antidotes to both the above. Sometimes they have been. But when the interpretation of knowledge-rich is little to do with knowledge, amounting to memorisation of isolated contextual facts, and when 'retrieval practice' means yet more skillification through the repeated rehearsal of structures for GCSE exam answers, one really does start to worry that the guardian angels of English have fled.

Other voices of concern have written recently and well about the above, but what strikes me about David Didau's new work is that he reserves equal fire for all of them. This includes his own book of nine years ago, and the former Ofsted regime that influenced it. It is not, however, a negative book. It is highly constructive and, despite his disavowal, highly practical. A detailed rationale for English teaching, it concludes with a sample curriculum exemplifying it.

This book stands out for me as significant among key works on English education for three main reasons.

First, Didau argues against short cuts. This is a book about going the long way round. A key reason each of the above three approaches is ineffective is that each is a cargo cult: each bypasses the whole point of the subject, both its pleasure and its effortful study. Didau goes the long way round on everything. At the level of simply reading a book, he is clear that there is no replacement for actually reading the book. Discussing Orwell for his suggested Year 9 programme, Didau recommends teachers 'forego extensive analysis for the benefit (and pleasure) of reading more'. And on the grander scale of the whole curriculum, his case for taking time with seemingly demanding classics, whether Chaucer, Behn or Austen, or for teaching the metalanguage of grammar or argument, is the pleasure and delight they later afford in changing what pupils subsequently notice and enjoy in other works. Delight, joy and pleasure feature large in this book. This is curriculum as narrative, one that lays foundations. We recognise the poetic, not through memorising ten features, but because of the vast array of poems we have read. Pupils need both immediate delight and the delight that is hard won, that arises through the way other texts have changed their ears.

Second, Didau's solution to historical clashes over the purpose of English is a rationale that unashamedly puts literature first in teaching language. When Bryan Cox sought to move English on from all the divisions of Holbrook *versus* Bullock, of personal growth *versus* functional communication, he did so by embracing all purposes and avoiding specification. Didau, by contrast, dives into that space with specificity, but what marks out his curricular thinking is a coherence that gets beyond the 'both...and...' solution. Yes, we encounter both Angelou and Shakespeare, both Charlotte Perkins Gilman and Shelley, both prescriptive and descriptive grammar, both the canon and its challenge; but Didau transcends these dichotomies by theorising disciplinary knowledge itself. And he finds it temporal: the English language is ancient. It is also medieval, modern and right now still changing. This journey of language itself needs serious study. Planning for all pupils to reap the riches of intertextuality requires the system and thoroughness of presenting intertextuality as story.

My final, abiding impression of this book is that it fosters a sense of higher purpose, the proper commitment of the English teacher to something even more important than the pupils in front of them: a sense of responsibility to the future as stewards of language and literature as a tradition, and precisely so that *anyone* can renew that tradition through challenge, creativity and debate. Canons are not there for ossification, but to furnish new and yet unknown ways of thinking, writing and being. By the concluding chapter, as Didau pours out how and why he would teach Toni Morrison and Achebe, he conveys breathless exhilaration that makes me wish I had been his Year 9 pupil. Here we feel the excitement from the kind of literary training that reveals the protean quality of language, its extraordinary capacity for reinvention, for mediating and for silencing, for empowerment and oppression.

This is a book for English teachers, but the group I most want to read it is headteachers, from all subjects. Subject community agency cannot thrive, nor be effective, without sponsors and guardians. We need those with power in the school situation to ensure that wider school policy is not the cause of cargo cults and we need them to empower English teachers with the professional incentives to debate the ambition of this book.

Christine Counsell

Christine Counsell serves on the boards of David Ross Education Trust, Now Teach and Ark Curriculum Partnerships. She taught in comprehensive schools for many years and has held positions as local authority adviser for primary and secondary schools, Senior Lecturer in the University of Cambridge Faculty of Education where she trained secondary teachers for nineteen years, and Director of Education of a Multi-Academy Trust in East Anglia. She now works nationally and internationally as an independent education consultant, especially in curriculum development and teacher development.

Introduction

The anxiety that there's something rotten in the state of English seems as old as the subject itself. When I trained in the 1990s, the fashion was to teach children creativity and empathy. We'd read young adult novels and ask, 'How do you think the characters *feel?* How would *you* feel in that situation?' Then we'd ask students to write letters to the characters expressing these feelings, or compose a diary entry from different characters' perspectives where they reveal their reactions to events. Other stuff – like sentence structure – we assumed children would just pick up if they read enough young adult novels and wrote enough diary entries.

With the era of accountability, results became ever more important. English lessons were increasingly focussed on checking off attainment targets, and students spent ever more time drilling skills as the curriculum became an extended rehearsal for examinations. If it was considered at all, the idea that a student should find meaning in their study of English was dismissed as risibly elitist.

More recently, we've become fascinated with cognitive science and begun to focus on building up students' stores of knowledge about literature and grammar. So, students learn lists of contextual facts, engage in retrieval practice quizzes

1

and answer multiple-choice questions. But in the rush to reinvent the subject as 'knowledge-rich' there's a risk that self-expression, empathy and meaning may be thrown out along with the admittedly filthy bathwater.

If English *should* be for passing on a body of knowledge – and I think it should – we need to think more deeply and critically about what this knowledge should be. Unlike most other school subjects English does not consist of an agreed, settled body of knowledge. We take our guidance from examination boards. We dwell on the detailed knowledge of a very few canonical texts and attempt to teach and assess a generic set of skills in the forlorn hope that this will equip young people for the vicissitudes they will face in life. But if this is not enough, if our students need more direction in navigating an uncertain world, we are often unprepared to guide them in making meaning.

I am no exception. My literature degree was gleefully focussed on literary theory, and tended to overlook the centrality of literature itself, except to diminish it. As a result, I embarked on my teaching career unaware of much of what the study of literature and language has to offer. In the fifteen years I spent as an English teacher, never once was it suggested I might want or need to expand my subject knowledge. All the training I received – pre- and in-service – was at the level of the pedagogic 'how,' and most of that was concerned with teaching as a generic act, with the same advice offered to teachers of all subjects. What specialist training there was focussed on teaching to examination specifications. How did it come to this?

At some point in the last half-century, English underwent seismic changes in higher education. It became common to hear that all language, no matter how transient or insubstantial, could be considered literature; that all texts are of equal worth; that the reason some texts are considered more important than others is the result of unfair power structures. We shouldn't seek to blame literary theorists; they were responding to the consensus that existed before them and sought to undermine overconfidence with some much-needed tentativity. Much of what they had to say has enlivened and enriched the subject, but the pendulum swung too far. Old certainties were replaced with new, equally dogmatic certainties. This new fervour eroded English's understanding of what it was. Now, wherever we look there is self-conscious hand-wringing. Is the author dead? Is the act of reading opaque and contentious? How do the concerns of identity, gender, ethnicity and class affect the processes of reading and writing? Is there such a thing as universal human nature? Is the aesthetic appeal of literature always subordinate to notions of power and prejudice? And what even *is* literature?

As English teachers we were left not just lacking expertise, but lacking conviction. Until recently, discussions about *what* to teach were sidelined by injunctions on *how* to teach. The curriculum became the business of exam boards and quangos; English teachers were shut out of the debate. Now, with a renewed focus on the curriculum, we are often unsure where to start or how to proceed. If we have been trying to build on a foundation of uncertainty we shouldn't be surprised if the resulting structure is rickety.

We've awakened to the idea that knowing things about language and literature is an essential part of the discipline, and that if students are going to enjoy the subject and do well in it, they need to be more knowledgeable. But lacking expertise, passionate intensity has resulted in all too predictable mistakes being loosed upon the world. English is in danger of becoming a clockwork version of itself with children learning lists of quotations and tables of techniques but with little sense of how to use these facts to create meaning.

Introduction

'Knowledge-rich' should – *can* – be much more than an anti-dote to 'knowledge-lite.' We need a third way, a path between the poorly conceived excesses of the 'skills-based' curriculum and the technocratic grip of the knowledge organiser; a path which teaches, "knowledge of a tradition that involves both knowing and doing,"[1] and conceives of the English curriculum as a conversation.

A guide to *Making Meaning*

Chapter 1: My search for a third way begins with an investigation of what English teachers have done in the past. This history tends not to be discussed in schools (or in university education departments) and so most English teachers have no way to learn from either the mistakes or successes of previous generations. I explore how English has been taught over the decades and find that what's studied today is surprisingly similar to what was studied in the 1890s. In considering 'traditional' and 'progressive' ideas about English the major shift has been from authority to impotence, leaving teachers and students cut off from the roots of what English was once believed to be about.

Chapter 2: Our collective lack of conviction has led to various endemic problems in the way reading, writing and literature are taught. Underlying all the problems considered is the issue that knowledge – specifically knowledge about literature and language – has been systematically undervalued, misunderstood or misapplied.

Chapter 3: Because there is little agreement about what knowledge in English actually is, it can be difficult for teachers to know how to take a genuinely knowledge-rich approach. I explore the tension between the need for English to be seen as an objective and rigorous academic subject and its concern

4

with the unquantifiable: feelings, beauty, values and meaning. Our focus will extend beyond knowledge; knowing is worthwhile when it helps us to shape our place in the world, to establish our relation to the knowledge we encounter and to be able to think about its significance.

Chapter 4: Our investigation into making meaning focusses on two processes: the ability to *notice* what is happening when readers read and writers write, and the ability to judiciously select from a store of knowledge to make *analogies*. These disciplinary actions of noticing what is happening on the page and making analogies to what has happened on other pages also benefit from learning the knowledge shaped by different modes of thought that I've called metaphor, story, argument, pattern, grammar and context. Each of these modes deals with the frames through which we 'see' meaning as well as what is 'seen' within the frame, the content itself.

Chapter 5: Metaphor plays a deep role in how we think: all subjects rely on metaphors to make meaning but in English, metaphors themselves are also the focus of meaning. I not only review how metaphor works and how our thinking changes as we become attuned to the connectedness between seemingly unconnected things, I also suggest what students might benefit from being taught to support their quest for meaning.

Chapter 6: Like metaphor, storytelling also seems to be a primary mode of thought. All subjects use stories to impose meaning on the substance of what they operate on, but in English we also study how different kinds of stories work and what makes them satisfying and successful. Here we focus on plot, character and thought as the most important aspects of story for students to understand.

Introduction

Chapter 7: Our instinct for argument is rooted in our need to cooperate with others; where we can we seek to persuade those around us using logic and reason instead of violence and intimidation. Here I discuss how students can analyse the arguments of others and improve their own in terms of rhetoric, dialectic, debate and conversation.

Chapter 8: We are instinctively drawn to patterns of similarity and difference. All subjects possess their own distinct patterns of meaning but, again, in English these patterns are also the object of study. Students need to become attuned to the patterns that proliferate in language and literature – sound, repetition, rhyme, metre, form – in order to understand and impose meaning on what they read and write.

Chapter 9: Grammar frames our thoughts as well as our speech and writing. Although we have an instinctive facility with morphology and syntax, learning metalanguage allows students to think more deeply about how they and others use language and, instead of being bound by half-understood 'rules,' are able to ask penetrating questions about the grammatical structures they encounter.

Chapter 10: There is an inherent tension between text and context; how much context is necessary or desirable in exploring a text? How much should students be taught about the circumstances in which texts were written and consumed? Two areas I explore in depth are the role and effects of literary theory, and the notion of 'the canon' and how canonical knowledge can be accommodated in schools. This role – as thoughtful curators of the canon – is something we owe to our students.

Chapter 11: The potential fruit of this 'knowledge-rich' approach to English is planted in curriculum plans but harvested in the classroom. In this chapter I discuss the tools and principles we can use to make decisions about what to teach.

Chapter 12: If what you're most interested in are practical resources, you may want to skip ahead to this final chapter. Here I imagine a curriculum that draws all the strands discussed in the book together in a framework that allows students to make sense of the knowledge they encounter.

Whether you agree with any or all of the suggestions offered is beside the point. What matters is that we take some tentative steps to being bolder about how best to help students make meaning within our subject.

The British-Hungarian polymath, Michael Polanyi warned, "Man lives in the meanings he is able to discern. He extends himself into that which he finds coherent and is at home there."[2] If we do not enlarge and extend the meanings our students are able to discern there will be no obvious tragedy. Our students will, on the whole, be at home with the limited glimpses of literature and language permitted them, but they will be prevented from entering and feeling comfortable in a larger, richer tradition of ideas and meaning.

This book is not a guide on how to teach English – there are several excellent such books already available – instead it is a book *about* English as a school subject. It is a plea to care about something only those who already know how to make meaning in English are able to discern. The aim is to reimagine English as a subject concerned primarily with significance. You may find ideas that strike you as too ambitious, too challenging, too rarefied for the students you teach, but I hope to persuade you to reconceive the curriculum as a place where old and new ideas clash, where the canon is wrestled with, and where students are given the intellectual wherewithal to impose their own judgements and meanings on what we lay before them.

The philosopher Michael Oakeshott once said, "As civilized human beings, we are the inheritors ... of a conversation, begun in the primeval forests and extended and made more articulate in the course of centuries."[3] If our students are to claim this inheritance, they need us to have higher expectations of ourselves. They need our guidance, our encouragement and our determination to share that to which we have been fortunate enough to be granted access.

1 What is English *for*?

What does the study of English – both in universities and schools – seek to achieve? Why do people engage in linguistic research or literary criticism? Maybe we should start by asking why, in the 'real world,' people read and write? Here, reading is either for recreation or is a purely functional activity designed to extract information as efficiently as possible. Writing, though, is rarely a leisure pursuit. In the 'real world' – although there is a tiny class of professional writers almost no one earns a living through the proceeds of writing[1] – people only write for practical purposes: to inform, persuade, instruct or explain. Should teaching reflect these utilitarian ends?

Like many English teachers before and since, George Sampson, writing in 1922, thought not.

> A very admirable, hard-working lady came one day to a London elementary school on Care Committee business, and found that the 'leavers' she wanted to interview had gone with their class to a performance of Twelfth Night. "Of course," she said, quite pleasantly, "it is very nice for the boys to go to the theatre, but Shakespeare won't help them to earn their living." This is profoundly true. Shakespeare

will not help anyone to earn a living, not even a modern actor-manager. Shakespeare is quite useless, as useless as Beauty and Love and Joy and Laughter, all of which many reputable persons would like to banish from the schools of the poor. Yet it is in beauty and love and joy and laughter that we must find the way of speaking to the soul — the soul, that does not appear in the statistics and is therefore always left out of account.[2]

This tension – between pragmatism and 'the soul' – has always been at the heart of debates about what English should be for.

It's revealing to compare the activities of academics with those of teachers in schools. The study of language varies enormously between universities and schools. Essentially, the professional study of language relates to a quasi-scientific investigation whereas the study of literature is more akin to the study of art or music, where texts are explored for their cultural or aesthetic value. Academics studying language explore how English changes, create models for the patterns it follows, and investigate how people use it, whereas the school subject is more narrowly focussed on technical competence. The study of literature in schools is more of a 'junior version' of the 'game' academics play, although one shorn of much of the trappings of theory.[3] Is this as it should be? Should students emulate the academic 'games' of English, or should we be satisfied with teaching them to master the foundations and prepare them for the 'real world'?

As it has many times over the past century, English is once again trying to remake itself. Typically, the arguments about what English should be – and what it is for – are simplistically presented in terms of 'traditionalist' versus 'progressive' positions (see Figure 1.1).

'Traditional'	'Progressive'
English for employment	English for 'life'
Vocational training in specialism	Education of whole person
Promotion of single standard language	Recognition of varieties
Emphasis on writing	Attention to speech
Formal written examinations	Mixed-mode assessment
Dictionary definitions & grammatical rules	Flexibility of usage
Canon of 'great works'	Open or no canon
National curriculum	Local syllabuses
Single dominant cultural identity	Multicultural differences

Figure 1.1 'Traditional' and 'progressive' views of English
Source: These lists are taken from Rob Pope, *The English Studies Book*, p. 31.

The idea that we can, or should, select from just one side of this dichotomous list is odd. Each of these opposed sets of views has something to offer but neither, taken alone, is satisfactory. This tension between the pragmatic and the idealistic is at the heart of debates about what English should be for. On one hand, there is the notion of functional English – that children must be able to read and write to an acceptable standard and capable of taking a useful part in society – and on the other, the belief that English ought to develop the 'whole child,' so that they become more empathetic, more cultured, more capable of participation in the 'conversation of humankind.'

In an attempt to bring together some of these polarised positions, here are *my* thoughts on what English should be for:

- English should exist to enlarge and extend children's capacity to think about the world. Naturally, this should equip them for employment as well as the rest of life.
- English teaching should both recognise and value the many varieties of English but also induct students into the opportunities afforded by the mastery of standard English.

- Whilst attention should be given to spoken English, the emphasis should be on written forms.
- Despite their many limitations, formal written examinations are, at the moment, the fairest way to ensure disadvantaged children are not further disadvantaged, but we should resist allowing assessment to warp the curriculum we teach.
- Children need both grammatical descriptions and metalinguistic knowledge in order to think flexibly about the use of English.
- Children should have access to the canon in order to develop their own ideas about taste and to be able to critique from a position of knowledge rather than ignorance.
- The National Curriculum should be viewed as offering a minimum standard that schools, if they intend to introduce their own curriculum, should seek to at least equal.
- We should recognise that although the subject derives from a dominant cultural identity, multicultural differences enrich and enlarge the English language and its literature.

Have a go at resolving each set of binaries to arrive at your own vision of what English should be for. Is English, as it's currently conceived, inclined more to the needs of employment, or more towards those of life? Place a cross on each of the continuums in Figure 1.2 to indicate where you think the subject sits.

Having done this, you may now have a better sense of whether English as it is currently taught and assessed is as it should be, or if it has lost its way.

Has English lost its way?

It seems widely accepted (or at least, widely discussed) that English as a school subject doesn't really know what it is, or

English for employment	English for 'life'
Vocational training in specialism	Education of whole person
Promotion of single standard language	Recognition of varieties
Emphasis on writing	Attention to speech
Formal written examinations	Mixed-mode assessment
Dictionary definitions and grammatical rules	Flexibility of usage
Canon of 'great works'	Open or no canon
National curriculum	Local syllabuses
Single dominant cultural identity	Multicultural differences

Figure 1.2   'Traditional' and 'progressive' continuum

has 'lost its way.' This is not a new idea. In *English for the English*, published in 1922, George Sampson railed against the education system of his day. He viewed English as the most important of all school subjects but understood that this depended on "an assumption that the purpose of ... school is really to develop the mind and soul of the children and not merely to provide tame and acquiescent 'labour fodder.'"[4]

In 1956, writing about academic selection, David Holbrook saw that the secondary modern was viewed as where 'the duds' went. The fact that over three quarters of children did not make the grammar school cut was of little importance; these unruly masses, it was assumed, could never be brought to appreciate the glories of English literature. Instead they must be taught something practical, something fitting for a life of labour. Echoing Sampson, Holbrook argued that the skills sought by employers should be the business of employers to teach. "We have no need to concern ourselves," he stated, "with education for 'earning a living': we educate for living."[5]

Sadly, his battle cry went unheard. Or at least, if English teachers ever rallied to its cause, they were roundly defeated by the forces of pragmatism. By 1979, responding to the

Bullock Report, Holbrook began *English for Meaning* with an introduction entitled, 'English has lost its way.' There is very little evidence to suggest it has made any great strides in finding itself in the intervening decades. Today some English teachers are more concerned with 'developing radicalism' than they are in overcoming the real injustice that children from disadvantaged backgrounds are disproportionately more likely to fail to learn to read and write fluently than their more affluent peers.[6] But *is* English actually lost? For it to be so it would once have had to have known where it was. Was there then some halcyon time or place when English was of a quality to which we would now like to return?

Maybe, instead of endlessly reinventing second-rate wheels, English teachers today might be better off knowing more about the history of their subject. I say this as someone who taught for fifteen years with only the haziest ideas about where the set of assumptions I had picked up about what English is and how it should be taught had come from. Some of these assumptions – as we'll discuss in chapter 2 – have revealed themselves to be based on faulty logic and flawed premises, but how much better if I had been aware of the tensions and debates that have preoccupied English teachers since English first came to take its place in the school curriculum.

How did we get here?

From our 21st-century vantage, it might seem that what was done in the past ought to remain there, but to dismiss the lessons of the past we ought to at least know what they are. Like most English teachers, I had only the vaguest notion of what previous generations of teachers had done or said. What I've come to learn is that we can, potentially, learn a lot about the difficulties and debates in which we're currently

entrenched by pondering mistakes and solutions v
the risk of being lost from our collective memory.

Despite its current domination of the curriculum
a latecomer to the suite of school subjects student
to master. Up until the late 19th century, 'English' ten
refer just to the basics of learning to read and write. Only
latterly has it come to mean learning to read and write *about
literature*. From the Middle Ages to the Renaissance, Latin
was the dominant medium of instruction in schools and universities. Even when English began to take over this role in
the 16th century, the languages and literatures studied were
classical. The emphasis in schools was on handwriting and
grammar and, as the effects of print began to make themselves felt from the 18th century onwards, standardised
spelling and punctuation. These were not taught with a concern for children's intellectual development, but to ensure
they could read and write sufficiently well to satisfy the
growing demands of the commercial world.

Only in the late 19th and early 20th centuries did the state
begin to take substantial responsibility for school education
of any kind, including schooling in English. At the same time,
English began to include English literature, and was increasingly charged with a variety of moral roles previously filled
by religion. Chief among these were the tasks of refining
sensibility, inculcating public morality, and promoting social
solidarity and national identity. One of the first and most
influential advocates of this use of literature was the school
inspector, poet and essayist Matthew Arnold. In *Culture and
Anarchy*, Arnold argued for the civilising effect of great literature. He was scathing of the idea that culture is little more
than a badge signifying membership of an elite. In his view,
true culture was "the study of perfection."[7] Arnold believed
that a full apprehension of the virtues of culture is attained
by induction into the best that human culture has to offer, by

the free play of the mind over these facts, and by developing a sympathetic attitude towards all that is beautiful.

In his thirty years as an inspector of schools (1851–1882) Arnold had much to say on what he saw as the parlous state of English teaching. In his 1852 report he wrote,

> Young men, whose knowledge of grammar, of the minutest details of geographical and historical facts, and above all, of mathematics, is surprising, often cannot para-phrase a plain passage of prose or poetry without totally misapprehending it, or write half a page of composition on any subject without falling into gross blunders of taste and expression.[8]

In his report for 1860, decrying the lack of literature taught in schools, he says,

> It is not enough remembered how, in many cases, his reading-book forms the whole literature, except his Bible, of the child attending a primary school. If, then, instead of literature, his reading-book, as is too often the case, presents him with a jejune encyclopaedia of positive information, the result is that he has, except his Bible, no literature, no humanising instruction at all.[9]

You can sense his despair when, in 1871, he made this observation:

> What is comprised under the word literature is in itself the greatest power available in education; of this power it is not too much to say that in our elementary schools at pre-sent no use is made at all.[10]

Arnold's high-minded ideal that children should be taught to appreciate truth and beauty was to be put severely to the test when the 1870 Education Act made schooling compulsory for all up to the age of 13. Suddenly, and for the first time, schools had to teach children from the very poorest and most disadvantaged margins of society not only how to read and write, but to appreciate literature. This was a daunting task and, perhaps inevitably, the more affluent a child's background, the broader and deeper the experience of studying English was likely to be.

By 1887 the study of English in schools had come to look like this:

Standard I: (i.e. about aged 7)

- Reading. To read a short paragraph from a book not confined to words of one syllable.
- Writing. Copy in manuscript characters a line of print, and write from dictation not more than ten easy words, commencing with capital letters. Copy books (large or half text hand) to be shown.
- English. To repeat twenty lines of simple verse.

Standard II: (i.e. about aged 8)

- Reading. To read a short paragraph from an elementary reading book.
- Writing. A passage of not more than six lines from the same book, slowly read once, and then dictated word by word. Copy books (large and half text hand) to be shown.
- English. To repeat forty lines of poetry and to know their meaning. To point out nouns and verbs.

Standard III: (i.e. about aged 9)

- Reading. To read a passage from a more advanced reading book, or from stories from English history.

What is English *for*?

- Writing. Six lines from one of the reading books of the Standard, slowly read once and then dictated. Copy books (capitals and figures, large and small hand) to be shown.
- English. To recite with intelligence and expression 60 lines of poetry, and to know their meaning. To point out nouns, verbs, adjectives, adverbs and personal pronouns, and to form simple sentences containing them.

Standard IV: (i.e. about aged 10)

- Reading. To read a few lines from a reading book or from a History of England.
- Writing. Eight lines of poetry or prose, slowly read once, and then dictated. Copy books to be shown.
- English. To recite 80 lines of poetry, and to explain the words and allusions. To parse easy sentences, and to show by examples the use of each of the parts of speech.

Standard V: (i.e. about aged 11)

- Reading. To read a passage from some standard author, or from a History of England.
- Writing. Writing from memory the substance of a short story read out twice; spelling, handwriting and correct expression to be considered. Copy books to be shown.
- English. To recite 100 lines from some standard poet, and to explain the words and allusions. To parse and analyse simple sentences, and to know the method of forming English nouns, adjectives and verbs from each other.

Standard VI: (i.e. about aged 12)

- Reading. To read a passage from one of Shakespeare's historical plays, or from some other standard author, or from a History of England.

- Writing. A short theme or letter on an easy subject: spelling, handwriting, and composition to be considered. Copy books to be shown.
- English. To recite 150 lines from Shakespeare or Milton, or some other standard author, and to explain the words and allusions. To parse and analyse a short complex sentence, and to know the meaning and use of Latin prefixes in the formation of English words.

Standard VII: (i.e. about aged 13)

- Reading. To read a passage from Shakespeare or Milton, or from some other standard author, or from a History of England.
- Writing. A theme or letter. Composition, spelling and handwriting to be considered. Note books and exercise books to be shown.
- English. To recite 150 lines from Shakespeare or Milton, or some other standard author, and to explain the words and allusions. To analyse sentences, and to know prefixes and terminations generally.[11]

Although English teachers today might be impressed that 13-year-olds were expected to learn 150 lines of Shakespeare by heart, the 'English' strand of the standards consisted of little more than the rote learning of lines of poetry and grammatical rules. Such was the frustration with this state of affairs that in 1888, the Cross Report recommended that 'English' should cease to be compulsory. Happily, the recommendation was never taken up.

It is interesting to note what the study of English today has retained and dispensed with. We can see that the idea of a national canon, which must include Shakespeare, can trace its origins back, but so can the practical concerns of transactional and discursive writing. Whilst we have largely ditched an interest in recitation – indeed the idea of learning poetry by heart, whilst it has made something of a resurgence in recent years, is widely considered quaintly old-fashioned – we are as focussed as ever on the need to teach spelling. Grammar teaching has gone in and out of fashion over the decades, and handwriting is now considered the sole pre-serve of primary schools.

The Newbolt Report

The publication of the Newbolt Report in 1921 underlined the continuing disagreements within and about English. Its brief was to consider the position the subject occupied in the curriculum, and to make recommendations about how its study could be strengthened and expanded. Prior to Newbolt, English was still seen as being of lesser importance than mathematics and the sciences, and many of the report's recommendations were designed to give English parity with other subjects and to occupy a more central place in the curriculum.

Many practices that have become the norm today began life in the Newbolt Report through such recommendations as the idea that children should be taught to speak standard English using phonetics; that children should be practised, not only in the art of speaking and reading, but also in the art of listening; the centrality of oral work as the foundation on which proficiency in the writing of English is based; and that exams should focus on English as a means of communication rather than on grammatical analysis and spelling. The report also recommended the reading and acting of plays, and that the teaching of literature should include reading aloud and dramatic performances. We can also find early roots for notions of teacher autonomy in the suggestion that literature teachers should be free to draw up their own syllabus and adopt their own methods. Importantly, Newbolt described 'commercial English' as "not only objectionable ... but also contrary to the true interests of commercial life,"[12] stating that "'the needs of business' must be strictly subordinated to those of a liberal education."[13]

One aspect of English that has persisted throughout its history as a school subject is the separation of reading, writing and literature. We continue to split English into two separate exam subjects: English Language and English Literature. Language has tended to focus on the more functional aspects of the subject, whilst Literature has been more concerned with character and culture. But are these sensible divisions or are we simply persisting with what we've always done? This somewhat uncomfortable carving up of English is borne of the tension between the practical roots of preparing children for employment in an increasingly literate world, and Arnold's interconnected notions of beauty and virtue.

The humanising effects of English

In the 1930s, Arnold's mantle was taken up by the literary critic and Cambridge don, F.R. Leavis. Leavis was opposed to the Victorian idea that appreciation of literature should be "the direct expression of simple emotions"[14] and instead saw the purpose of studying literature as developing students' intellectual and imaginative faculties in order to make critical judgements. Leavis argued that appreciation of literature led to a growth of intelligence and sensibility that marked the educated out from a debased majority, corrupted by the evils of democratic industrial society. This elitist view had some currency with English teachers during the 1950s and 1960s but had largely fallen out of favour by the 1970s. One of the main objections was to Leavis' notion that culture and the arts were undemocratic. The idea that culture was inherently civilising was challenged, amongst others, by George Steiner who saw that the certainties of Arnold and Leavis seemed absurd when faced with the knowledge that a "man can read Goethe or Rilke in the evening, that he can play Bach and Schubert, and go to his day's work at Auschwitz in the morning."[15] One of the big claims for studying English – that it makes us more empathetic, more rounded human beings – falters in the face of such damning evidence.

The Bullock Report

From the 1970s onwards, this uncomfortable tension between the demands of culture and employment was also expected to accommodate concepts from linguistics. Alan Bullock, appointed by Margaret Thatcher when Education Secretary in 1972, published his report, *A Language for Life*, in 1975. The Bullock Report recommended that children should learn about the nature and function of language, language acquisition, and speaking and writing as social processes, as well as a whole host of other scientific-sounding elements. While the explicit teaching of most of these linguistic infiltrations only made their way onto A-level language courses, they still exert a considerable gravitational pull on English language teaching throughout secondary school. The inclusion of linguistics was intended to give the subject much-needed objective and scientific rigour. At the same time, Bullock explicitly resisted the idea that English should be concerned with encouraging children's personal growth and development as members of a civilised society.

Although Bullock recommended including concepts from linguistics, it wasn't made very clear how this might work in practice. Some thought was given to adopting the approach pioneered by Noam Chomsky, but transformational – or generative – grammar was too abstract to be of much use in the classroom. When asked how his work might help English teachers, Chomsky himself said,

> I'm hesitant even to suggest an answer to this question. Practitioners have to decide for themselves what is useful in the sciences, and what is not. As a linguist, I have no particular qualifications or knowledge that enables or entitles me to prescribe methods of language instruction.[16]

Bullock agreed saying, "In our view linguistics has a great contribution to make to the teaching of English, but not in this form." Instead, the report made this suggestion:

> Linguistics and other specialist studies of language have a considerable contribution to make to the teaching of English, and they should be used to emphasise the inseparability of language and the human situation. *Linguistics should not enter schools in the form of the teaching of descriptive grammar.*[17]

> [emphasis added]

To understand why this was controversial, we need to know something of the grammar wars of the early 20th century. The teaching of grammar had always been entirely *prescriptive*. It was taught as a series of abstract rules about what students must and must not do and, as such, was exceedingly unpopular. Tellingly, the Newbolt Report had noted that "English Grammar has disappeared in all but a few schools, to the joy of children and teacher."[18]

But, instead of attempting to prescribe rules for spoken and written English, the *descriptive* approach attempted to describe how people actually use English. A descriptive approach might observe, for instance, that articles precede nouns, but not to then insist that this *must* be so, just that this is what ordinary speakers actually do. It included the study of semantics and pragmatics to work out why English speakers and writers make the choices they do and what the effects of their choices might be. Descriptive grammar was a direct product of linguistics research; to decide that it must be excluded from schools was, by extension, to exclude the backbone of linguistics. In the words of David Crystal, this was "a remarkable contradiction."[19]

So, despite arguing for a linguistic approach to the teaching of language, Bullock had no meaningful advice for English teachers about what to do in the classroom. On the other side of the argument, David Holbrook argued that the Bullock Report was a "dead end." English, he argued, should be about much more than teaching language; instead it ought to focus on teaching 'significance': "we cannot merely stick at the language, but must see what it points to 'beyond.'"[20] He goes on,

> The hidden planet we have been searching for is meaning: once we accept that man's primary aim is for meaning, then we can find a better basis for our work.[21]

Holbrook was less interested in promoting a national literary culture where people read and know books, but was concerned with English as a mechanism for populating society with people who think, reflect and use language as a means to explore identity and the wider world. Because the Bullock Report gave so little attention to literature, Holbrook branded it as "illiterate."[22] Predictably, his criticisms were dismissed as elitist.

Back to basics

Following Bullock, Labour Prime Minister James Callaghan called for a return to teaching 'the three Rs' because, "In today's world, higher standards are demanded than were required yesterday and there are simply fewer jobs for those without skill."[23] The subsequent political preoccupation – especially

during the years of Margaret Thatcher's Conservative government – was for a much more concrete and practical approach
to teaching English, a move 'back to basics.'

Bullock's recommendations have echoed across the years
and into the present. It is in his report that we discover the
seeds of Ofsted; the notion of whole school policies for language across the curriculum; the systematic teaching of
reading, and additional assistance for struggling readers and
those with English as a second language.

Over a decade later, in 1988, the Thatcher government
commissioned another report into the teaching of English
language. The committee was chaired by the mathematician,
John Kingman, who, in his introduction to the report, wrote
that while mastery of English could be,

> ... achieved without an explicit knowledge of the structure
> of the language ... there is no positive advantage in such
> ignorance. And the worst reason for avoiding teaching
> about language is that teachers are not confident in their
> own knowledge.[24]

The report made explicit its rejection of Bullock's odd dis-
missal of descriptive grammar, arguing that English should
provide "a sound and accessible description of the structure
and uses of the English language." The greatest barrier to this
aim was that the practical knowledge of how to go about this
no longer existed. The reason children were not taught anything of grammar was because grammar teaching had all but
vanished in the 1970s and 80s and few teachers had learned
anything themselves.

The National Curriculum

A year later, Professor Bryan Cox's report into how English
should look in the new National Curriculum was published.

This was an enormous endeavour, not least because of the breadth of the subject:

> It includes, for example, language use; language study; literature; drama; and media education; it ranges from the teaching of a skill like handwriting, through the development of the imagination and of competence in reading, writing, speaking and listening, to the academic study of the greatest literature in English.[25]

As the report acknowledged, "such broadness poses problems." The Cox Report decided that it was impossible to specify exactly what the subject should be composed of, and instead settled for offering guiding principles to help teachers make better decisions. Cox saw the danger of polarised views on what English teaching should be and consequently the National Curriculum for English was always intended as a compromise between extreme positions. Cox explicitly attempted to resolve the rifts between the competing aims of English: the subject should contribute to children's personal growth *and* prepare them for adult life; English should encompass cultural heritage *and* cultural analysis.[26] These were worthy aims. The future of English looked more secure than it perhaps ever had. But the long shadow of Ofsted was set to fall across the subject.

The effects of Ofsted

Between 2009 and 2012, Ofsted published three subject reports on the teaching of English: *English at the Crossroads*, *Excellence in English* and *Moving English Forward*. Together they set out a vision of what English should be for and how it ought to be taught. These reports sum up the orthodoxy on English teaching throughout the first decade of the 21st century and, as the consequences for displeasing inspectors became ever greater, were hugely influential. The main concern of all three reports was the quality of teaching and learning as observed in the classroom. Increasingly, *what* was taught in English became of secondary importance to *how* it was taught. This was in stark contrast to an earlier Ofsted report, *English 2000–05*, which made almost no mention of teaching methods, but instead concentrated on the actions needing to be taken at a national and local level. The only recommendation to schools on English teaching in this earlier report was to "develop varied and engaging approaches to learning in the classroom that are flexible enough to stimulate and meet the needs of pupils."[27]

Published in June 2009, *English at the Crossroads* was the culmination of visits to over 240 primary and secondary schools. The report claimed to have isolated the key ingredients of success, and urged all schools to adopt "practical and creative approaches" which "engage pupils by giving them good opportunities to express ideas." English teachers were advised to "find ways to develop pupils' initiative and independent learning" and to "help pupils think for themselves." Teachers were explicitly told to "Resist dictating the form and context of students' work" and to avoid "too much direction." Lessons were outstanding where, "imaginative activities and varied approaches engaged and maintained pupils' interest. Most importantly [pupils should be] actively involved: discussing, trying out ideas, working with others and learning." Unsatisfactory lessons were those where teaching was "passive" and "not all students enjoyed their learning." The English curriculum was praised in those schools where there was a focus on "generic learning skills."

If *English at the Crossroads* provided a baseline picture of what the ideals of teaching of English were considered to be, its follow-up, *Excellence in English*, published in May 2011, addressed ways to improve practice across *all* schools. The report's recommendations emerged from visits to twelve schools deemed to be 'outstanding' and, although it acknowledged, "there are many routes to excellence" and that "there is no simple formula that will make a school outstanding in English," the recommendations were increasingly seen as prescribing 'what Ofsted wanted.'

The report praised departments where teachers "listened very carefully to what pupils said about English, what they enjoyed doing and how they learnt best" and "involved the pupils in constructing the English curriculum." All the departments praised in the report, "offered a lively and engaging curriculum, supported by active approaches in the classroom with substantial emphasis on discussion and well-managed group work."

A clear connection was established between low standards and an "inappropriate or dull curriculum" where "teaching is held in check" by an "identity" for English that has not been generated or shared by the school. In other words, as there was (and still is) no established consensus on what English was or should be, it was incumbent on English departments to work this out for themselves, presumably with help from their pupils. In this shared vision, anything "inappropriate or dull" should be swapped out for what is relevant and exciting. In the best schools, pupils were "stimulated" and teaching "engaged all the senses." Rather than establishing a curriculum founded on subject expertise and the underlying concepts that open up the subject, effective departments were considered to be those that continually reinvented themselves with whatever was new and exciting.

For instance, one English department was praised for its 'Mr Men' scheme of work for Key Stage Three pupils:

> The unit begins with an exploration of the notion of stereotypes. Students then review and extend their knowledge of

grammar focusing on the use of adjectives, onomatopoeia and alliteration. This leads into an analysis of Mr Men characters, analysing the author's use of these techniques before students create their own new character.[28]

In another outstanding English department,

> [S]tudents applied their knowledge of TV programmes such as the Jeremy Kyle show to JB Priestley's An Inspector Calls. Characters from the play appeared in turn to be grilled by the presenter. Their work combined good understanding of the play alongside very good knowledge of the TV programme. 'Mr Birling' revealed all his characteristic pugnacity, arguing with the presenter: 'I don't appreciate you insulting my daughter ... remember that life is hard,' before storming out of the 'studio' exclaiming that 'I've got better things to do with my time.' The class booed and hissed, as appropriate.[29]

This is all very well, but if students are restricted to those ideas and formats with which they are already familiar, when will they encounter those which lie outside of their experience? And if students are asked to think about Mr Men and Jeremy Kyle, are they less likely to think about grammar and literature? Where does all this leave English as an academic discipline?

Where the two earlier reports were focussed on a particular view of what exemplary teaching and learning looked like, the focus of 2012's *Moving English Forward* was on how to raise attainment. As a result, it dealt more with what was wrong in classrooms than what was right. Improvement, the report claimed, had been too slow or variable across the age groups and blamed this on the many 'myths' that had grown up about what made a good lesson. The suggestion was that English teachers had made erroneous assumptions "about what inspectors 'want' to see in a lesson or what constitutes effective teaching." These assumptions led to a variety of unintended consequences including excessive pace; an overload of activities; inflexible and unresponsive planning; lack of time for independent reading and writing; and too great and too early a concentration on examination skills. A key criticism was that "the person who worked hardest ... was the teacher!"

Like many English teachers, I assumed that inspection was based on the most up-to-date research on how children learn and uncritically adopted many of Ofsted's recommendations. In 2012 I published *The Perfect Ofsted English Lesson,* which while not wholly awful, hopelessly of its time. Although much of my teaching remained didactic this was a source of shame, and only took place behind safely closed doors.

The curriculum – particularly at Key Stage 3 – was still a cause for concern. English departments were praised for focussing on 'emotional literacy.' One lesson singled out for praise,

> explored the relationship between Pip's adoptive parents in *Great Expectations.* The teacher's plan included family relationships and resolution of family issues. Students chose to explore these ideas by role-playing marriage guidance sessions and hot-seating different characters.[30]

In another school, a department described as "innovative" had developed schemes of work focussed on 'independent learning':

> Planned units in Year 7 include: organising a lunchtime or after-school club; improving the English department; and planning and teaching a unit of work for Year 6 pupils. The unit on 'improving the English department,' for example, aims to give students the opportunity to

consider the best way to use an allocated amount of money in order to improve the department. As part of this work, students are expected to research and audit the resources currently available and to conduct a survey to discover how teachers and students would like to see the department improved. The unit includes meetings of students in order to narrow the range of options, research possible cross-curricular initiatives, and prepare proposals for the chosen projects to include costings and technical advice. Groups of students will present their ideas to the rest of the class. This will lead to a whole-class decision about the best proposals which will then be presented formally by students to the rest of Year 7 and to the school's senior leadership team and English department.[31]

In this school, a teacher was praised because they "withdrew from the learning and handed responsibility to the students" for deciding how they would complete a task. "Inevitably, there were disagreements and time was wasted but the students came to realise that they would have to compromise, agree and accept different roles, listen to others, and work effectively together." This wasted time was deemed acceptable because, presumably, children never got to compromise, listen and discuss anywhere except in English classrooms.

As late as February 2014, Ofsted continued to recommend that English lessons should be "engaging" and "fun":

The fun elements to all lessons switch students on. Verbal and pictorial references to students' cultural knowledge and experience humorously engage students and encourage creative and active thinking. ... The active tasks involve physical movement and are embedded in the presentation, highlighted by the humorous reference to the dance song, 'I like to move it, move it'. Thinking skills activities, like the use of boggle boxes, are included in all lessons.[32]

There is clear, unambiguous praise for "creative and active thinking," and "active tasks" that "involve physical movement" are considered desirable. Ofsted's continued preference for the content of lessons to be culturally familiar rather than culturally rich was made clear. "Detective reader, murder mystery, and crime scene investigation approaches engage students and draw on their cultural experience." Teachers were praised for "combining high-quality visual stimulus and active learning methods to engage all levels of learners." And, rather than working to produce a curriculum to stand the test of time, "the team is always updating schemes of work and incorporating new things they come across."

Since then, Ofsted's focus has altered sharply. As teachers' presence on social media grew, so too did vocal criticism of Ofsted's approach to inspection. In February 2014, I and several other 'teacher bloggers' met with senior Ofsted officials which heralded a new era of openness and a concerted attempt to communicate with teachers.[33] I was consulted on an update to the inspection handbook published in July 2014 which did away with lesson grading once and for all and since then the trajectory has been to minimise the harm caused by teachers trying to replicate 'what Ofsted want.'

When Amanda Spielman took over as Chief Inspector in 2017 this process accelerated further and, with the introduction of a new inspection framework in 2019, the inspectorate has stopped making judgements on 'Teaching and Learning' and is instead judging schools on the 'Quality of Education' offered. The focus is now on what pupils are remembering over time. Not only that, a new appreciation of evidence from cognitive science has led to an acknowledgement that children need to learn knowledge. Schools are praised when "curriculum leaders have planned what pupils will learn in each subject in detail … detailed planning supports current pupils to remember the knowledge they need."[34] And schools are criticised where the curriculum has not been carefully sequenced: "The order of topics is random. Pupils struggle with this because they have not remembered the vocabulary from previous lessons."[35]

Gove's reforms

Michael Gove, Secretary of State for Education from 2010–2014, succeeded in making sweeping (if unpopular) changes to the curriculum, public examinations and the ranking of schools on performance tables. Gove saw an academic, subject-based education as the right of every child, regardless of background or perceived ability. The 2015 National Curriculum was conceived as a 'knowledge-rich' alternative to the 'knowledge-lite' version that had preceded it. Any who objected were dismissed as 'enemies of promise.'

Gove's vision for English was for authors such as Byron, Keats, Austen, Dickens and Hardy to be reinstated and that there would be a renewed emphasis on the teaching of spelling, punctuation and grammar. Arguably, Gove was justified in his reaction to the excesses of what had gone before, with its emphasis on vaguely defined 'personal learning and thinking skills,' but, perhaps understandably, his reforms were widely criticised as 'backward looking' and 'elitist.'

The new National Curriculum for English states its aim as promoting,

> … high standards of language and literacy by equipping pupils with a strong command of the spoken and written language … and … developing their love of literature through widespread reading for enjoyment … the national curriculum for English aims to ensure that all pupils:

- read easily, fluently and with good understanding
- develop the habit of reading widely and often, for both pleasure and information
- acquire a wide vocabulary, an understanding of grammar and knowledge of linguistic conventions for reading, writing and spoken language
- appreciate our rich and varied literary heritage
- write clearly, accurately and coherently, adapting their language and style in and for a range of contexts, purposes and audiences
- use discussion in order to learn; they should be able to elaborate and explain clearly their understanding and ideas
- are competent in the arts of speaking and listening, making formal presentations, demonstrating to others and participating in debate.[36]

Compare this with the advice from 2009 given in *English at the Crossroads*:

- Use practical and creative approaches; engage pupils by giving them good opportunities to express ideas.
- Find ways to develop pupils' initiative and independent learning.
- Use speaking and listening activities to help pupils think for themselves.
- Resist dictating the form and context of students' work.
- Find effective ways to identify and share good practice within and between schools.

Apart from a marked change of tone, there is a clear change of intent. In 2009, English was about 'practical and creative approaches'; fostering 'initiative and independent learning' and resisting 'dictating the form and context of students' work.' By the time we reach 2015, however, there is a growing concern to ensure that teachers of English deliver what the sociologist Pierre Bourdieu called 'cultural capital,' to provide a common, 'knowledge-rich' curriculum to all students. In fact, Matthew Arnold's proposal that children must be taught "the best of what has been thought and said"[37] is now explicitly enshrined in the current National Curriculum.

Figure 1.3 summarises some of this history of English as a school subject.

Where are we now?

Different ideas of what English should be for have pulled the subject in a number of competing directions:

1. Learning how to read and analyse increasingly sophisticated fiction and non-fiction texts.
2. Learning how to write accurately and fluently in a range of different contexts.
3. Developing empathy and imagination both by reading about the lives of others and by expressing ideas and writing imaginatively in a range of genres.
4. The study of a canon of 'great works' including Shakespeare, as well as more modern examples of literature.
5. The study of language as a vehicle for conceptual thought.

It is hard to see that these aims are all united by one neat, unifying purpose. What potential inconsistencies or conflict do you notice between the various aims of English?

Gove's curriculum reforms failed to ask, let alone answer, important questions about how to help teachers ensure students grasp the curriculum sufficiently to think beyond it and help schools create a curriculum that engages students

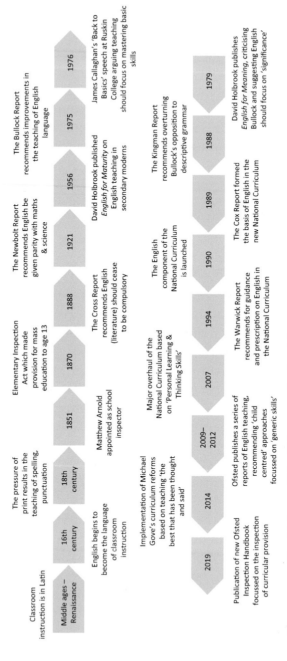

Figure 1.3 The history of English as a school subject

before they have lost interest in acquiring new knowledge. Some of these questions are:

- What subject knowledge is essential to making meaning in English?
- How do we prevent an English curriculum degenerating into lists of knowledge to be learned or skills to be acquired?
- How are judgements made in English?
- How do students make progress in English?
- What is the 'how to' knowledge students need to make meaning in English?
- What connections are there between English and other subjects?[38]

Addressing these concerns requires that teachers have access to curricular expertise on the form knowledge should take in English and how to support students in acquiring that knowledge. But, as yet, these questions have gone largely unasked and wholly unanswered.

This chapter has sought to answer the question, what is English for? Well, it's more than adding to the store of students' knowledge; it's also an attempt to confront young people with something beautiful, moving and profound. Although English should strive for them to become knowledgeable about the story of English literature, and skilled and fluent readers and writers, we should also value children's ability to think critically and creatively. As well as helping students master the discipline, we must also, as Sampson put it, "find the way of speaking to the soul." The approach outlined in the pages ahead is rooted in a belief that literature can nourish the soul and that language can fire the imagination, even though these aims will always be "absent from statistics."

> ## KEY POINTS
>
> - Although polarised 'traditional' and 'progressive' ideas about English tend to be unhelpful, understanding them helps us to work out what we believe English should be for.
> - Too many English teachers are unaware of the forces that have shaped the subject; it's helpful to understand how and why English has developed as it has.
> - In many respects, the substance of the subject has remained unchanged since the 1890s, although the emphasis of what and how we teach has altered radically.
> - The current emphasis on knowledge and cognitive science is a reaction to the excesses of the recent past: generic skills, the undermining of teachers' authority and the insistence on 'engagement,' 'relevance' and 'authenticity.'
> - There are still important questions to ask about what the English curriculum should be and how it should be taught.

The next chapter will address some of the problems that have accumulated as a result of the troubled history of English. Only once this debris is cleared from our path can we hope to build something more sustainable and fit for purpose.

Further reading

- The website www.educationengland.org.uk was invaluable in writing this chapter. It is an incredible resource containing pretty much every official document concerning the history of education in England you could hope to find.

- David Crystal's book, *Making Sense* (and especially his supplementary essay, "English Grammar in the UK: A Political History"), helped to bring together some of the ideas about the history of English as they relate to grammar teaching.
- I also found George Sampson's *English for the English* a fascinating insight into education in the early 1920s. It is available as a free download here: https://archive.org/details/englishforenglis00samprich/page/n6/mode/2up

2 Problems in English

If we're not entirely sure what English is for, then we are even less confident about how it should be taught. For the sake of argument, let's agree that the aims of the current National Curriculum are the right ones (see pages 33–34). How then can these aims be achieved? Some are perhaps more straightforward to tackle than others, but all require careful thought. How, for instance, would you get a child who is not currently reading fluently to do so? What is the process required to ensure children develop the habit of reading widely and often? Do we know how to teach children to understand grammar and to appreciate our literary heritage? Maybe you feel surer about how to go about teaching children to write clearly, accurately and coherently, but are you equally clear about how to get them to elaborate and explain their ideas?

The point is, we don't have a codified body of knowledge of how to achieve these aims. To be sure, pieces of the puzzle are out there, scattered across the blogosphere, hidden in little- known academic papers and mouldering books, but they haven't been collated and placed in the hands of English teachers in an easily digestible form. Instead, English has become a folk discipline with craft knowledge passed down in individual departments without much recourse to empirical observation or evaluation.

As a result, a great deal of poorly understood and ill-thought through ideas continue to be passed off as 'best practice,' and many excellent ideas are lost or forgotten.

For example, the Newbolt Report made this observation on marking in 1921:

> Teachers, as a rule, show themselves most painstaking in the correction of all the errors of punctuation, spelling and grammar. This is a tedious task, but a plain and straight-forward one, and *there is a danger that some of them may absorb all the available time in its performance and cherish the illusion that nothing more needs to be done.* The correction of perhaps 50 or 60 exercise books is, indeed, a heavy burden, and if the children write as, strange to say, they sometimes do, several 'Compositions' in the week, it will take the teacher all his time merely to keep up with them. ... The teacher who limits his teaching to correction is asking for little, and he will get but little. He will seldom get a genuine attempt by the pupil to express as well as he can what he is really capable of thinking and saying. *The pupil knows what will pass muster and does not offer more. His own past work becomes his model*, and so, to the end, perhaps, of his school life, he may continue to serve up as composition what is as to the matter the mere froth of his mind, and as to the manner, painfully lacking in style and arrangement.[1]
>
> [emphasis added]

One hundred years later and this seems acutely prescient. As many English teachers have recently come to suspect, one of the foundations of English teaching – regular correction of students' work – may not just be time-consuming drudgery, it may actually be counterproductive. The purpose of marking and correcting students' work is that it should provide them with feedback on how to improve, but writing extended comments for each student is a particularly inefficient and ineffective way of going about this. Thankfully, teachers have started rejecting the orthodoxy that students must have work marked, individually and at length, and are moving towards systems for providing whole class feedback. But, the fact that this information disappeared from our collective pool of knowledge sometime in the past century is both a frustration and a concern. How do we ensure that what we currently know is passed on to future generations of teachers?

Some of the problems English teachers have faced and continue to contend with are reactions against similar axiomatic beliefs about English. The most pernicious of these beliefs is this:

> *The 'skills-based' subject assumption*: because English is made up of transferable disciplinary skills it doesn't much matter what students read or write about.

This assumption is at the root of a great many problems encountered in teaching English. If English is 'skills-based' then it obviously makes sense to teach these skills, and specific content is more or less irrelevant. This being the case, it makes sense to get students to practise the skills we want them to develop by providing them with the most accessible and familiar texts and prompts to practise on. In this way, students up and down the country are taught English day in, day out. How do we know it works? Because some children are successful. What about the ones who aren't? Well, what can you do with kids like that?

This is precisely the same kind of critical analysis that led doctors to believe that by bleeding patients their humours would be rebalanced: it obviously worked because so many patients recovered. It was all too easy to ignore all the dead ones because they don't have much to say on the matter. Like reluctant medics who slowly became aware that the world wasn't organised the way they supposed, we need to understand that skill in English is based on knowledge.

Michael Oakeshott understood that the knowledge needed to make meaning in any field "cannot be learned or taught in principle, only in detail."[2] Chasing general principles is to take a short cut that doesn't exist. Oakeshott saw teaching as any approach that would impart knowledge and show how it could be used to make meaning, such as,

> ... hinting, suggesting, urging, coaxing, encouraging, guiding, pointing out, conversing, instructing, informing, narrating, lecturing, demonstrating, exercising, testing, examining, criticizing, correcting, tutoring, drilling and so on – everything, indeed, which does not belie the engagement to impart an understanding.[3]

The sadness is that a great deal of what goes on in English lessons does, in fact, belie that engagement.

We can't teach skill; we can *only* teach knowledge

Let's say you want to teach the skill of punctuation, or the skill of selecting textual evidence. Or maybe something broader like the skill of reading. Where would you begin? You might think that you can teach a skill by showing somebody how to *do* something.

Let's say you decide to teach the skill of punctuation by showing your students how to end a sentence with a full stop. You write your sentence and then at the end add a full stop.

Look everyone, the full stop shows where you have ended the sentence.

You could then go through a few more examples and get children to add their own full stops, first to some pre-prepared examples and then to a few sentences of their own. What will they have learned? Well, perhaps they will now know that at the end of something called a sentence comes a dot which can be made by pressing a pencil onto paper or by tapping a key on a keyboard. Can they punctuate? Of course not. And the reason they can't is because they don't know *enough*. To avoid just scattering dots throughout their writing they need to know what a sentence is. (*Even English teachers sometimes struggle to explain what a sentence is, although they know one when they see one; it becomes an instinctive, intuitive sense picked up from doing lots of reading or writing.*)

But, teachers' lived experience is that these sorts of exercises result in some children learning the skill of basic punctuation. Is this proof you *can* teach a skill? The children who seem to acquire skills quickly already possess much of the knowledge they need to make sense of instruction. What they already know acts like intellectual Velcro; new knowledge sticks easily. The students who seem most resistant to this type of teaching are, on average, the less advantaged. They fail to acquire the skills we teach not because they're less able but because they've done a lot less reading. Because they don't have as much relevant prior knowledge they sometimes seem to possess the equivalent of intellectual Teflon: new knowledge has little relevant to grip onto.

If we take instead the example of teaching a skill like juggling, things are likely to go differently. Few, if any, children possess much prior juggling knowledge but all will have the basic folk knowledge of what happens if you throw objects in the air and then try to catch them. Juggling requires you to keep track of at least three objects at once, but anyone who wants to teach juggling is likely to start by showing how to throw and catch just one ball. When juggling three balls, only one ball is thrown at a time, while holding the other two. The ball should pop off your hand rather than rolling off your fingertips. If the ball spins, it has been thrown incorrectly. Balls must travel in a figure 8 pattern, with the hand carrying them from outside to inside, so that they don't hit each other. This is not instinctive and the vast majority of people need it carefully explained and patiently demonstrated before they begin to get it.

If you continued your juggling tutorial, children would, eventually, know enough to be able to practise. With practice they would start to acquire skill; the more they practise, the more skilled they become. Eventually, with effort and determination, they will have acquired the skill of juggling. Of course, some children are likely to be better jugglers than others – all abilities tend to distribute normally – but pretty much anyone in possession of the requisite physical attributes can learn to juggle. Or to read, punctuate and select textual evidence.

Although students need to acquire a range of skills, we can only teach them knowledge. Different kinds of knowledge may be taught differently: some things you can explain, others you have to point out during practice, but as all this knowledge accumulates, it begins to chunk together. To start, each item of knowledge is known inflexibly but, through repetition and practice, items become increasingly flexible the more they cohere with other related knowledge. *Knowledge becomes skill through application within the area in which we hope to become skilled.*

Let's imagine you want to teach the skill of using quotations to support an argument. What knowledge needs to be imparted?

- What a quotation is and is not (providing non-examples is a helpful way of bolstering understanding).

- The purpose of using quotations (to attribute ideas to the original author; as supporting evidence; to provide material on which to demonstrate a theory).
- The punctuation needed to separate a quotation from the rest of a text (commas, quotations marks and, possibly, ellipses and square brackets).
- Embedding quotation within sentences (attribution within subordinate clauses).
- The dangers of plagiarism.
- Selecting relevant quotations.

All of this needs to be demonstrated and discussed using a variety of examples (and non-examples). Once students have had all this explained, they can start practising. Practice, as we'll see shortly, has some limitations, but for the most part, what we practise we get better at.

Most of the items on this list are relatively straightforward but the last item, selecting relevant quotations, is much harder to teach as it cannot be directly explained. The ability to select a relevant quote relies on the tacit knowledge of what is relevant in *this particular instance* and needs to be shown in the moment. For this reason, teachers have to be alert for examples of relevant and irrelevant selection during practice and bring these instances to all students' attention. In the same way, it would be difficult for a chef to explain the perfect consistency of a soufflé, but much easier to point to perfection as and when it occurs.

Once a skill has been acquired, we stop being able to see the joins between the items of knowledge that went into its creation. Selecting an apt quotation begins to feel intuitive and effortless. The more expert we become, the more invisible and automatic our skills become until, eventually, they become tacit. Michael Polanyi suggested that the closest we could get to articulating our tacit understanding is to come up with proxies or maxims:

Maxims are rules, the correct application of which is part of the art which they govern. The true maxims of golfing or of poetry increase our insight into golfing or poetry and may even give valuable guidance to golfers and poets; but these maxims would instantly condemn themselves to absurdity if they tried to replace the golfer's skill or the poet's art. *Maxims cannot be understood, still less applied by anyone not already possessing a good practical knowledge of the art.* They derive their interest from our appreciation of the art and cannot themselves either replace or establish that appreciation.[4]

[emphasis added]

Everything we know explicitly depends on a more tacit understanding. Eventually, we may start to believe that the skill (which for us has become so natural and straightforward) can be taught to others as a complete edifice. This is like presenting someone with a meal and telling them to cook their own without giving them the ingredients or a recipe. It's possible for another expert to see how this might be done, but frustratingly difficult for a novice. The idea that skill can be imparted without the hard work of teaching all the requisite knowledge is an illusion born from being unable to remember how *we* went about acquiring our own expertise.

Taking a 'skills-based' approach is like trying to build on sand. If we want students – *all students* – to become skilled, teach them the knowledge they need to be able to practise. Skill requires knowledge and the will to practise. This leads us to another overarching assumption that creates all sorts of difficulties in English.

> *The practice assumption*: we know that improvement comes through practice, but what happens if students are practising the wrong things?

Practice makes permanent, not perfect; whatever we practise, we get better at. If we practise doing the wrong things then we'll get better at doing those things badly. While pretty much anything we do can be improved through practice, students spend many hours in lessons practising the skills of reading and writing, and although some seem to fly, others fail to improve. Why is this?

I'd predict that those students who are successful within a skills-based English curriculum overwhelmingly come from more affluent backgrounds. They already possess enough background knowledge to be able to make better inferences and analyse meaning more deftly. Their vocabulary and implicit understanding of academic English allows them to write well because they're also more able to use academic English in their speech. They do well *despite* the way they're taught, not because of it. Less advantaged students are less likely to have the kind of background knowledge and cultural literacy that allows for making inferences and analysing meaning. They are less likely to have experienced formal academic register outside school and so their writing is often cruder and clunkier. As we'll see, the role of practice changes depending on whether you think English is a skills-based subject or not.

These assumptions – that English is 'skills-based,' and that these skills can be acquired through practice – explain so much of what has gone wrong:

Q: Why are so many children poor at selecting textual evidence, reading or punctuation?
A: They don't practise enough.
Q: Why don't children practise enough?
A: Because they learn early on that they 'can't do it.'
Q: Why do they learn that they 'can't do it'?
A: Because they've not had the skill broken down into teachable units of knowledge.

Problems with reading

The ability to read is composed of many thousands of individual pieces of knowledge which allow us to automatise a hugely complex process. As reading is automatised it becomes increasingly effortless, and children are likely to read more. The more they read the more they learn about texts and the wider world. The more knowledge students possess, the easier it is for them to connect new ideas to things they already know about. This virtuous cycle is how skill is acquired.

If students fail to automatise the 'mechanical' aspects of reading – decoding and word recognition – progress in reading stalls. Comprehension depends on fluent and accurate decoding; if a student cannot understand something written down that they would understand if heard, they probably have a decoding problem, but they will also be unfamiliar with orthography.

> ## ORTHOGRAPHY
>
> Greek: *orthographia* 'correct writing,' from orthos 'correct' + graphein 'to write.'
>
> Conventions of a written language including spelling and punctuation.

Written text contains many words people don't use in speech; style and syntax tend to be more demanding which places greater burdens on students' attention. You might be persuaded that the best way to improve students' reading comprehension is to teach oral comprehension skills but there is no evidence that this makes any difference to children's reading skill.[5] The best bet for improving comprehension is to spend more time reading. This way students not only get lots of orthographic experience, they also encounter a wider range of vocabulary in a wider range of contexts.

However, following a skills-based approach it makes sense to practise comprehension skills because by practising you'll improve. But, if there are no such things as comprehension skills, you can't practise them. To be clear, I'm not saying inference, analysis and evaluation don't exist – obviously you can tell students what an inference is, show them lots of examples of analysis and make them practise evaluating the effects of writing – just that these are not skills that can be practised. Let's see if I can explain why by focussing on inference.

An inference is 'a conclusion reached on the basis of evidence and reasoning.' So, to think about whether we can practise making inferences we need to consider whether by drawing conclusions based on evidence and reason we'll become better at drawing conclusions based on evidence on reason. This sounds logical, but we need to consider *what* we're actually practising. How do you actually draw a conclusion from evidence and reason? Well, first you need to weigh the specific evidence. How do you know what the evidence is telling you? How do you know the importance of the evidence? Then, how do we apply reason to this evidence? Are these generalities that can be learned, or do they depend on specific instances?

Robert Marzano suggests we can teach inference by posing four questions to students:

1. *What is my inference?* This question helps students become aware that they may have just made an inference by filling in information that wasn't directly presented.
2. *What information did I use to make this inference?* It's important for students to understand the various types of information they use to make inferences. This may include information presented in the text, or it may be background knowledge that a student brings to the learning setting.
3. *How good was my thinking?* According to Marzano, once students have identified the premises on which they've based their inferences, they can engage in the most

50

powerful part of the process – examining the validity of their thinking.

4. *Do I need to change my thinking?* The final step in the process is for students to consider possible changes in their thinking. The point here is not to invalidate students' original inferences, but rather to help them develop the habit of continually updating their thinking as they gather new information.[6]

I'm going to assume that readers will consider themselves reasonably practised at making inferences. Let's try applying these four questions to a short passage from *Finnegans Wake*:

> riverrun, past Eve and Adam's, from swerve of shore to bend of bay, brings us by a commodius vicus of recirculation back to Howth Castle and Environs.

> Sir Tristram, violer d'amores, fr'over the short sea, had passencore rearrived from North Armorica on this side the scraggy isthmus of Europe Minor to wielderfight his penisolate war: nor had topsawyer's rocks by the stream Oconee exaggerated themselse to Laurens County's gorgios while they went doublin their mumper all the time: nor avoice from afire bellowsed mishe mishe totauftauf thuartpeatrick: not yet, though venissoon after, had a kidscad buttended a bland old isaac: not yet, though all's fair in vanessy, were sosie sesthers wroth with twone nathandjoe. Rot a peck of pa's malt had Jhem or Shen brewed by arclight and rory end to the regginbrow was to be seen ringsome on the aquaface.

Was your skill in making inferences any help? Did the questions help you in your thinking?

Admittedly, this is an extreme example but it makes the point that if I wanted to improve my ability to make an inference I would need to know more about what Joyce was trying to achieve. It's not that these kinds of metacognitive strategies don't have value, it's that they only ever take you part of the way. Once you know that inferences can be made you can start trying to make them. But you will always struggle to make a worthwhile inference unless you know something about the content and context of the text you're reading, and the more you know, the more insightful your inferences are likely to be.

All inferences depend on knowledge. Students may spend hours of lesson time successfully practising the skill of inference only to come completely unstuck when they encounter a text about which they know little. If we genuinely want children to become better at inferring, analysing, evaluating or any of the other so-called 'skills' on which success in English depends then they need to read much more widely, acquire a greater breadth of vocabulary and generally know more about the world around them. Being skilled is indistinguishable from being knowledgeable.

Strategies not skills

This is not to say that there's *no* merit to giving children some instruction on strategies that might make it easier for them to understand written texts. For instance, it's probably useful to teach children that the conventions of fiction and non-fiction are very different.

The sort of strategy I think it's worth spending *some* time on is to explicitly teach students how to skim and scan. Confident readers do these things without thinking but for struggling readers they're likely to be more alien. So, for instance, it's worth telling students that the key to unlocking the meaning of a paragraph of non-fiction text is to pick out the head noun in the topic sentence. Quickly skim the following passage from a GCSE geography textbook to work out what it's about:

> The Laki eruption was one of the most devastating eruptions in human history. Iceland lies on the mid-Atlantic ridge and its volcanoes pose a constant threat, although very few of them produce violent eruptions because the magma is usually basaltic and relatively free-flowing. In 1783–84, a major eruption from the Laki fissure poured out an estimated 14 km3 of basaltic lava and clouds of poisonous compounds. The volcano is located in a remote part of Iceland and no one was killed by the event itself. However, the secondary effects were devastating because the poisonous cloud killed over half of Iceland's livestock population, leading to a famine which killed approximately a quarter of the population.[7]

In this example, the head noun is the phrase 'The Laki eruption.' Able readers don't even notice the definite article and are hardly slowed down by the fact they probably have no idea what Laki is. Their attention latches onto 'eruption.' If this were a passage of fiction the word could relate to an angry teacher but because it's non-fiction the list of things likely to erupt is strictly limited. Even if only given two seconds to read the whole passage, able readers are developing a volcano hypothesis long before they actually see the word, but this is because a skilled reader is, in reality, a knowledgeable reader.

Struggling readers will attempt to read the passage very differently. Unless specifically told not to, they're likely to spend as much time trying to decode 'the' as any other word and, because they're so used to encountering unfamiliar vocabulary the word 'Laki' is likely to convince them the text is 'too hard.' They may give up before reaching 'eruption' but even if they do persevere they're far less likely to be familiar with its meaning.

One important tip is for teachers to ensure that students know at least the head nouns before being asked to read a passage, but it's also worth modelling the process of skimming. Students who don't read much need to be shown they can ignore 'the' and that it doesn't matter that they don't know what 'Laki' is. If they need to know, it will become clear later.

There's a similar body of knowledge we can share on how to scan for information. Try to locate the answers to the following questions in the extract below:

1. What was the only form of schooling available to women in the 17th century?
2. When did England experience a period of growth in social awareness?
3. What was the name of Defoe's essay arguing that women should be educated?

Although the education of women in 17th century England was not entirely neglected, the only schooling available to them was private tutoring, which was usually shared with siblings or cousins. Such tutoring was an option only for the upper classes, and then only if the father or husband allowed it. Despite their limited education, a few women began to express themselves publicly during the 1600s. Some called for more rights for women, including the right to an education. In most circles, however, such ideas were ignored or ridiculed. Following the Restoration, England experienced a period of growth in social awareness as well as in industry and commerce. More and more individuals looked for practical ways to correct what they saw as society's flaws. One of those individuals was Daniel Defoe. Best known today as a novelist, Defoe was also involved in both commerce and social reform. One of his first publications, written in 1697, was An Essay on Projects, a series of proposals advocating, among other things, the establishment of banks, insurance companies, and credit unions – and in 'An Academy for Women,' the education of females.[8]

For many struggling readers this is a daunting task. The reason you found it easy was because you implicitly knew the first answer would be near the beginning, the second would be in the middle and the third at the end. Once you located the answer to the second question there was no way you would have gone back to the beginning to look for number 3. You *just knew* that the answers would be presented sequentially. This makes the process of scanning very efficient. The reason why some students take forever to complete these kinds of comprehension activities is that they go back to the beginning of the text for every single new question!

If students knew that, in the context of school, the answers to comprehension questions emerge sequentially, reading becomes less onerous. The answer to the first question is likely to be in the first paragraph and the answer to the second question in the second paragraph. Able readers seem to know this instinctively, struggling readers do not.

Problems with writing

Students often have only a vague idea of what academic writing is supposed to look like – they know the sorts of words and phrases they should use – but they may have little understanding of the underlying content and therefore whatever they write is likely to be superficial at best and fatuous at worst.

In *Death in the Afternoon*, Hemingway wrote,

If a writer of prose knows enough of what he is writing about he may omit things that he knows and the reader, if the writer is writing truly enough, will have a feeling of those things as strongly as though the writer had stated them. The dignity of movement of an ice-berg is due to only one-eighth of it being above water. A writer who omits things because he does not know them only makes hollow places in his writing.[9]

Similarly, the 'holes' in students' writing are caused by not knowing enough about the subject they're writing about. Of course, knowing lots of facts about a text is not the same thing as being able to write an essay but it is this knowledge that gives students' work the 'dignity of movement' it needs to be successful. It has come to seem reasonable to ask students to spend time practising writing essays rather than teaching them what they omit through ignorance.

Much essay writing practice consists of teaching students some sort of structural device (PEE – Point Evidence Explain – or one of its many variants) and getting them to write paragraphs in which they give an opinion, provide textual evidence to support their opinion, and then go into detail about precisely why the evidence supports their opinion. On the face of it, this seems to work because some students seem to get better at writing such paragraphs, but for every student who seems to gain increasing confidence there is always another who slavishly follows the structure without saying anything of any interest or originality. I've come to think of this as cargo cult writing.

Cargo cult writing

Cargo cults grew up on some of the Melanesian islands during the first half of the 20th century. Amazed islanders watched as Westerners arrived on their islands, built landing strips and then unloaded precious cargo from the aeroplanes which duly landed. That looks easy enough, some canny shaman must have reasoned, if we knock up a bamboo airport then the metal birds will come and lay their cargo eggs for us too. Despite the islanders' best efforts, no cargo arrived. Not only had they no understanding of global geopolitics and modern science, they'd fundamentally misunderstood the causal relationship between cargo and airports.

Richard Feynman famously appropriated the cargo cult metaphor to describe bad science. He referred to the social sciences as Cargo Cult Science, because "they follow all the apparent precepts and forms of scientific investigation, but they're missing something essential, because the planes don't land."[10] Melanesian islanders had a good theory about how to attract cargo but made very little progress. As a result, most cargo cults died out fairly quickly because it was really hard to continue fooling themselves: the planes didn't land. We don't always have this advantage because, depending on the kind of 'cargo' we desire, it can be much easier to convince ourselves that it has arrived. After all, an essay gets written – no matter how poor – so what we're doing must be working, right?

It's clear that many students approach exams like cargo cultists. They know how to imitate the form and structure of a good response but the planes don't land. As Christine Counsell observes, "English teaching sometimes bypasses its own purposes to such an extent that we can see the sad irony of pupils trained to answer the ubiquitous exam question, 'What's the effect on the reader...?' without a hope of the text having had an effect on the reader."[11]

Figure 2.1 is an extract from an essay written by a student who's been taught about how to structure writing to resemble an academic essay, but it's full of 'hollow places.' What would this student have to practise in order to improve?

How does the writer use language here to
describe the teacher and her class?

You could include the writer's choice of:

• Words and phrases
• Language features and techniques
• Sentence forms

[8 marks]

*Miss brodie looked hard at the door
for a long time – this sentence is
a simple sentence however they have added
the word hard this makes the sentence
better they have added an adverb to make
it stand out.*

Figure 2.1   An example from a student's essay

They already know what simple sentences and adverbs are,
what they appear not to know is their *significance*: what do
these things 'point to,' what do they *mean*?

Developing stamina

Too many students spend too much time filling up exercise
books in English lessons. They write page after page of low-
quality answers to comprehension questions and endless
awful 'analytic' paragraphs. What do you suppose they are
getting better at?

The main justification for this approach is that because
students will be judged on their ability to write essays, they need
to spend as much time as possible writing essays. But in many
domains, practice looks very different to final performance. Just
as the best way to prepare to run a marathon is by slowly and
incrementally building up to ever longer distances until in the
final stages of training 26 miles become possible, the best way to
get better at essay writing is to practise acquiring the components
of knowledge needed to be skilled at writing essays.

A radical-sounding suggestion for solving the stamina
problem is for students to write less for longer. There's small
value in spending time writing essays if you don't know how

to develop thoughts within a paragraph. Similarly, there's little point writing paragraphs if the sentence has not been mastered. As we've seen, this is likely to lead to cargo cult writing. Daisy Christodoulou argues that writing an essay – or a paragraph – is a summative task, and giving formative feedback on that task is only useful if the student then repeats the same task. Instead, she suggests, we ought to give formative feedback on genuinely formative tasks.[12]

Retrieval of information about the texts being studied can be a genuinely useful formative task. It's easy for both teachers and students to believe that just because information has been encountered previously it has been learned. If we tell students something we've previously told them they'll nod with familiarity. We mistake this familiarity for the ability to independently recall information elsewhere and later.

To help students acquire more flexible knowledge we could start by asking them multiple-choice questions, like this one about the character of Arthur Birling from J.B. Priestley's play, *An Inspector Calls*:

What does the word "portentous" imply about Mr Birling?

a) He is overweight.
b) He is self-important.
c) He is good at predicting what will happen in the future.
d) He worries about the future.

Here, students' effort goes into trying to recall an answer they have previously learned. This kind of question has two important functions. First, it provides excellent feedback on what students have forgotten. Second, it provides retrieval practice which improves students' ability to bring information to mind when they need it. Thus, if they're asked to write an essay about Mr Birling, or the opening scene of

An Inspector Calls in an exam, they will have less trouble remembering that Birling is a pompous boor who likes to look like he knows things other people don't.

Of course, whilst this kind of knowledge is necessary it's insufficient. Students also need to integrate what they know to venture and challenge opinions. But instead of writing lengthy, summative paragraphs, time would be better spent in debating ideas and practising writing excellent sentences. Regularly writing analytical sentences about the content being studied demands that reasons are provided and consequences explained, and it provides excellent opportunities for expressing ideas clearly and succinctly. (See pages 287–91 for some examples of what this might look like in practice.)

As students learn more about the texts they're studying, they will become increasingly able to add information to analytic sentences. And, as they become increasingly knowledgeable about how sentences structure content, they will become ever more confident in expressing what they know. By practising the smaller components that make up monolithic 'skills,' students become more skilled.

The capital letter problem

I have almost never met a secondary age child who doesn't conceptually understand how to use a capital letter. But, you'd never know. Students regularly hand in work liberally sprinkled with missing – or extraneous – capitals, and conscientious teachers spend hours circling the errors and patiently reexplaining the rules. In return, students say, 'I know. It's just the way I write.'

Giving someone feedback about something they already know is pointless. Dr Johnson once said, "It is not sufficiently considered that men more frequently require to be reminded than informed."[13] Lack of knowledge is not the problem; the problem is caused by practice. The more we practise something the more automatic it becomes. If we practise doing something badly we get better at doing it badly. Many students have become superb at not using capital letters. For practice to be effective, it must *remind* them of what they know.

When students are writing they have to remember what they know about the subject, as well as having to remember spelling and punctuation conventions *and* trying to make what they know sound interesting. If there's too much to remember something has to give. Although students may *know* how to use a capital letter or how to spell 'necessary,' if it's not automatic, they'll forget to do it. If we don't automatise the technical aspects of writing, we'll automatise *not* using them to make space in working memory to think about more interesting things.

The answer is, of course, to practise using capital letters (and all the other boring technical aspects of writing) correctly. It's not enough to practise until students get it right, they need to practise until they can no longer fail. So, why don't we? It's certainly not that teachers don't care, it's that what we do doesn't apply appropriate pressure. Whenever *we* correct or even identify students' mistakes we're signalling *they* don't have to. When we circle missing capital letters children become dependent on us to do it for them. Students need consequences for neglecting to do what they know how to do; otherwise why would they bother?

The solution is to expect students to proofread work before it's handed in. If this is a minimum standard there can be no argument about it. If work makes it through to the teacher and there are still missing capital letters there should be some sort of sanction that makes it clear that missing out the basics first time round is more onerous in the long term. If you knew that the consequence of not proofreading was being made to copy out your work again, you might think twice.

Using appropriate pressure is not about cruelly forcing children to use capital letters, it's about creating conditions where they become more responsive and more willing. It's about never lowering our expectations and saying, 'That'll do.' It's about teaching children to take pride in their work and that the little things matter. It's about explaining that while *you* may know what they mean and will judge their work charitably, there's no guarantee anyone else will. The world is biased against those who misspell common words and fail to punctuate correctly.

Knowing when to stop applying pressure is key to helping students learn to get things right independently. This means that when students start doing the right thing you stand back and let them show you what they can do. Releasing pressure too early means students may not have automatised the basics; too late may mean they might become bored or frustrated. When pressure has been applied carefully enough students won't have to think about when to use capital letters, they'll do it automatically. When spelling and punctuation rules are made automatic students have so much more capacity to think about meaning.

The clockwork curriculum

While I'm absolutely in favour of making English a 'knowledge-rich' subject, some of the backlash against the 'knowledge-lite' skills-based approach has tended towards a mechanistic conception of English in which texts are in danger of being reduced to lists of facts to learn and retrieve. For a long while I considered these kinds of criticisms to be a straw man lacking any substance, but in my visits to many schools over the past few years some of my worst fears have been confirmed. In the well-intentioned search for greater objectivity, the importance of making meaning risks being neglected or ignored.

The two problems discussed in the following section are reasonably typical of the sorts of things than can go awry in a classroom prioritising knowledge at the expense of meaning.

The history lesson problem

The first time I taught *Julius Caesar*, I spent a couple of weeks filling in the history of the late Roman Republic from Sulla's dictatorship right up until the events at the start of the play. Some of it might even have helped my students to better understand the events and references in the play, but it almost certainly wasn't worth the time. I've made similar mistakes in teaching the Cold War as background to *The Crucible*, and the Bolshevik Revolution as context for *Animal Farm*. It's not that these things aren't interesting or worth knowing, it's that they're not English.

What often goes wrong with the teaching of historical context is that it fails to be properly integrated into students' thought and work. Students need to know that Shakespeare was born during the reign of Elizabeth I with all that would have entailed about religion, antipathy with the Catholic nations of Europe and concerns about the succession. It's important for students to know that Shakespeare is the inheritor of a European tradition which reaches back to classical Greece, and the English verse of Chaucer and Spenser as well as the dramatic traditions of the mystery plays, but no one wants to see all that weight of context dragging down the introductions to essays.

Students learn all this context, but do they learn its significance? The trick, or art, to the deft use of contextual information is to know a lot and to be able to *judiciously* select from all we know. And to do this, we have to know the impact and effect of contextual details. Is it significant that Shakespeare was born in 1564? Not on its own, no. Is it significant to an analysis of *Julius Caesar* that he was writing late in Elizabeth's reign? Potentially, yes. Knowing, and being able to explain, the significance of the parallels between the political context of Caesar's Rome and Elizabethan England is worthwhile. *Julius Caesar* can be read as an allegory for Shakespeare's own time. Caesar is the undisputed master of Rome, just as Elizabeth is of England; both states have endured civil strife and political turmoil in the recent past; in both it is unclear what plans there are for the smooth transition of power after the death of their aging rulers. Why wouldn't Shakespeare just come out and frankly discuss his concerns about the English succession? Because it was treason to do so!

Similarly, if students are going to have any understanding beyond the literal when reading Arthur Miller's play, *The Crucible*, it's vital that they know something of the 'Reds under the beds' panic that swept through 1950s America cynically fanned by the flames of McCarthyism. Miller's original audience would have been all too painfully aware of what was going on, but our students won't. They need to know that Miller's retelling of the Salem witch trials of the 1690s is an allegory for the activities of the House of Representatives Committee of Un-American Activities and that Miller himself was convicted of contempt for refusing to give the Committee the names of supposed communists. That should be enough, but the problem is, when you tell students this stuff they want to know *why*. And then you end up, if you're not careful, telling them about the Cold War, then the Bolshevik Revolution, and then the events that led up to that. And so it goes.

So, when does providing essential context turn into a history lesson? As with many potential problems, this can be avoided with careful planning. First, list the background that's essential to understand the text being studied, then, when teaching context, model how it would be integrated into a critical analysis, demonstrating the conventions of how context is woven into an academic essay.

Our search for essential context should consider the place the text we're studying has in the wider literary conversation. Is it part of a particular tradition, or is it responding to other texts? Many works of English literature consciously refer back to Greek myths and classical literature as well as Bible stories. Can the text be categorised as metaphysical, neo-classical, Romantic, modernist or part of the post-modern period? If students are studying Wordsworth's 'Prelude' then it will help them to know something of the Romantic notion of the sublime. This might also be useful if they are reading Mary Shelley's *Frankenstein* but students will also benefit from knowing something about the cares and conventions of the Gothic tradition within which the text can also be located.

We should also consider what else a writer has written: is this text typical of their output? Can we see the development of particular themes throughout their oeuvre? Dickens, for instance, was always interested in social reform and the plight of orphans, and we can see these ideas develop through early works like *Oliver Twist* to later works like *Great Expectations*. Similarly, Austen's writing was always concerned with marriage and the precarious position of women in society, but we can trace the increase in sophistication with which these ideas were treated from *Sense and Sensibility* to *Persuasion*. If we've thought about context like this, we can show how it informs the whole text rather than taking it on as an afterthought.

The problem with knowledge organisers

Lists of 'essential' context have been recently popularised as 'knowledge organisers.' The idea is that everything that students ought to memorise about a text should be set out on a single sheet of A4 paper. There's nothing wrong with the desire to organise the contextual knowledge you wish students to learn about a given text but my criticism of very many of the knowledge organisers I've encountered is that they suffer from being crammed with stuff that is unlikely to be particularly helpful. Take a look at the example in Figure 2.2 of a knowledge organiser for Dickens' *A Christmas Carol.**

Are all those stylistic features necessary? Do we really want to teach students about Jeremy Bentham and Malthusian economics? Will their interpretation and understanding be enhanced by knowing about 'Sabbatarianism'? And I'm fairly sure there's no need to go into the sublime when considering *A Christmas Carol*. It might be worth teaching students about 'pursued protagonists' or the grotesque, but it would be

> Remarkably, writing in 1891, John Churton Collins anticipated the development of knowledge organisers saying, "An elaborate apparatus of mnemonic aids would be devised [summarizing texts] into tables for facts and … reduced to epitomes for generalisations. Criticism … would be got by heart."
>
> *The Study of English Literature*, p. 27

more helpful to focus on how these ideas relate to this particular text. I'm sceptical of the expectation that students' ability to think and write about the novel will be improved by memorising details of the various pieces of legislation passed in the 1830s, and I'm positive that little good will

* I'm allowed to be critical as I'm responsible for its existence.

A Christmas Carol – Knowledge Organiser

Plot summary:

1. Ebenezer Scrooge is at work in his counting house. Despite the Christmas Eve cold, he refuses to spend money on coals for the fire. Scrooge turns down his nephew, Fred's, invitation to his Christmas party and the request of two men who want money for charity.

2. Scrooge is visited by the ghost of his dead partner, Jacob Marley, who tells Scrooge that, due to his greedy life, he has to wander the Earth wearing heavy chains. Marley tries to stop Scrooge from doing the same. He tells Scrooge that three spirits will visit him during the next three nights. Scrooge falls asleep.

3. He wakes and the Ghost of Christmas Past takes Scrooge into the past. Invisible to those he watches, Scrooge revisits his childhood school days, his apprenticeship with a jolly merchant named Fezziwig, and his engagement to Belle, who leaves Scrooge as he loves money too much to love another human being. Scrooge sheds tears of regret before being returned to his bed.

4. The Ghost of Christmas Present shows Scrooge Christmas as it will happen that year. Scrooge watches the Cratchit family eat a tiny meal in their little home. He sees Bob Cratchit's crippled son, Tiny Tim, whose kindness and humility warm Scrooge's heart. The spectre shows Scrooge his nephew's Christmas party. Scrooge asks the spirit to stay until the very end. Toward the end of the day the ghost shows Scrooge two starved children, Ignorance and Want. He vanishes as Scrooge notices a dark, hooded figure coming.

5. The Ghost of Christmas Yet to Come takes Scrooge through a sequence of scenes linked to an unnamed man's death. Scrooge, is keen to learn the lesson. He begs to know the name of the dead man. He finds himself in a churchyard with the spirit pointing to a grave. Scrooge looks at the headstone and is shocked to read his own name. He is desperate to change his fate and promises to change his ways. He suddenly finds himself safely tucked in his bed.

6. Scrooge rushes out onto the street hoping to share his newfound Christmas spirit. He sends a turkey to the Cratchit house and goes to Fred's party. As the years go by, he continues to celebrate Christmas with all his heart. He treats Tiny Tim as if he were his own child, gives gifts for the poor and is kind, generous and warm.

Key characters	Key themes	Historical context	Dickens' stylistic features and terms
Ebenezer Scrooge – A se fish business man who transforms into a charitable philanthropist. **Fred** – Scrooge's nephew whose party invitation he declines **Jacob Marley** – Scrooge's dead partner who returns as a ghost to warn scrooge to change his ways. **Bob Cratchit** – Scrooge's clerk **Tiny Tim** – Bob's son whose story plays a part in inspiring Scrooge s transformation. **Mrs Cratchit** – Bob's wife **The Ghosts of Christmas Past, Present and Future** – Spirits who visit Scrooge and show him scenes which make him reconsider his behaviour. **Fezziwig** – Scrooge's ex-employer **Belle** – A woman who scrooge was in love with who left him in due to his greed. **Fan** – Scrooge's sister	Greed Predestination/ fate vs. free will Poverty & class stratification Isolation Transformation The passage of time Family Guilt Generosity Redemption Capitalism & social responsibility Justice	- During Dickens' childhood, his father was imprisoned for debt. - Dickens was put to work in a warehouse, pasting labels on bottles. He had experience of poverty. - Dickens became a writer of fiction and journalism, reporting on court cases and working for radical newspapers on his disillusionment with politics and the class system. - 1832 – The Great Reform Bill gave many middle-class property owners the right to vote for the first time. Large sections of the middle classes, the working classes and women still didn't have the right to vote. - 1834 – Poor Law Amendment Act – Led to a cut in aid given to paupers to help them stay in their own homes. Workhouses were created which poor people would have to live and work in, if they were unable to pay for their own housing. - December 1840 and February 1843 – Children's Employment Commission reports. - September 1843 – Dickens visits a 'Ragged School.' - October 1843 – Dickens speaks at an event for Manchester Athenaeum, an organisation bringing education and culture to the working masses. - December 1843 Dickens writes *A Christmas Carol*, focusing on how many of society's ills can be blamed on greed for money and status.	**Allegory** – a story which can be interpreted to reveal a hidden meaning, typically a moral or political one. **Ambiguity** – having more than one meaning. **Analepsis** – a form of anachrony by which some of the events of a story are related at a point in the narrative after later story-events have already been recounted. **Antihero** – a protagonist who lacks the attributes that make a heroic figure **Benthamism** – the utilitarian philosophy of Jeremy Bentham. **Gothic** – a style of literature characterised by a gloomy setting, grotesque, mysterious, or violent events, and an atmosphere of degeneration and decay **Grotesque** – odd or unnatural in shape, appearance, or character; fantastically ugly or absurd; bizarre. **Malthusian economics** – the belief that the population is out of control and that the world will run out of resources. **Morality tale** – a story using allegorical characters to portray the soul's struggle to achieve salvation. **Non-chronological narrative** – a story not told in the order the events occur. **Pathetic fallacy** – the attribution of human feelings and responses to inanimate things or animals. **Personification** – the attribution of human nature or character to inanimate objects, or abstract notions, especially as a rhetorical figure. **Prolepsis** – an anticipation, either in rhetoric or in narrative: the use of a descriptive term prior to the circumstances that would make it truly applicable **Pursued protagonist** – a central character who is threatened or chased. **Sabbatarianism** – excessive strictness in the observance of the Divinely ordained day of rest. **The sublime** – associated with ideas of awe, intensity ruggedness, terror, and vastness emphasising Man's insignificance in the face of Nature.

Figure 2.2   A Christmas Carol Knowledge Organiser

67

come from students learning by heart that in September 1843 Dickens visited a Ragged School. The plot summary and the list of dramatis personae may or may not prove useful, but what's the point of memorising a list of themes? And that brings us to what is often supposed to be the point of a knowledge organiser: to provide a list of those essential elements of study which a student should memorise. What here is *actually* essential?

Arguably, these ideas might be the most essential:

Historical context
- Dickens had personal experience of poverty as a child which may have motivated his interest in social reform.
- Those in financial difficulty were required to enter workhouses which had awful living conditions.
- Many of Dickens' novels address the lives of poor children (*Oliver Twist, David Copperfield, Great Expectations*) and this is reflected in the character of Tiny Tim.
- Christmas was an increasingly popular festival in Victorian England but *A Christmas Carol* did much to influence the idea that Christmas should be a time for giving and charity.

Stylistic features and terms
- *Gothic*: the novel borrows familiar elements from the Gothic tradition such as ghosts.
- *Grotesque*: Dickens regularly exaggerated the worst qualities of his characters' appearance and mannerisms to make them repulsive and memorable.
- *Allegory*: Scrooge's transformation is an allegory for the kind of societal transformation Dickens hopes for.
- *Non-chronological structure*: the story shifts between different time periods with flashbacks and flashforwards to tell the story of Scrooge's past and future.

Themes

- *Social responsibility*: Dickens was concerned that the middle classes should be aware of the suffering of the poor and wrote to push forward an agenda of social reform.
- *Greed vs generosity*: Scrooge's behaviour and attitudes are an exaggeration of those which created unfair conditions for the poor.
- *Redemption*: Scrooge's journey of self-discovery and transformation offers the possibility for society to change.

There may well be more contextual information which ends up leaking naturally into lessons but this is probably plenty for students to memorise. As you can see, each of the items above has been made relevant to the text, but students will still require explicit modelling for what the inclusion of context should look like in practice. For example:

> Dickens' interest in social reform and the plight of the poor is reflected in the allegory of Scrooge's transformation. At the start of the novel he is the personification of greed and selfishness, but through its non-chronological structure the novel shows us both Scrooge's sad childhood and the mistakes he made as a young man as well as offering a dystopian view of the future where he is made to face the consequences of his neglect of social responsibility.

There's a lot of contextual knowledge compressed into this brief paragraph but it's included for its significance and in service to an interpretation of the text. By giving careful thought to the precise extent of contextual baggage we want students to carry around, as well as clearly modelling how to pack it into the neatest and smallest of spaces, we will avoid some of the worst excesses of teaching context poorly.

KEY POINTS

- English is, to a large extent, a folk discipline with knowledge passed between individuals with limited understanding of which approaches are likely to be most effective for most students.
- English is more likely to be taught poorly if it is understood as a 'skills-based' subject. Such things as inference or analysis are functions of having sufficient textual and background knowledge.
- Instead, teachers need to teach the knowledge that makes up skill and then allow students time to practise in order to turn this knowledge into skill.
- Too often, students are asked to practise the wrong things with the result that they get better at doing these things badly.
- Practice should focus on mastering basics to the point that students can no longer get them wrong.
- Practice provides an essential opportunity to share the tacit knowledge of what skilled performance feels like.
- Teaching knowledge can easily backfire if we have not thought carefully enough about what we want students to learn and why.
- Avoid teaching context for its own sake; instead focus on its significance.

Having addressed some of the more egregious problems in English, it is now time to turn our attention to how we could reconceptualise the subject as one rooted in its own unique system of specialised knowledge.

Further reading

- Some of the problems discussed in this chapter have also been addressed by Daisy Christodoulou in her book, *Making Good Progress?*
- Many of the issues around reading are discussed with great insight in James and Diane Murphy's *Thinking Reading* and Alex Quigley's *Closing the Reading Gap.*
- For a general overview on how to teach English I can recommend a number of books written by English teachers in the last few years: Andy Tharby's *Making Every English Lesson Count*, Jennifer Webb's *How to Teach English Literature*, Chris Curtis' *How to Teach English* and Joe Nutt's *Teaching English for the Real World.*

3 An epistemology of English

As teachers, we build on what our students know to induct them into the patterns and precepts others have already established but which, to them, may seem startlingly, dangerously alien. While we may want our students to get good grades, we also strive for them to appreciate beauty, to perceive profundity, to be able to make sense of their experiences and spin new knowledge from the straw of ignorance. Writing about humanity's search for meaning Michael Polanyi said,

> The image of man's destiny, as derived from his mythical origins, is much nearer to our own experience of our own lives, to our experience of human greatness, to our perception of the course of our history since history began, and to our experience of the shattering forces of our utopias than is the image of the barren atomic topography to which the ideal of detached observation seeks to reduce these matters.[1]

But where is the line between 'the barren atomic topography' of chasing grades and the 'shattering forces of our utopia'? Can we hold the 'detached ideal' in creative tension with our subjective impressions of what is valuable? To what extent can this topography be made fertile? If English is to be more than a 'skills-based' subject, if it is to be reconceived as something 'knowledge-rich,' we need to grapple with what we mean by 'knowledge.' As we shall see, this leads us into a well-trodden field of conflict.

Knowledge, I should make clear, is more than facts. Philosophers have been trying to work out what knowledge is for millennia and facts are

> ## ARISTOTLE – 385–323 BC
>
> Aristotle was a Greek philosopher and polymath during the classical period in ancient Greece. Taught by Plato, he is still one of the most influential thinkers on the disciple of English. Two of his most important works are *Poetics* (the earliest work of literary theory) and *Rhetoric* (a treatise on the art of persuasion).

just one part of a much greater whole. When Greece was still ancient, Aristotle divided knowledge into three components he called *episteme, techne* and *phronesis*. We can think of *episteme* as what we know – factual knowledge – whereas *techne*, know-how, is broadly synonymous with craft or skill.* *Phronesis* can perhaps best be thought of as tacit knowledge and is made up of those things we're unable to articulate and don't necessarily know we know. From *episteme* we get epistemology – the study of knowledge and how meaning is made.

The struggle for an epistemology of English

Working out the epistemology of English has long been a site of skirmish. In order to prove itself worthy of entry to the

---

*   Aristotle actually defines *techne* as 'a productive capacity informed by an understanding of its intrinsic rationale' but this doesn't easily trip from the tongue.

halls of academia, English had to demonstrate that it consisted of content that could be examined. The study of language (or philology as it used to be known) was considered dispassionate enough to qualify as a university subject, but how could literature be taught and examined in a way that was suitably objective? Speaking against the establishment of a Chair in English at Oxford University, the historian Edward Freeman notoriously dismissed the study of literature as "chatter about Shelley." He went on to say,

> There are many things fit for a man's personal study that are not fit for University examinations. One of these is 'literature' ... [We are told] that it 'cultivates taste, educates the sympathies and enlarges the mind'. Excellent results against which no one has a word to say. Only we cannot examine tastes and sympathies. The examiner, in any branch of knowledge, must stick to the duller range of that 'technical and positive information'.[2]

What is the 'technical and positive information' that can be examined in English? John Churton Collins, writing in response to Freeman, argued that the study of English literature could, if it were properly systematised, meet the objective standards necessary for an academic subject and become "positive and tangible."[3] His suggestions included such ideas as establishing an agreed historical framework of literature, the study of the historical contexts in which literature was written, and close critical reading of individual texts and other pursuits that are still today given the scientific sounding title of 'research.'

In opposition to this 'sciencing' of English – an Enlightenment ideal – is the Romantic tradition of aesthetic knowledge, expressed most famously in the closing lines of John Keats' 'Ode on a Grecian Urn':

Beauty is truth, truth beauty, —that is all
Ye know on earth, and all ye need to know.

We might take issue with whether this is *all* we need to
know, but the value of beauty is certainly *something* students
of English should know. English is, or should be, concerned
with the creation of art. Keats warned that if all our efforts
are expended trying to "unweave a rainbow" and explain precisely how *this* technique has been used to create *that* effect,
we will, to use Wordsworth's phrase, "murder to dissect." In
A Defence of Poetry, Shelley wrote that literature "strips the
veil of familiarity from the world [compelling us] to feel that
which we perceive, and to imagine that which we know."[4] Can
we retain this more numinous sense of what English might be
in the classroom?

The way English has been taught in schools is a piecemeal of
scientific and Romantic beliefs. The discipline is broken down
into areas of skill within which students can develop, with
objective-sounding assessment criteria to capture students'
progression. Conversely, we are interested in developing
students' personal growth and empathetic responses to the
texts they read. Creativity and empathy are to be assessed
scientifically; students are expected to write about linguistic
and structural devices but we are largely uninterested in
their feelings about writers and texts. In trying to accommodate both extremes of a dichotomy we have instead opted for
dismal compromise.

That said, an epistemology of English does need to strike
a balance between, on the one hand, 'technical and positive
information,' and on the other, 'taste and sympathy.' This is
no easy task, but examining some of the ways knowledge
can be categorised and considered might help us find a way
forward.

Substantive and disciplinary knowledge

Substantive knowledge is the agreed upon facts within a discipline, its substance. For English, knowledge of literary texts and traditions is substantive, as is the specialised vocabulary used to discuss features of these texts. The historical development of the language, its grammar and its various forms are all substantive, as are the claims made about literature and language by literary critics and language theorists. Some elements may be subject to criticism or scholarly debate (for instance the teaching of grammar and reading have long been ideological battlegrounds, and the concept of a literary canon is very much up for debate) but such substantive knowledge tends to be produced either by those working within the academic discipline, or by those who have made, or are making, a living from writing. So, literature itself is substantive – the plays of Miller, the poetry of Wordsworth, the novels of Dickens – but so are the works of literary scholarship that surround literature; literary biography, criticism and theory all enable us to think in new ways about language and literature.

One of the difficulties for English teachers – certainly as compared to teachers of science or mathematics – is that there is surprisingly little substantive knowledge which we agree *must* be taught. Shakespeare's plays are about as close as we get and most English teachers, whatever their personal misgivings, will, reluctantly or otherwise, accept that students have to encounter at least one from a fairly short list of plays. Beyond Shakespeare, any convergence tends to be due to the pressures of exam specifications. Today all students are studying *A Christmas Carol* or *Jekyll and Hyde,* yesterday it was *Of Mice and Men,* when I was a lad it was *A Kestrel for a Knave.* The staples of poetry anthologies move on too: once it was Hughes and Harrison, now it's Duffy and Dharker. Where once students routinely studied Milton and Chaucer, they now read J.B. Priestley and Willy Russell. The choice demanded by exam boards, especially at GCSE, seems to inspire a race to the bottom for the simplest, shortest texts possible. Whilst this is an understandable response to perverse incentives, it's perhaps not the best way to arrive at a consensus of what represents substantive knowledge in literature.

With language, substantive knowledge is possibly a *little* easier to pin down and includes spelling, vocabulary, grammar, the evolution and etymology of English, rhetorical figures, non-fiction genres, ideas about character, plot,

> ## ETYMOLOGY
>
> Greek: *etymologia* 'study of the true sense' from *etymon*, 'original meaning' + *-logia* 'study of.'
>
> Study of the origin of words.

theme, structure and form. But for every English teacher who espouses an item on this short list there will probably be another happy to condemn it.

Disciplinary knowledge, in contrast, is that which is used to analyse existing substantive knowledge and create new knowledge. It's a toolkit of ideas and approaches with which students can ask questions of the claims made by others and frame their own responses to the substantive knowledge they encounter. In a subject so potentially infinite in its scope as English, disciplinary knowledge – the tools of enquiry – is the mechanism by which students come to appreciate that although they are studying *this*, they could equally be following very similar lines of enquiry were they studying *that*.

As we saw in the previous chapter, English is not (or at least, not necessarily) a 'skills-based' subject. The supposedly transferable skills that are so often the object of English teaching – inference, analysis, evaluation – are not the same as disciplinary knowledge. For the student of English, such disciplinary knowledge includes how to construct a critical response and peruse a line of argument; how to incorporate contextual detail; how to analyse the use of structural and linguistic devices; how to use textual evidence to support an argument; how to express and connect ideas persuasively; how to manipulate readers' responses, and so on. We will discuss two disciplinary approaches to making meaning in English in the following chapter.

Propositional and procedural knowledge

Propositional knowledge is that which can be recalled and considered, whereas procedural knowledge (knowledge of how to perform procedures) is what we usually call skill. There's clearly some overlap between propositional and substantive knowledge, just as there is between disciplinary and procedural knowledge, but are they just different ways of saying the same things?

A proposition might be either substantive or disciplinary. For instance, it's clearly factual to say 'Gradgrind was a fictional character that Dickens invented as a caricature of what was doubtless some fairly awful teaching in Victorian England.' Likewise, it's factual to say that an argument will be strengthened by the inclusion of supporting textual detail. But neither of these are quite the timeless, immutable truths Aristotle had in mind when he developed his ideas of episteme. Propositions don't have to be justified, true or believed (although it's helpful if they are), they just have to be statements that can be brought to mind and ruminated upon.

Similarly, the disciplinary knowledge of how to write a critical essay is closely linked to the skill of being able to write such essays, but it is *not the same*. One must precede the other. The knowledge of how to write critical essays is made up of lots of smaller items of disciplinary knowledge (making thesis statements, incorporating quotations, conventions about using writers' names, the knowledge of specialist terminology as well as the substantive, propositional knowledge of what the essays will be about). As we've seen, when this disciplinary knowledge is practised on a wide enough range of substantive or propositional knowledge, it becomes skill. The more essays we write, the more skilled we become at writing essays, just as the more lines of iambic pentameter we write, the more skilled we become at writing lines of iambic pentameter. To reiterate, for procedural knowledge to become skill, it must be practised. If practice continues beyond being able to perform an action to the point where we can no longer *not* perform that action, we have become fluent.

Tacit knowledge

The difficulty English teachers often have is that once fluency has been acquired, it's very difficult to separate all that propositional and procedural knowledge to be able to see clearly what we had to learn to get where we are now. This 'expertise induced blindness' can make it seem reasonable to attempt teaching students to acquire skills without providing the underlying propositional and procedural knowledge they need to do what we can do. The more skilled we become, the more we rely on tacit knowledge. We 'just know' what to do when reading and writing and so assume this knowledge is simply the result of practice: read more, write more and you too can do what I do. In Michael Polayni's words, "We know more than we can tell."[5] But as we've seen, if we practise the wrong things we get better at doing them badly. Expertise induced blindness is a curse. We begin to systematically overestimate what others already know and pitch our explanations over students' heads.

There's a delightful psychological experiment that illustrates this 'curse of knowledge' beautifully. Volunteers are randomly divided into two groups to recreate a game you may have played yourself. One group is designated as experts. They are given a list of popular songs and told they will tap out the rhythms of these songs for a partner to guess. The second group are novices. They have no access to the list and must listen to the rhythm of their partners' taps to guess the song being communicated. If you've tried this yourself you'll know how hard it is. Unsurprisingly, the 'listeners' did poorly, correctly guessing an average of three out of 120 songs. What was most interesting about this study was that the 'tappers' guessed their partners had got 50% right. A massive overestimation. To understand this mismatch, try tapping out a song you know well; as you do so you'll hear the song's melody in your mind's ear. The rhythm you tap out will feel so obvious that it becomes hard to imagine anyone failing to guess it. But if all you get to hear are taps, it's far from obvious. In fact, it can be almost impossible: Tchaikovsky's *1812 Overture* can sound pretty similar to The Rolling Stone's 'Satisfaction.' Tappers possess 'expert' knowledge of which listeners are ignorant.[6]

This is the same for teachers. We confidently tap out the rhythms of what we know well only for our novice students to stare at us blankly, desperately trying to guess what we might mean. Not only do our students not know what we know, they may not even understand the words on which our explanations depend. How then can we communicate our tacit understandings of English? By breaking it down into easy to understand chunks.

Chunking procedures

When we attempt to 'chunk' our tacit knowledge it loses most of its vibrancy and elegance. We may feel that we're teaching

An epistemology of English

students something that 'feels wrong,' but we should trust that we too once saw the world in disparate, disconnected parts. The advantage of these chunks is that they become propositions and procedures that can be discussed, practised and learned. The PEE paragraph is an attempt to chunk the style of literary criticism into something learnable: first we make a point about the text we're discussing, then we provide textual evidence to support this point, before explaining why this evidence makes our point. Neat, easy to understand and *nothing whatever like actual literary criticism.* If students only practise this, they're unlikely to acquire our tacit skill. We can see how the propositions of point, evidence and explanation are turned into a practicable procedure, but how do we return this into something approximating well-written critical style?

The grammarian William Strunk advised that "vigorous writing," should be "concise."

> A sentence should contain no unnecessary words, a paragraph no unnecessary sentences, for the same reason that a drawing should have no unnecessary lines and a machine no unnecessary parts. This requires not that the writer make all his sentences short, or that he should avoid all detail and treat his subjects only in outline, but that every word tell.[7]

In all the time we spend teaching students to write academic essays, do we ever show them to make every word 'tell'? The scaffolds we employ contain stock phrases which students use as glue to hold their thoughts in place and provide their work with structure. But, more often than not, the phrases become redundant; students continue to use them long after their usefulness has been exhausted. Consider such gems as 'The first point I am making is ...' or 'The writer is using the phrase ... because ...'. These might be initially helpful,

81

but quickly become a constraint. In our efforts to return the implicit into students' writing, we need to show them how to remove the redundant chunks.

Consider this extract from a student's essay on *Julius Caesar*:

> Act 3 scene 2 is important because Brutus lets Antony speak to the people of Rome which is the turning point of the play. Antony makes what could be the best persuasive speech in English literature. It fits into the play because before Antony's speech Cassius tricks Brutus into joining the conspiracy to kill Caesar. Brutus then lets Antony speak at Caesar's funeral because he trusts him: 'I know that we shall have him well to friend'. This shows that Brutus is wrong to trust Antony because he turns the people of Rome to his side and gets them to riot. Antony says, 'Cry havoc! And let slip the dogs of war'. This shows that he is deliberately making the people riot.

The bones of PEE are jarringly visible: both the writing and the writer appear less impressive than they might. To improve it we need to excise anything that isn't absolutely essential to the meaning of the paragraph:

> ~~Act 3 scene 2 is important because~~ Brutus lets Antony speak to the people of Rome ~~which is~~ the turning point of the play. ~~Antony makes what could be the best persuasive speech in English literature. It fits into the play because~~ before Antony's speech Cassius tricks Brutus into joining the conspiracy to kill Caesar. Brutus then lets Antony speak at Caesar's funeral because he trusts him: 'I know that we shall have him well to friend.' ~~This shows that~~ Brutus is wrong to trust Antony ~~because~~ he turns the people of Rome to his side and gets them to riot. Antony says, 'Cry havoc! And let slip the dogs of war.' ~~This shows that~~ he is deliberately making the people riot.

But *just* getting rid of these stock phrases means the paragraph no longer makes sense. It now requires redrafting.

> The turning point of the play comes when Brutus lets Antony speak to the people of Rome. Earlier in the play, Cassius tricks Brutus into joining the conspiracy to kill Caesar, but Brutus also trusts Antony: 'I know that we shall have him well to friend.' Brutus is wrong about both Cassius and Antony. The line 'Cry havoc! And let slip the dogs of war' shows that Antony wants revenge and intends to turn the people of Rome to his side and get them to riot.

This last example is far from perfect but it's more economical and expresses the writer's thoughts with more sophistication. Fewer words, but more that 'tell.' When students are encouraged to black out their own scaffolding, the acres of black space help them see just how much of what they write is unnecessary.

Going through this sort of procedure – making the implicit explicit and then back to implicit – helps students acquire the kind of tacit knowledge needed to make meaning with confidence and sophistication.

Powerful knowledge

While we can make a case that 'all knowledge is precious,' it's not all equally precious. The problem with Matthew Arnold's urge that we should teach 'the best that has been thought and known' is that there's little direction provided for determining what is the 'best.' The assumption is that this is a given, and not the outcome of social forces and debates within disciplines. The sociologist Michael Young has advanced the idea of a 'social realist' view of knowledge as a means of making decisions about what to include in a school curriculum. Social realism suggests that some knowledge has more power than

An epistemology of English

other knowledge and that access to 'powerful knowledge' should be an entitlement for all children.

Knowledge is considered powerful if it:

- provides reliable explanations, a sound basis for making judgements and generalisations about the world beyond the narrow limits of experience
- is developed systematically by specialists within subject disciplines
- changes our perceptions, values or understanding
- provides a language for engaging in political, moral and other kinds of debates
- allows us to think the 'unthinkable' and the 'not yet thought.'[8,9]

If knowing something causes you to ask new questions and explore different explanations, then that knowledge is powerful.

But where does English fit in? Does our subject possess knowledge that can make reliable predictions and universal generalisations? Not really. Young argues that the power possessed by the arts permits us to imagine alternatives which, while not representing the kind of reliable generalisations offered by the sciences, "may be universal in the sense of connecting people to a larger humanity."[10] Although knowledge in English is different to that of the sciences it is still able to transcend its origins in particular social contexts. Our focus of study is on our subjective perceptions of human experience; in reading and writing we make claims about specific forms and particular texts. Young says,

> There are good reasons why we still want young people to read Jane Austen's novels, which are not weakened by the narrow community that she wrote about. Her novels are

84

situated in time and context, but they are also timeless in the moral and relationship issues that they explore.[11]

English in schools is certainly shaped by specialists, for better or worse, and it can most definitely change the way we see and understand the world. For instance, the aesthetic knowledge of literature allows us to make more informed judgements on matters of taste. We hope the study of English can provide a set of cognitive tools that may, in time, allow some of our students to move beyond the knowledge of literature and language in the past and present to take the next steps in shaping the possibilities of the future.

English also relies on a specialised language for discussing the subject that is crucial in school but which might be out of place at home. Young sees this distinction between 'school knowledge' and 'everyday knowledge' as important. Everyday knowledge is very useful in navigating the familiar landscape of our day-to-day experiences, but it's less useful at school. Likewise, school knowledge may be really useful in English lessons but of little use in working out what to do when confronted by a tearful friend or an irate shopkeeper. Everyday knowledge is dependent on the context in which it was learned, whereas school knowledge – powerful knowledge – can help us move beyond the confines of our personal experiences and open up new ways of thinking about aspects of the world which would otherwise be unknown and inaccessible.

A common misconception is that for knowledge to be powerful it must be widely shared and used. But knowledge isn't powerful because we use it a lot or because it's commonly discussed, but because it transforms our conceptual understanding of the world. Powerful knowledge invites us to consider what has the greatest potential to explain the world and provide new ways for thinking about it. Specific examples of powerful knowledge in English are discussed in Chapter 11.

Ways of making meaning in English

Most of the problems in English stem from lack of knowledge. Too often, English teachers (and I include myself) don't know enough to teach aspects of the subject in ways that make sense to students. One glaring instance of this is the thorny issue of grammar. Because almost all grammar teaching disappeared from the 1970s onwards, English teachers today have largely managed to muddle through without knowing much. It may be possible to teach something you have only rudimentary knowledge of, but it's hard to teach it well. Metre is also poorly taught. Many English teachers are unsure of what a metrical foot might be (although all are able to confidently point out – often incorrectly – that Shakespeare writes in iambic pentameter). As a result, students are rarely able to do anything other than feature spot when it comes to aspects of metre because they've never learned about the different choices available to writers and why they may have decided on *this* rather than *that*. If our students don't know enough to make meaning in English then it's possible that neither do we their teachers.

So, what *do* students need to know to make meaning in English? Although there's little agreement within the field, I suggest there are perhaps six overlapping but distinct areas which are central to the study of language and literature. I've chosen to call these disciplinary ways of knowing metaphor, story, argument, pattern, grammar and context. They each offer a different conceptual lens through which literature and language can be viewed. When combined with the substantive knowledge of the subject, these disciplinary lenses enable students to make meaning in English. Each is discussed at length in the following chapters, but here's a brief explanation:

- *Metaphor*: Our direct experience is of the concrete, tangible world. In order to think about abstract ideas, we draw comparisons between what we have directly experienced and what we cannot. This figurative way of seeing permeates the way we think as much as it does language and literature.
- *Pattern*: Everything around us is composed of rhythms of similarity and difference, discord and harmony, variation and repetition. In perceiving these patterns, we turn chaos into order. This body of knowledge deals with the various ways we use structure to impose meaning on texts.
- *Story*: In order to make sense of our experiences we tell stories. Stories and storytelling have evolved with us as a primary means of describing the world. By examining how storytelling developed from its origins in myth and legend to its modern bewildering array of forms and expressions, students learn to appreciate their place in a conversation that has been unfolding throughout history.
- *Argument*: In order to communicate, discuss and persuade with clarity and force we require formal structures of thought and expression. By analysing the ways arguments are structured and made persuasive, we can start to take part in shaping the world in a more deliberate way.
- *Grammar*: Our instinct for rapidly acquiring grammatical knowledge in order to impose meaning and order on the words we use appears to be innate, but an ability to notice, understand and play with grammatical structures requires learning a new language about language.
- *Context*: The more students know of the broad sweep of literature, the better they can interpret any individual text. If they have some idea of what a writer has read, what concerns they are responding to, how the assumptions they would have taken for granted would have been very different from our own, then their judgement is better informed, more refined.

Each of these areas of knowledge deals with the idea that the object of study in English is both what is displayed and its means of display: the frame and what is framed. Metaphor and pattern (and therefore grammar which is a subcategory of pattern) are the modes of thought most concerned with 'framing' reality in ways we think of as literary or linguistic. Story and argument are more concerned with filling these frames, providing the content of literature and language. The content without the frame is either random or naïve; the frame without the content is unsatisfying or solipsistic. Only by combining content and frames do we arrive at the substantive knowledge of our subject, what Polanyi called "objects of the imagination."[12]

Whilst each of these epistemic lenses has distinct characteristics, the boundaries between them are blurred. Metaphor, for instance, is an important element of story-telling; metaphorical figures are an essential part of the art of argument and metaphors are both composed of linguistic patterns and create patterns. Story and argument are mutually dependent: stories contain arguments and arguments are expressed through stories. Grammar is a subset of pattern, concerned as it is with making patterns with syntax and morphology. Grammar is also intimately connected with both story and argument. And, of course, both stories and arguments follow predictable patterns. But, despite this blurring, each of these areas supplies us with a different way to think about and make meaning with language and literature.

It should be made clear that none of these epistemological angles presupposes anything about the activity of 'doing' English. However, it stands to reason that students will come to understand and, hopefully, master English, through the mediums of reading the work of others, writing their own critical and creative responses, and through discussion, dialogue and debate.

KEY POINTS

- Knowledge is far more than just facts: it includes experience, emotions, the know how to perform actions, and wisdom.
- There is a tension in English between knowledge that can be assessed and measured and taste, judgement and aesthetic appreciation.
- There is little clarity about the substantive knowledge of English, especially in literature.
- Disciplinary knowledge, propositional knowledge and skill are all closely related. It might be more useful to think of this as 'know-how.'
- Procedural knowledge is often tacit – it can be pointed out during practice but not explained directly. The best way to acquire it is through guided practice.
- Powerful knowledge is that which gives us the ability to ask new questions, make explanations and think new thoughts.
- Culturally rich knowledge is that which is shared amongst the widest number of people.
- In English there are, perhaps, several distinct ways of knowing: metaphor, story, argument, pattern, grammar and context.

What I hope to show in the following chapters is that, woven together, these disparate strands can be spun into a broad cloth from which an English curriculum can be cut and stitched. Together they offer the potential of a progression model in which the mastery of English can be planned, taught and assessed, but first we need to explore the disciplinary practices of noticing and analogising.

Further reading

The following texts, all written by different Michaels, are fairly dense but if you can persevere they're well worth the effort:

- Michael Oakeshott, *The Voice of Liberal Learning*
- Michel Polanyi, *Meaning*
- Michael Young and Johan Muller, *Curriculum and the Specialization of Knowledge*

4 Noticing and analogising

If students' experience of English is to proceed beyond the most superficial, they need some ownership of the disciplinary tools with which meaning is made. The view of English to which I subscribe is beautifully expressed by the philosopher, Michael Oakeshott:

> ... languages recognized, not as the means of contemporary communication but as investments in thought and records of perceptions and analogical understandings; literatures recognized as the contemplative exploration of beliefs, emotions, human characters and relationships in imagined situations, liberated from the confused, cliché ridden, generalized conditions of commonplace life and constituting a world of ideal human expressions inviting neither approval nor disapproval but the exact attention and understanding of those who read ...[1]

Oakeshott's view of English as requiring 'exact attention' and 'analogical understandings' provides a way through the thicket of

ANALOGY

Greek: *analogia* 'proportion,' from *ana* 'upon, according to'+ *logos* 'ratio,' also 'word, speech, reckoning.'

A thing which is comparable to something else.

exam technique and assessment objectives that blight much of what the study of English has become. By exploring language as a 'record of perception' and an 'investment in thought,' and in contemplating literature as the imagined story of humanity in all its aspects, students can begin to amass the tools to hew meaning from the edifice of words with which they are confronted. The study of English requires that we pay attention in particular, specialised ways and, once we have learned to focus, to be able to experience new insights through seeing that what we are attending to is connected to things we have experienced previously. From here on I will refer to these aspects of disciplinary knowledge as *noticing* and *analogising*.

Noticing

By 'noticing' I mean reading and writing whilst being attuned to the choices and effects of everything that language has to offer: punctuation, sounds, diction, syntax, patterns of form, imagery and the ways each of these combine to make narratives and arguments. If we read or write without awareness of the effects of language we are doing so naïvely. If we're not noticing, we're likely to see the writer's choices as merely coincidental and view our own efforts at writing as the product of happy, or unhappy, chance. But if we notice as we read and write then we're alive to possibilities, able to make informed choices and consider multiple interpretations.

Our ability to pay attention is strictly limited. We can see metaphor alive in the phrasing: attention is the currency we 'pay' in order to 'purchase' new information and insight. As a scarce resource we cannot attend to everything; as William James, the grandfather of psychology, observed, attention "implies withdrawal from some things in order to deal effect-ively with others."[2]

In order to survive, our ancestors needed to solve a par-ticular problem: how to focus on finding the resources needed to survive – gathering roots and berries; searching for signs of prey – whilst simultaneously staying alert for threats and opportunities. Our brains appear to be arranged to enable us to focus on details whilst at the same time remaining aware of our surroundings.[3] But, whilst this is possible, these two kinds of attention – the narrow focus on detail and the broad awareness of the environment – provide mutually incompat-ible data. The more closely we examine a tree, the less aware we become of the woods; the more we stand back to survey the woods, the harder it becomes to focus on individual trees.

Close attention on what we already know enables us to see vital details, but standing back provides us with a vantage to survey the unknown, allowing us, as Iain McGilchrist puts it, to:

> ... see the world as separate from ourselves as something we can *use*, or as quite the opposite – as connected to our-selves more deeply: we can see others, for the first time, as beings like ourselves, the ground of empathy.[4]

By focussing we are able to explain the world around us, by standing back, we become open to intuitions and insights. Michael Polanyi explains that our ability to focus makes use of what he terms 'subsidiary attention.' Essentially, although attention implies a withdrawal of focus from one set of things in order to concentrate on another, we nevertheless retain our subsidiary senses. So, for instance, if you were probing a tooth for a morsel of trapped food most of your attention would be on the food but you would retain the subsidiary awareness of your tongue. If you were to switch focus onto your tongue you would become less aware of the food morsel's presence.

Noticing and analogising

When we read or write, we usually focus all our attention on meaning, but then we might notice a particularly interesting turn of phrase (or we might become confused) and our attention switches to focus on the subsidiarity of the texture of sounds/letters/syntax to resolve the difficulty, or enjoy the sensation, before we switch back to the text as a whole.[5]

When confronted with something unfamiliar our instinct is often to shut down and back away. If we can't perceive a 'way in' then we're likely to assume that this is 'not for me.' When students try to make sense of, say, a Shakespeare play, their attention is directed at its unfamiliarity. They focus on what they don't know and struggle to find points of reference. Similarly, poetry often presents an impenetrable façade but when we hear it read aloud – and when we see Shakespeare performed – we become better able to focus on meaning and shift the difficulties of the text into the background.

In order to explain or 'make sense' of something we must direct our focussed attention on to it. What we perceive with our subsidiary senses – what's in the background – is known tacitly. As Polanyi puts it, this kind of perception "constitutes an observation of external facts without recourse to formal argument."[6] We may notice something but be unable to explain it. This tacit understanding can feel intuitive; insights feel mysterious *because* we're unable to explain them but are really just the emergence of half-remembered fragments from the undistilled depths of memory. The act of noticing can – sometimes – trigger a subsidiary awareness of 'unknown knowns' in long-term memory without conscious retrieval. This flash of insight causes us to take in the detail *and* perceive the whole, but we can only explain our insight by losing sight of the whole to focus again on the detail.

This openness to insight caused by noticing the relationship between the whole and its parts is akin to the state John Keats called 'negative capability': a state in which "a man is capable of being in uncertainties, Mysteries, doubts, without any irritable reaching after fact and reason."[7] As R.S. Thomas wrote, "poetry [and in this we'll include all literature] is that which arrives at the intellect by way of the heart."[8]

The key is, perhaps, to help students pay attention to insight, to help them notice the qualities of words and ideas without worrying about whether they 'get it,' or reaching after the facts and certainties needed to pin down and explain their thoughts. These things should come, but we can help students defer the need to switch back to that close attention to detail which precludes them from the tacit experience – the uncertainties, mysteries and doubts – of the whole.

In 'The American Scholar', Emerson discusses what he refers to as 'creative reading.' He says,

> When the mind is braced by labor and invention, the page of whatever book we read becomes luminous with manifold allusion. Every sentence is doubly significant, and the sense of our author is as broad as the world. We then see, what is always true, that as the seer's hour of vision is short and rare among heavy days and months, so is its record, perchance, the least part of his volume. The discerning will read, in his Plato or Shakespeare, only that least part,—only the authentic utterances of the oracle;— all the rest he rejects, were it never so many times Plato's and Shakespeare's.[9]

In order to practise noticing, students (and teachers) should get into the habit of annotating as they read. As Andrew Bennett and Nicholas Royle say, if you don't annotate as you read, "you will forget what it was you found interesting or funny or sad or perplexing, and you won't be able to find those particularly exciting, enticing, intriguing passages or moments again so easily. You may think you will, but you won't."[10] I can attest to the truth of this observation.

Noticing and analogising

Teachers, as relatively expert readers, can find it difficult to give explicit instruction to novice literary readers
on *how* or *what* to notice. Sometimes, the best we can do is to
explicitly model the process and articulate why we are paying
attention to particular aspects of texts. Helpfully, Bennett and
Royle augment this general advice with some suggestions
as to what novice students of literature ought to be looking
out for:

- striking phrases, arresting metaphors, unusual wordings;
- significant events or changes in the direction of the
  narrative;
- the recurrence of a motif, topic or figures that intrigue you
  (flowers, say, or telephones, or moments of humour);
- moments of self-reflexivity – moments where a text seems
  to be referring to itself, for example where a poem says
  something about the poem you are reading or about poetry
  or language more generally;
- significant alterations in narrative perspective (you might,
  for example, mark places where you feel that the voice of a
  narrator falters or shifts, perhaps by feigning not to know
  something, or by moving suddenly into the point of view
  of one or other of the characters);
- significant alterations in temporal perspective (you might
  mark a flashback or analepsis, a flashforward or prolepsis,
  the incursion of a scene of memory or the past in the midst
  of the present, and so on).[11]

These strike me as very useful pointers (and, coincidentally,
very much in line with the kind of close reading required for
exam success).

Noticing can be directed towards any aspect of a text, but
it is felt in the meaning we make as individual readers and
writers. This is in danger of sounding too otherworldly to

fit into the curriculum but the meaning we make is always a product of what we *know*. We can help students cultivate a feel for noticing by guiding their attention and carefully adding to their knowledge *just at the point that they need it most*, allowing them to arrive at an analogical understanding.*

Analogising

The judicious application of analogies and allusions – analogising – requires that we know as much as possible. The more we know – and, in particular, the more we know about language and literature – the better able we are to recognise that *this* piece of knowledge fits *just there*, or that the word, image or structural device over which we're currently poised reminds us of something we've seen elsewhere. This knowledge is not always literary. When Julia is first introduced in Orwell's *1984*, we're told, "Winston disliked her from the very first moment of seeing her. … He disliked nearly all women, and especially the young pretty ones." On reading this a student who happened to be an aficionado of the 60s rock band The Doors said this reminded her of the line from 'People Are Strange,' that refers to women seeming wicked if you're not wanted. This is precisely how we use analogies to make meaning.

The literary critic and professor of English, I.A. Richards once said, "All thinking from the lowest to the highest – whatever else it may be – is sorting."[12] Meaning in English is built up by analogies with all we have read and experienced. The broader our literary knowledge, the more attuned we are to intertextual references, the conversations between texts. The more our students know of literary texts and their history

---

* For instance, if I wanted students to notice the quality of sounds a writer uses I would remind them of the associations and effects of different consonants. (See page 222.)

and traditions, the greater their facility for comparing what they are studying now with everything else they have read. Developing literary knowledge helps students to hone a sense of connoisseurship with which they can move from naïve responses to the exercise of taste and the stating of educated opinions. Without it, students are limited to the most basic and banal of ideas.

So, all thought is concerned with finding analogies between concepts and categories. Words point to meanings, to categories we hold in mind, and we find our way in the world by seeing connections, overlaps between one category and another. A dictionary definition merely grazes the surface of these meanings; most of what we know is tacit. We 'just know' what we mean when we point to a dog, or a pencil, or a poem. Strictly defining these categories may seem superficially satisfying but there are inevitably blurred boundaries between, for instance, what is and is not a dog. Is a picture of a dog a dog? Is a dead dog still a dog? If we hear barking are we hearing a dog? What about a recording of a dog's bark? And this becomes much more difficult when trying to pin down the essence of something less precise: what is and is not a poem? Should it rhyme? Contain metaphorical language? Does it have to 'look like' a poem? Is a song a poem?

Thinking about language – as with thinking about anything – is about placing new information within existing categories or recognising layers of abstraction and placing more concrete ideas into more abstract 'boxes.' Consider this:

> My mistress' eyes are nothing like the sun;
> Coral is far more red than her lips' red;
> If snow be white, why then her breasts are dun;
> If hairs be wires, black wires grow on her head.
> I have seen roses damask'd, red and white,
> But no such roses see I in her cheeks;

And in some perfumes is there more delight
Than in the breath that from my mistress reeks.
I love to hear her speak, yet well I know
That music hath a far more pleasing sound;
I grant I never saw a goddess go;
My mistress, when she walks, treads on the ground:
And yet, by heaven, I think my love as rare
As any she belied with false compare.

We might read this and place it into the category 'poem,' or we might recognise that it's a sonnet, a type of poem, and categorise it accordingly. We might place it into the category of 'rhyming poem,' or 'love poem,' or 'old-fashioned poem.' But to do any of these things we must have something to compare it *to*; there needs to be a pre-existing category that meshes with the features we have spotted. Depending on the sophistication of the categories we possess, something else might happen. We might notice that the poet is being a bit rude about the object of his affections ("her breasts are dun"; "black wires grow on her head"; her breath "reeks"*). It doesn't fit tidily into the category of 'love poem.' If we're familiar with Shakespeare's sonnet sequence we might recognise this as 'Sonnet 130,' and, if we have the category 'Elizabethan love sonnet' fairly well fleshed out with examples from Wyatt, Sidney and Spenser – as well as other examples from Shakespeare – we might be able to draw the conclusion that *this* – despite many superficial similarities – is not exactly like *that*. We might decide that this poem's essence is different and label it accordingly. We might conclude from the final couplet that Shakespeare is commenting on the entire tradition of the love sonnet – that sonnets falsely compare their subjects and therefore being

---

* Not quite as rude as you might think. In Elizabethan English 'reeks' meant 'smokes.'

blunt and honest in writing is a more trustworthy way of conveying emotion. Maybe it's a more sophisticated example of the category, or maybe it deserves to be labelled as 'satire.' Either way, two things are true:

1. Thinking is allegorical and new ideas arrive via comparisons with existing ones, and;
2. You need a firm foundation of relevant categories to see anything beyond the most superficial.[13]

Noticing and analogising in practice

These two processes, noticing and analogising, are the cornerstones of being able to make meaning with literature and language. For a masterclass I recommend Terry Eagleton's *How to Read Literature*. At one point, Eagleton dissects the first sentence of E.M. Forster's critique of British imperialism, *A Passage to India*:

> Except for the Marabar Caves – and they are twenty miles off – the city of Chandrapore presents nothing extraordinary.

He notes that the novel sidles into being with a throwaway qualification, rather than a trumpet fanfare. Restructuring the sentence as 'The city of Chandrapore presents nothing extra-ordinary, except for the Marabar Caves, and they are twenty miles off,' would be ungraceful and spoil the syntactic elegance, but more importantly the meaning would subtly shift.

As it stands, the reader has to work through two subordinate clauses before confronting the sentence's subject, 'the city of Chandrapore.' This raises our expectations only to dash them against the rocks of anti-climax as there is 'nothing extraordinary' about the city. The only remarkable thing is the Caves, and they're not even in the city. The syntax downplays their importance, but, as readers of the novel will know, the Caves are where the central action takes place (or, more precisely, where it *may* have taken place). The sentence then is a microcosm of the ambiguity at the heart of the novel: the centrality of the Caves is asserted and then denied.

Eagleton points out that the first three phrases of this sentence are "almost metrical," and that they can be read as lines of verse, each with three stresses:

Except for the Marabar Caves

And they are twenty miles off

The city of Chandrapore

Presents nothing extraordinary.

Pointing out the stress patterns created by the sentence concentrates us on the artistry of Forster's prose. Forster himself may, or may not, have been aware of this pleasing pattern, but that matters little. What we see, as readers, is that the sentence gives the narrative a coolly aloof, dismissive tone, like that of a "rather snooty guidebook." But a disdainful tone is, perhaps, at odds with what we know about the author – Forster was anything but disdainful of India and Indians – so this suggests that the narrator, although given the authority of a disembodied third person voice, is not the same 'character' as Forster himself.[14]

The sheer quantity that one has to *know* to notice these details and make these analogies – knowledge of both grammar and metre, the textual and contextual knowledge of Forster's novel, theories of narrative, not to mention the disciplinary knowledge of literary criticism – is vast. This merely scratches the surface of what Eagleton knows but it would be quite beyond school students and may well defeat their teachers.

Grasping the world and changing it

Teachers can guide students' attention to notice particular aspects of a text and build up the pool of available analogies by introducing just the right knowledge at just the point where it will be most useful to make links and connections, but we also have to stand back and turn students' attention from the parts to the whole. Our awareness of the components – metaphor, story, argument, pattern, grammar, context – must fade into the background in order to make meaning.

We guide our students' attention to what we hope they will find meaningful, but if the act of guiding becomes the focus, then students will struggle to see what we want them to see. If I point my finger, students will look at what I'm pointing at, but if I wave my finger around ostentatiously it becomes the focus of attention. The act of *teaching the content we want students to learn* is the pointing finger; what we point *at* is meaning. The content – the curriculum – is not an inert block of knowledge to be consumed, rather it is something from which we 'make sense.' What we *know* determines what this sense will be.

Noticing and analogising are not just ways to grasp the world, they also change it. What we notice comes alive. For us to inspect the parts we must first see the whole. As Wordsworth warns, in spreading out the component parts of a poem to admire its tricks and techniques, we lose the ability to feel its beating heart. This is certainly a danger, but only if we dissect too soon. First, we must appreciate the whole, to let our attention dapple a text, to contemplate its power and beauty and delight in the images we find.

In Richard Feynman's famous monologue, 'Ode to a Flower,' an artist friend holds up a flower and says, "I as an artist can see how beautiful this is but you as a scientist take this all apart and it becomes a dull thing." Feynman responds that as a scientist he is able to appreciate more:

> I could imagine the cells in there, the complicated actions inside, which also have a beauty. I mean it's not just beauty at this dimension, at one centimeter; there's also beauty at smaller dimensions, the inner structure, also the processes. The fact that the colors in the flower evolved in order to attract insects to pollinate it is interesting; it means that insects can see the color. It adds a question: does this aesthetic sense also exist in the lower forms? Why is it aesthetic? All kinds of interesting questions which the science knowledge only adds to the excitement, the mystery and the awe of a flower. It only adds. I don't understand how it subtracts.[15]

Students often overthink comparisons and contrasts and end up with something clunky and grating; they labour to find the seams of their ideas, then stitch them clumsily together. But the more they know, the more they bathe in literature and language, the more instinctively they'll see the links that underlie everything they read and write. The best of these realisations come in flashes which then have to be artfully reconstructed as we work out just why *this* reminded us of *that*. The knowledge of how to notice and analogise gives us the tools to see the mystery and awe inside.

Literature relies on the implicit, the tacit, for much of its power to speak to us. A writer, fired with ideas, does not necessarily weigh every word; sometimes they 'just know' what's exactly right. In reading over what they have written they may well polish and correct, but skilled writing is a groove that can be more easily slipped into if we have the habit of careful reading. Reading teaches us how to write, but it does so implicitly. Very often these lessons must be made explicit for us to learn them. Holding together our ability to notice – to appreciate the whole as well as notice the parts – with our tendency to drift and keep one eye on all else we've read is how meaning is made in English. In the words of the art historian H.W. Janson, "it is a game of find-and-seek in which the seeker is not sure what he is looking for until he has found it."[16]

KEY POINTS

- To make meaning in English students need to know how to pay attention so that they *notice* details as well as their significance.
- Teachers can train students' attention by guiding them to notice what is most pertinent.
- To make meaning, students also need to be able to make judicious analogies between what they are attending to and what they have experienced before.
- Teachers can kickstart the process of noticing and analogising by supplying the precise information students need at the point they need it.
- Noticing and analogising can result in insight which can be almost impossible to explain. Students should be encouraged to feel their way into a text and not to be overly concerned about 'getting it.'
- Explaining insight should be allowed to come later as students become more attuned to noticing details and making links and connections to other knowledge.

Further reading

- Terry Eagleton's book *How to Read Literature* is a very readable example of how noticing and analogising operate at a high level.
- I.A. Richard's *Practical Criticism,* although dated in some ways, provides some excellent examples of how to guide students' attention.
- Iain McGilchrist's book *The Master and His Emissary* is a long read which looks at the effects of noticing and analogising (although he doesn't use these terms) over the history of Western culture. He's also written a much shorter book called *Ways of Attending.*

5 Metaphor

All English teachers are well-versed in the basics of metaphor, but, typically, what gets taught in lessons does little more than scratch the surface of what is a rich and fascinating area of study. The argument made in this chapter is that metaphor is much more than literary imagery; it offers us a particular way of seeing, knowing and making meaning. As the Spanish philosopher and essayist, José Ortega y Gasset put it, "The metaphor is perhaps one of man's most fruitful potentialities. Its efficacy verges on magic, and it seems a tool for creation which God forgot inside one of His creatures when He made him."[1] Metaphor provides a frame through which to see and understand not just our subject but, well, everything.

Whenever we substitute a concrete meaning to shed light on an abstract concept we are thinking in metaphor. ['Shed light' is a good example: no actual light is being employed, but the quality of shining a light on something concrete makes it easier to see that thing.] Similarly, metaphor makes it easier to understand abstraction. Metaphor is a subset of trope, a 'turning away' from

> ## TROPE
>
> Greek: *tropos* 'a turn,' or 'change of direction.'
>
> Metaphorical use of language.

the literal towards the figurative. The literal meaning of metaphor – both in ancient and modern Greek – is to transport.* Metaphorically, meaning is transported from one idea to another. So, when Romeo says, "Juliet is the sun," certain (but by no means all) ideas about the sun are transferred to Juliet. We know that Romeo means that she shines, she puts everything else in the shade, or that her beauty may be too bright to stare at directly. (We also know he's not suggesting she's a giant ball of superheated gas!)

One of the oldest and most common definitions of metaphor is Aristotle's: "metaphor consists in giving something a name that belongs to something else,"[2] but this is to sell the concept short. Gasset went much further, saying that metaphor is a tool we use to alter reality. Anxiety about taboos led primitive peoples to rename what they feared so as not to invite the unwanted attention of jealous gods: "metaphor disposes of an object by having it masquerade as something else."[3] Today, we regularly use euphemisms for similar reasons. According to Gasset's reasoning, if we avoid mentioning death and instead say our loved ones have 'passed away' or 'kicked the bucket' we are, at some level, attempting to forestall the same fate for ourselves.

Aristotle also suggested that metaphors possess, "clarity and sweetness and strangeness."[4] It's sometimes said that metaphor acts to defamiliarise language, to express something in a new or surprising way; it should at once explain something and at the same time be unfamiliar. The pleasure we take in metaphors comes from *noticing* the connection between the known and the unknown. This is what the best metaphors do; when Emily Dickinson wrote, "Hope is the

---

*   There's something rather exquisite about the fact that lorries in modern Greece are still called *metaphores* from *meta* (between or among) and *phoros* (carrying or bearing).

thing with feathers – that perches in the soul," we are both startled by the originality of the image and at the same time we nod and think, *yes, that* is *what hope's like.*

In Gabriel García Márquez's novel *Love in the Time of Cholera,* Dr Urbino complains to his wife about the chamomile tea he has been served, saying,

> "This stuff tastes of window." Both she and the servants were surprised because they had never heard of anyone who had drunk boiled window, but when they tried the tea in an effort to understand, they understood: it did taste of window.

It might seem absurd to suggest tea can taste like window, but sometimes an apt metaphor is the closest we can come to describing something for which we have no words. Nietzsche saw metaphor as a way to glimpse truth. He famously described truth as, "a mobile army of metaphors" that with long use "seem firm, canonical, and obligatory." He warned that truth, like metaphor, can become "worn out and without sensuous power; coins which have lost their pictures and now matter only as metal, no longer as coins."[5] As metaphors lose their "sensuous power," they fade into the background of thought and language, until we can no longer differentiate between what's 'true' and what's metaphorical. As Ralph Waldo Emerson observed, everyday language is strewn with 'dead' metaphors,

> The etymologist finds the deadest word to have been once a brilliant picture. Language is fossil poetry. As the limestone of the continent consists of infinite masses of the shells of animalcules, so language is made up of images, or tropes, which now, in their secondary use, have long ceased to remind us of their poetic origin.[6]

The image of language as 'fossil poetry' is vividly alive, but when we say or hear 'wake up,' 'feeling down,' 'black mood,' 'white hot,' we longer 'turn away' from the literal. We learn these once fresh metaphorical phrases almost as complete units of sense with firmly anchored meanings. The presence of these layers of fossilised metaphor in language means it is almost impossible to communicate anything complex without employing metaphor, although most often we are unaware of so doing. But, as we'll see, some of these 'dead' metaphors are very much alive in the way we think about the world and our place in it.

There is a tension between the way metaphor is conceived in language and in literature. To linguists, metaphor is symbolic and conceptual; it 'infects' the way we think; it is a product not of words but of thought that merely recognises and makes use of natural or conventional correspondences. As Oakeshott says, "Metaphors here are like counters which may carry an attractive design upon their face but it is a design which merely indicates (and does not constitute) their value." In literature, "there is no room for stereotypical images." Literary metaphors are self-contained fictions rather than "coins of fixed value." Instead, their value is a negotiation between a writer and a reader. Conventional, symbolic meanings have to be "'dissolved' before poetry can appear."[7]

If we cast back to the origins of literature in English we find language being put to innovative use to create an array of 'brilliant pictures,' but the way Anglo-Saxons used metaphor feels strikingly different to the way we use it now. In Old English, metaphors – or *kennings* – were created by compounding two or more words together to describe

> **KENNING**
>
> Old Norse: *kenning* 'teaching, mark of recognition,' from *kenna* 'to know, to recognize, to name.'
>
> Anglo-Saxon metaphor compounding two or more words.

something ordinary and commonplace in a way that causes us to experience it differently. The meaning of kennings has to be inferred. Because many kennings are, as far as we know, unique coinages, an imaginative leap is required to interpret them; they *always* dissolve the literal allowing the poetic to emerge. In *Beowulf*, the oldest example of literature in English, blood is "battle-sweat," the sea is a "whale-road" and a king is a "ring-giver." The *Beowulf* poet refers to the eponymous hero's "word-hoard." The first part of the compound, 'word,' clearly refers to language, but the second part, 'hoard,' refers to treasure, or something collected and guarded. This gives the impression that words have power and importance, suggesting much more than mere 'vocabulary.' It's reasonable to suppose that the metaphor *language = currency*, utilised by both Nietzsche and Oakeshott, has its origins in the Anglo-Saxon 'word-hoard.'

What makes a metaphor?

I.A. Richards saw metaphor as "a transaction between contexts."[8] In order to analyse the operations of metaphor he saw the necessity of naming these contexts and proposed the terms 'tenor'

> **TENOR**
>
> Latin: *tenorem* 'a course' or 'direction.' From 13th century: 'general meaning, prevailing course, purpose, drift.'
>
> Subject of a metaphor.

and 'vehicle': the tenor is the subject of the metaphor, the vehicle the source of its imagery.* Without names for the parts

---

* There have been various attempts to replace Richards' terms such as 'metaphier' and 'metaphand.' Those who study conceptual metaphor prefer 'target' and 'source' but these are too prosaic for my taste and turn us away from the richness and strangeness of metaphor.

of metaphor we run the risk of confusing the relationship between tenor and vehicle for the relationship between the whole metaphor and its meaning.

We can also add the concept of 'ground,' the relationship between literal

> **VEHICLE**
>
> Latin: *vehere* 'to bear, carry, convey.'
>
> Image that 'carries' or embodies the tenor of a metaphor.

and metaphorical meanings. Considering tenor, vehicle and ground allows us to explain why a metaphor is (or is not) successful.

- Tenor = the subject of the metaphor and its intended meaning
- Vehicle = the source of the comparison or substitution being made
- Ground = the relationship between the tenor and the vehicle

We can see how this works by analysing the metaphor in Wordsworth's famous poem, 'I wandered lonely as a cloud':

- Tenor = Wordsworth's wanderings
- Vehicle = a cloud
- Ground = just as clouds are randomly blown by the wind, so Wordsworth's wandering is directionless and without intent

By examining the ground of a metaphor, we can work out what qualities of the vehicle are being transferred to the topic. For instance, clouds can be dark and result in rain, but unless otherwise stated we think of them as white and fluffy.

Metaphor

This is the quality that is transferred from the vehicle to the tenor in Wordsworth's metaphor.

Here's a more complex example, this time from *Macbeth*: "I have no spur to prick the sides of my intent, but only vaulting ambition."

- Tenor = Macbeth's ambition to be king
- Vehicle = a spur jabbed into the sides of a horse
- Ground = Macbeth's desire to be king is compared to riding a horse. The only justification for the murder of Duncan is his ambition which is described as a spur to make the horse of his desire go faster.

Sometimes metaphors work despite the disharmony of tenor and vehicle. Although metaphors struggle to work where there is little or no point of similarity, sometimes greater tension is produced by the 'unlikeness' than the 'likeness' of tenor and vehicle. Consider this line from *Othello*: "Steep'd me in poverty to the very lips."

- Tenor = poverty
- Vehicle = the sea, or a vat of liquid
- Ground = poverty, which should be a state of deprivation, is conceived of as being so much in abundance that Othello is at the point of drowning in it. This disharmony underlines Othello's disturbed state of mind as he frets over Desdemona's supposed infidelity.

We shouldn't be able to drown in the lack of something, but Shakespeare's startling combination of unlikenesses captures Othello's predicament and carries us away without being troubled by the 'irritable reaching after certainty' Keats warns us against. Polanyi, articulating how the process of being 'carried away' by metaphor works, said, "those inchoate experiences in our own lives that are related to the two parts of a metaphor are integrated into the meaning of a tenor and a vehicle as they are related to each other in a focal object."[9] The result is that we 'get' the connection. When a metaphor 'works,' tenor and vehicle reinforce each other; meanings are transferred in both directions, enriching each other. In Othello's case, the tenor (his poverty) takes on a liquid, clinging viscosity, while the vehicle (a liquid) becomes an oxymoron that could never quench thirst.

We should always recall that however well we describe the workings of a metaphor, our explanations tend to reduce the sense or surprise, delight and recognition produced by the original. Richards warned that "a metaphor may work admirably without our being able ... to say how it works or what is the ground of the shift."[10] Nevertheless, thinking in terms of topic, vehicle and grounds can be a useful way for students to think about the relationship between the components of a metaphor and will help prompt them to move beyond noticing into more analytic analogising.

Metaphors within words and as words

At the closest magnification, metaphors work at the level of individual words, even at the level of morphemes (the units of meaning from which words are built). Take a word like 'involve.' It comes from the Latin *in* + *volvere* (to roll) so a word we use quite literally to say, for instance, 'reading involves decoding and comprehension,' has a metaphor at work at an etymological level: decoding and comprehension are 'rolled together' to create reading. Or what about 'eradicate'? Its origins are again Latin: the prefix *e* means out, whereas the root comes from *radix* meaning ... root. Combined, they mean 'to tear out by the roots.' Clearly, the word 'root' is metaphorical here – the origin being the literal roots of a plant, but it's fascinating to note that the roots of words have been metaphorical for many thousands of years.

Many words provide similarly interesting origin stories: sully (from the French *soullier*, 'to soil'); sarcasm (from the Greek *sarkazein*, 'to tear the flesh'); poppycock (from Dutch *pappekak*, 'soft dung'); or harbour (from the Old English *here*, 'to occupy' and *beorg*, 'shelter'). If you feel enthusiastic about this sort of metaphorical digging, then the word 'enthuse' is itself an excellent subject: the Greek *en theos* means, literally, 'possessed by a god.' To be filled with enthusiasm is to be in a divine frenzy. Both the definition of enthusiasm and the metaphorical substrata of its etymology make it the fuel of emotional commitment, outward looking enthralment and fascination.[11]

Words seem to regularly travel from the literal to the figurative. Where 'root' has come to mean origin, 'branch' has transferred its meaning from something covered in leaves that sticks out of trees, to smaller subdivisions or categories of a larger whole. Words like root and branch can be said to be *polysemous*; that is, they have at least two senses in which they can be employed, one literal the other metaphorical. Other examples include cream, fossil, stream, float and magnetic. For all these words, their core meanings

> ## POLYSEMY
>
> Greek: *polysemos* 'of many senses,' from *poly-* 'many' + *sema* 'sign.'
>
> Existence of multiple possible meanings for a word.

are concrete and describe an object or observable phenomenon. Their metaphorical meanings have evolved with use. As speakers of English groped about to describe more abstract concepts they used the concrete words they had at hand (cream becomes the best; fossil becomes an old person; stream becomes a steady flow of anything, not just water; float becomes the buoyancy of a new idea; and magnetic becomes any form of attraction).

Some domains seem to provide particularly fertile vehicles for metaphor, 'literally' creating new objects and ideas. For instance, the human body: think of *heads* of steam, *heads* of households or nails; *legs* of voyages and tables; *faces* of clocks or cards; *eyes* of needles and storms; the *foot* of a page; the *tongue* of a shoe; a *body* of literature and so on. These metaphors are so deeply embedded in the way we think and speak that it's hard to remember their figurative origins.

We can even observe the metaphorical at work in the most insignificant of words. Grammatical words like 'in' transfer their meaning from the literal – '*in* a box' or 'to allow visitors *in*' – to the more abstract '*in* love' or '*in* haste.' As it's impossible to physically occupy an abstract quality, we can only be *in* love metaphorically. Similarly, 'at' transfers its meaning from space to time; I can literally 'meet you *at* the corner,' or, metaphorically, I can meet you '*at* ten o'clock.'

When students become attuned to the idea that all words reverberate with echoes of metaphoric meaning, language becomes much more than a mechanism for transactional communication, and is revealed as an infinitely malleable plaything in which analogies can be hidden, hinted at and transformed.

Systematic metaphors

One of the most interesting aspects of metaphor to introduce to students is the idea that metaphors can be systematised; that whole fields systematically borrow language from different domains in order to describe ideas in their own domain. For instance, medicine has borrowed vehicles from warfare; viruses *invade* our bodies; we *fight* diseases; patients lose the *battle* against illness; we fall *victim* to illnesses; our bodies have *defence* mechanisms; we try to *combat* depression; we suffer heart *attacks* and *bouts* of illness. And so on. We have come to see medicine as waging a war against ill health and disease.

In their 1980 book, *Metaphors We Live By*, George Lakoff and Mark Johnson introduced the study of metaphor as a tool for thought, saying, "Our ordinary conceptual system, in terms of which we both think and act, is fundamentally metaphorical in nature."[12] They pointed out that, like medicine, argument is also conceived as battle: your idea is *indefensible*; we *attack* the *weak points* of an argument; criticisms are *on target*; arguments are *demolished, shot down* or *won*. According to Lakoff and Johnson, this isn't a coincidence, it reveals an important fact about the confrontational way English speakers think about and conduct themselves in arguments.

Other systematised metaphors include:

- Time = Resource (don't *waste* my time; are you *free*? I've *invested* so much time in this; we're *running out* of time)
- Understanding = Seeing or Holding (I *see* what you mean; *look* at the facts; he struggled to *grasp* the idea; getting to *grips* with a problem)
- Communication = Sending (it's hard to get that idea *across*; she *gave* me an excellent idea; *pack* more thought *into* fewer words; his words *carried* no meaning)
- Anger = Heat (a *heated* debate; his temper *flared* up; my blood was *boiling*; I saw *red*)
- Life = Journey (take each day one *step* at a time; she was at a *crossroads* in her life; you've got to *move on*; my life took an unexpected *turn*)

We can see systematised conceptual metaphors at work in the idea that while positives are up, high or light, negatives are down, low and dark:

- wages have *risen*
- on a *high*
- *brigh*t eyes
- I'm very *low*
- prices *plummeted*
- *dark* thoughts

Systematic and conventional metaphors shape the way we perceive the world. It is difficult for our minds not to run along the deeply embedded tracks and plough fresh furrows. In this way, metaphors have the power to constrain our imagination in ways that are difficult to notice. Because of the way metaphor is systematised it's almost impossible to associate down with good or, more controversially, dark or black with positivity. Look at this passage from Chinua Achebe's novel *Things Fall Apart* (published in 1958 but set in the 1890s) about a European missionary's impact on the Ibo community in what is now Nigeria:

> He saw things in black and white. And black was evil. He saw the world as a battlefield in which the children of the light were locked in mortal combat with the sons of darkness.

The systematic metaphor that black = evil is difficult to dis-lodge and it's not hard to see why this might make it easier for some people to espouse racist beliefs.

Any abstract concept will be shaped by the concrete metaphors we use to conceptualise it. For instance, it can be hard for teachers to think themselves out of the metaphors used to conceptualise learning. We can't help using metaphors because we have no idea what learning actually looks like. So, we think of learning as a staircase which pupils steadily ascend or as a line on a graph. Cognitive psychologist, Robert Siegler offers an alternative metaphor in which learning is envisaged as,

> ... a gradual ebbing and flowing of the frequencies of alternative ways of thinking, with new approaches being added and old ones being eliminated as well. To capture this perspective in a visual metaphor, think of a series of overlapping waves, with each wave corresponding to a different rule, strategy, theory, or way of thinking.[13]

This might be a more useful way to frame our thinking about progress. Siegler's image of surging and receding waves helps explain the seemingly random retreats and swells we experience as we grapple to make meaning and why progress is rarely linear.

Noticing metaphor

So how can we train ourselves to notice metaphors and their significance? Robert Eaglestone argues that 'metaphor-spotting' is a craft. Just as we can become increasingly aware of the analogies we use to think with, we can train ourselves to see the unfamiliar in the everyday and, by becoming attuned to new ways of restating old ideas, we can connect *here* with *elsewhere*. Many English teachers may recoil at the thought of teaching children to spot metaphors but this is to misunderstand the state of mind with which a student of English should read and write. The fear is that if students are focussed on spotting metaphors they'll miss out on engaging with the text, but in noticing what's around us we are more, not less, aware of our environments.

Only when we are receptive to the possible meanings of the words around us can we feel our way through what is being communicated. Without the craft of 'metaphor-noticing', readers only attend to superficialities and writers just plop down the first words to come to mind. But a practised metaphor-spotter can see past the surface to the essence; can see past the tree to the wood. Rather than merely picking a flower you are, in Eaglestone's words, "having your attention drawn to the whole ecosystem."[14]

Think about the metaphors at work in Seamus Heaney's poem 'Storm on the Island.' One obvious metaphor that is extended over several lines is storm = war: "exploding," "dives and strafes," "salvo" and "bombarded." There is the vivid one-off image "spits like a tame cat / Turned savage." The use of caesura here makes us feel the jump of the spitting cat viscerally. We also have several subtler comparisons: the earth is "wizened" (made wise?) with age, and the sounds of leaves and trees can be a "tragic chorus" – commenting on the unfolding drama, invoking the 'fear and pity' felt when experiencing a Greek tragedy – but there are no leaves or trees, therefore no chorus and no catharsis. Then there's the beautifully spare image, "space is a salvo"; that although there's nothing for the storm to blow away or destroy, "we" are fearful of a "huge nothingness" and "empty air." In noticing Heaney's stark use of language, we are also drawn to the barren landscape of the island.

Modelling this kind of noticing is an essential part of the process of tuning students in to metaphor. But, while metaphor-spotting may well be a craft, it can be enhanced by learning some of the hard-won knowledge about how metaphors work, where they're likely to appear and the ways we use them to think and live.

The 'major tropes'

Linguist, Zoltán Kövecses argues that although literary metaphors can offer new and distinctive perspectives on reality, they are simply extensions and elaborations of the ordinary conceptual metaphors that shape our thought. The difference is of degree not of kind: literary metaphors are "less clear but richer in meaning."[15]

Michael Oakeshott disagreed, maintaining that to view literary images as something to be grasped and used was to fail to think in a 'poetic' mode. He warns against mistaking the kind of systematic analysis of metaphor in linguistics as anything like the way metaphor works in literature. Instead, literary metaphors are "made, remade, observed, turned about, played with, meditated upon, and delighted in."[16] In his view, the kind of symbolic analysis Lakoff and Johnson engage in is the enemy of the literary metaphor as the "symbolic language of practical activity offers a strong and continuous resistance to the appearance of poetry."[17]

Metaphors are more easily understood as 'poetic' when they appear in works of literature. Unlike 'dead' or systematic metaphors, images like Yeats' "sea-starved hungry sea" or Whitman's "Earth of the slumbering and liquid trees" are impossible to mistake as anything other than poetic. But memorable characters – Mercutio, Falstaff, Elizabeth Bennett, Miss Havisham, Atticus Finch, Harry Potter – or moments – the storm in which Frankenstein's monster is brought to life, the gas attack in 'Dulce Et Decorum Est,' Scrooge waking up delighted that "the time before him was his own, to make amends in" – are all also varieties of metaphor: poetic images composed of words.

Literary metaphors – imagery, or figurative language – are tropes, linguistic pivots away from the ordinary or literal. The so-called 'major tropes' are metaphor (of which we have already heard rather a lot), simile, personification, metonymy and irony. The relationship between these figures is depicted in Figure 5.1.

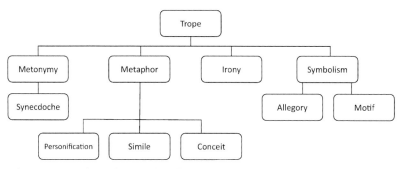

Figure 5.1 The relationship between tropes

Simile

Treating similes as being distinct to metaphors produces very marginal returns. I've nothing against similes: they can be enormously effective and refreshingly direct as well as surprisingly subtle. Here are four choice examples:

> Elderly American ladies leaning on their canes listed toward me like towers of Pisa.
>
> *Lolita*, Vladimir Nabokov

> Time has not stood still. It has washed over me, washed me away, as if I'm nothing more than a woman of sand, left by a careless child too near the water.
>
> *The Handmaid's Tale*, Margaret Atwood

> ... impressions poured in upon her of those two men, and to follow her thought was like following a voice which speaks too quickly to be taken down by one's pencil ...
>
> *To the Lighthouse*, Virginia Woolf

> When the minted gold in the vault smiles like the night-
> watchman's daughter ...
> > 'A Song for Occupations #6,' Walt Whitman

But similes are merely metaphors with the scaffolding still visible. Where metaphor can hide in the shadows, simile is more explicit. The only point of departure worth troubling ourselves over is the observation that metaphors are literally untrue whereas a simile can be literally possible, if implausible. They also have the advantage of being more noticeable due to the presence of the comparative phrasing *like, as* or whatever. The big danger is that students sometimes mistake these words for simile signposts when they're not. And sometimes it can be hard to tell. Is this a simile?

> She walks in beauty, like the night
> Of cloudless climes and starry skies

Well, yes, but what's being compared? Is Byron saying 'beauty is like the night,' 'she is like the night,' 'her walk is like the night,' or 'the way she walks is like a beautiful clear night'? Or, perhaps, all of these? Being 'right' is irrelevant, it's the noticing that tells.

A rule of thumb to bear in mind is that similes can – if handled carelessly – lose all power to surprise or delight and descend to the prosaic. W.H. Auden, on being shown a poem containing the line 'Women swaying their long hair, like trees,' crossly observed, "You can have trees swaying their long hair or women swaying their long hair, but one swaying its long hair like the other won't do."[18]

Personification

Personification is another subset of metaphor where the inanimate is given the properties of human action or thought. Sometimes this can be subtle (to describe troubles as possessing "outrageous fortune" is to suggest some troubles can be unluckier than others), and sometimes explicit as in this gem from Emily Dickinson:

> Because I could not stop for Death –
> He kindly stopped for me –
> The Carriage held but just Ourselves –
> And Immortality.

Here both Death and Immortality are conceived as physically embodied. We picture them as characters able to take seats in a carriage and engage in conversation. Usually, though, personification is less overt. These lines from the opening of Robert Browning's dramatic monologue, 'Porphyria's Lover' provide a textbook example of personification:

> The rain set early in to-night,
> The sullen wind was soon awake,
> It tore the elm-tops down for spite,
> And did its worst to vex the lake.

The wind is conceived as a "sullen" teenager, smashing windows out of boredom. After the spiteful act of tearing down the elms, the idea that it "did its worst to vex the lake" is something of an anti-climax and gives the impression that for all the wind's violence, when it comes to something as deep and permanent as a lake it's as ineffectual as a sulky child.

Personification can be darker and stranger, such as in, "The yellow smoke that rubs its muzzle on the window-panes" and "Licked its tongue into the corners of the evening," from Eliot's 'The Love Song of J Alfred Prufrock.' The image of fog behaving like a predator is unpleasantly intimate. Its intrusions feel directed by a disturbingly alien intelligence, until the moment of anti-climax when it "curled once about the house, and fell asleep," like a harmless household pet.

In this passage from *The Great Gatsby* the effects of personification are more restrained but equally effective:

> The eyes of Doctor T. J. Eckleburg are blue and gigantic— their retinas are one yard high. They look out of no face but, instead, from a pair of enormous yellow spectacles which pass over a nonexistent nose. Evidently some wild wag of an oculist set them there to fatten his practice in the borough of Queens, and then sank down himself into eternal blindness or forgot them and moved away. But his eyes, dimmed a little by many paintless days under sun and rain, brood on over the solemn dumping ground.
>
> ...
>
> I followed [Tom] over a low white-washed railroad fence and we walked back a hundred yards along the road under Doctor Eckleburg's persistent stare. ... "Terrible place, isn't it," said Tom, exchanging a frown with Doctor Eckleburg.

There's a lot going on here. We have eyes that "brood" and "solemn" ground, but the fact that 'Doctor Eckleburg' – a stylised image on an advertising hoarding – is capable of exchanging frowns with Tom Buchanan only adds to the image's mesmeric, baleful power.

Metonymy

Another less well-known trope is metaphor's cousin, metonymy. If metaphor transfers meaning between

METONYMY

Greek: *metōnymia*, 'to call by a new name,' from *meta* 'change'+ *onyma*, 'name.'

Trope in which an attribute is substituted for the thing meant, e.g. 'suit' to mean 'executive.'

different things, metonymy finds and connects similar things. Here's an example from William Blake's 'Jerusalem':

> And did those feet in ancient time
> Walk upon England's mountains green?

Blake was speculating that Jesus may have visited England during his lifetime, but instead of asking 'did *Jesus* walk upon England's mountains green,' he only asks about his feet. Obviously enough, he's not implying that Jesus' feet had been amputated and reanimated; he's expecting us to assume that if Jesus' feet were wandering about in England, so was the rest of him. Likewise, when Mark Antony asks that the Roman mob lend him their ears, at no point is he expecting anyone to hack them off, but simply that they listen with them. Similarly, when a teacher asks for 'Eyes on me,' we know she's using eyes as a metonym for attention.

This is what metonymy does; it takes a part as representative of the whole. This is a common feature of the way we use language:

- hands = workers
- wheels = vehicle
- bricks and mortar = house
- dish = meal
- pen = writing
- tongue = language
- stage = theatre

These metonyms* provide a cognitive shorthand for thinking about larger, more abstract ideas by their most recognisable,

---

* Technically, some of these are examples of synecdoche. Where synecdoche uses a part to refer to a whole (feet = Jesus)
[*cont. on next page*]

concrete aspects. Lakoff and Johnson point out that metonymy is systematised in exactly the same ways metaphor is:

- Part for whole (get your *butt* over here; lend me your *ears*; I don't like *red necks*)
- Producer for product (I fancy a *Guinness*; she's got a new *Toyota*; is that a *Van Gogh?*)
- Object used for user (the *first violin* can't play a note; he's a hired *gun*; the *trains* are on strike)
- Controller for controlled (*Nelson* was victorious at Trafalgar; a *Porsche* crashed into me; *Blair* invaded Iraq)
- Institution for people responsible (*Arsenal* were awful last night; the *university* won't agree to that; the *government*'s policy is immoral)
- The place for the institution (*Downing Street* made no comment; *Hollywood* has gone downhill; the people hate *Washington*'s policies)
- The place for the event (don't let Iraq become another *Vietnam*; *Watergate* has changed politics; it's another *Twin Towers!*)

Kövecses suggested that the way conceptual metaphors find their way into language is through metonymy. He argues that the idea of 'body heat produced by anger' can be viewed as a metonym in which body heat stands for anger. Thus, we have the following chain of conceptualisation: anger produces body heat (metonymy); body heat becomes heat (generalisation); heat is used to understand anger (metaphor). The metaphor anger = heat is a case where the vehicle (heat) emerges from the tenor (anger) through a metonymic process.[19]

> . . . metonymy refers to the process of naming by association (the Crown = the institution of monarchy). As you can see, the distinction is subtle and the convention for referring to both cases as metonymy makes for a simpler and happier life.

Whatever the case, metonymy in everyday language – like metaphor – largely passes unnoticed and a phrase like "our top brains are working on the problem" is unremarkable. It's only when metonymy is employed to confront us with new ways of perceiving or understanding the world around us that it becomes vivid and vital. In Marlowe's play, Faustus trades his soul for, amongst other things, the love of Helen of Troy, reputedly the most beautiful woman who ever lived. When he sees her he asks,

> Was this the face that launched a thousand ships
> And burnt the topless towers of Ilium?

We recognise that not only is Helen's face the most important part of her (at least to Faustus) but that the Greek army can be quickly understood by reference to their ships and that the sacking of Troy is summed up in the burning of its towers. As Mark Forsyth puts it, "Ten years of elaborate Greek mythology in three clear images: a face, a flotilla, and turrets set ablaze."[20]

Irony

The last of the 'major tropes' we'll deal with here is irony. Defining irony can be the bane of the unwary English teacher's life, so here's my attempt: irony is a mismatch between

> **IRONY**
>
> Greek: *eironeia* 'dissimulation, assumed ignorance.'
>
> When the opposite of what is meant is said.

appearance and reality. That is to say, the words used are intended to be interpreted as meaning something different, often the opposite, of what is directly stated. There are three types of irony: verbal, situational and dramatic.

Metaphor

One of the most famous examples of verbal irony is the opening sentence to Jane Austen's *Pride and Prejudice*:

> It is a truth universally acknowledged that a single man in possession of a good fortune must be in want of a wife.

Of course, this 'truth' is anything but universally acknowledged. Those who most want it to be true, at least in the context of Austen's milieu, are the mothers of unmarried daughters, which neatly encapsulates a major theme of the novel.

Another much celebrated example comes from *Julius Caesar*, when Mark Antony subtly turns the Roman mob against his adversary, Brutus:

> But Brutus says he was ambitious;
> And Brutus is an honourable man.

There's also a situational irony here. Situational irony occurs when actions have the opposite effect to what was intended. Brutus really *is* honourable and Caesar really *was* ambitious, but Antony is not one to let inconvenient facts get in the way of his schemes. Another well-known example occurs in Coleridge's 'The Rime of the Ancient Mariner,' where the doomed sailors are dying of thirst on a giant ship in the middle of the ocean:

> Water, water, everywhere,
> And all the boards did shrink:
> Water, water, everywhere,
> Yet not a drop to drink.

It's easy to confuse bad luck with situational irony as Alanis Morissette discovered to her cost. Rain on your wedding day is just unfortunate, but holding your wedding indoors to avoid bad weather only for the sprinkler system to open up on you: that *is* ironic.

The last form of irony – dramatic irony – has a long and honourable tradition and occurs when the reader possesses information that characters do not. The ancient Greeks saw the meddling of gods in the lives of men as the irony of fate. Odysseus knows his travails are due to the interference of Poseidon, but we know so much more than he does as we are privy to the gods' conversations. We know Athena persuades Zeus to force Calypso to release Odysseus from his sexual slavery, even if she presents the decision to Odysseus as if it is her own. Similarly, Achilles is unaware of the gods' discussion about whether to help or hinder him in his duel with Hector, even though Hector realises, at the end, that he has been abandoned.

More recently, we have Mr Birling praising the Titanic as "unsinkable, absolutely unsinkable," in Priestley's *An Inspector Calls*. This is a clear cue to the audience that here is a man on the wrong side of history. The play, written in 1945 but set in 1912, months before the unsinkable ship sank, uses our foreknowledge to tip us off that Birling's pronouncements are not to be valued or trusted.

Noticing extended metaphors

Metaphors don't have to be one-off explosions of significance and surprise, they can be slowly unwound over several sentences or lines in a poem. Here's one of the most well-known examples from *As You Like It*:

> All the world's a stage,
> And all the men and women merely players;
> They have their exits and their entrances;

Metaphor

> And one man in his time plays many parts,
> His acts being seven ages.

The metaphor here is that the world = a theatre, but, just to be sure we get the point, Shakespeare also tells us that people = actors, their comings and goings = stage directions, and the stages of human life = the acts of a play. Extending a metaphor like this allows us to explore all the different ways in which *this* is like *that* and also serves to make it more memorable.

The metaphor of financial credit as a vehicle for the tenor of trust was extended by Martin Luther King in his famous 'I have a dream' speech. He begins by saying he has "come to our nation's capital to cash a check" and then compares the writing of the US Constitution as "a promissory note to which every American was to fall heir" before making the point that "America has defaulted on this promissory note, insofar as her citizens of color are concerned" giving a "bad check, a check which has come back marked 'insufficient funds.'" He refuses to accept that "the bank of justice is bankrupt" or that "there are insufficient funds in the great vaults of opportunity of this nation." He describes his campaign for civil rights as an attempt "to cash this check, a check that will give us upon demand the riches of freedom and the security of justice."

A "check" (cheque in British English) is a promise to pay a sum of money. The cheque that King has come to cash is the promise made in the American Constitution that all men (and by implication, all women too) have the right to, "Life, Liberty and the pursuit of Happiness." But if a bank defaults on a cheque, they refuse to pay what is promised. A 'bad cheque' is a faithless promise. Normally, banks only default on cheques when there are "insufficient funds" in the payer's account, but King refuses to accept that this can be the case for the "great vaults" of the "bank of justice," and so he demands to be paid the freedom and justice all people of colour are owed.

Conceit

A *conceit* is a particularly clever or convoluted extended metaphor in which the tenor and vehicle seem completely unrelated. This challenges us to see the topic in a new and surprising light. Conceits were used to great effect by the so-called 'metaphysical poets' such as John Donne. In Donne's poem 'The Flea' he compares sex to the bite of a blood-sucking parasite:

CONCEIT

Late 14c., 'a thought, a notion, that which is mentally conceived,' based on analogy of *deceit/deceive* and *receipt/ receive*. Sense evolved from 'something formed in the mind' to 'fanciful or witty notion, ingenious thought.'

An elaborate extended metaphor in which two very dissimilar things are compared.

> Mark but this flea, and mark in this,
> How little that which thou deniest me is;
> It suck'd me first, and now sucks thee,
> And in this flea our two bloods mingled be.

Our immediate reaction is one of disgust, but Donne's argument is that a flea bite is so trivial, so negligible an event, that we don't even notice it and soon forget it. Further, it's obviously not shameful or sinful to be bitten by a flea:

> Thou know'st that this cannot be said
> A sin, nor shame, nor loss of maidenhead.

Metaphor

Then, Donne asks the object of his affections, will she not make love to him? After all, there'll be no more loss of honour in making love than in being bitten:

> Just so much honour, when thou yield'st to me,
> Will waste, as this flea's death took life from thee.

Posterity does not record whether Donne's argument was successful.

Symbolism

Symbols are another type of extended metaphor. We use symbols as shorthand for complex ideas and abstract qualities. Everyone knows that a rose is rarely just a rose. For many people, roses – especially red ones – have become a rather trite symbol of romantic love, with their thorns representing the hidden dangers inherent in romance: love hurts. For sports fans, the red rose is a more prosaic symbol for the England rugby team. If you're Chinese, then a red rose is likely to symbolise wealth and prosperity. Other flowers – lilies for instance – are sometimes used to represent death, but they can also be a symbol of the Virgin Mary's purity and, to the ancient Romans, the lily symbolised majesty as the flower was sacred to Juno, queen of the gods.

Colours themselves are common symbols; here's a variety of their possible meanings:

> **SYMBOLISM**
>
> Greek: *symbolon* 'token,' literally 'that which is thrown or cast together,' from *syn-* 'together' + *bole* 'a throwing, or casting.'
>
> Use of an object to represent ideas or qualities.

- Red – love, danger, Christmas, passion, aggression, blood
- White – purity, winter, marriage, peace
- Black – death, power, mystery, evil
- Yellow – joy, warmth, sickness, cowardice
- Blue – sadness, tranquillity, trust, water, sky
- Green – youth, nature, health, poison, jealousy

All this is to point out the obvious, that symbols shift meaning with context.

Trying to pin down the difference between a metaphor and a symbol is not straightforward. Obviously, symbols are a category of metaphor, but generally metaphors are used to draw a comparison between two distinct objects or ideas, whereas symbols are readily understood stand-ins. Metaphors rely on freshness and originality, symbols rely on widespread understandings that a symbol always (in a particular context) represents the same thing. A metaphor might be used once, symbols must endure to have symbolic power.

In the poem, 'My Heart Leaps Up When I Behold,' Wordsworth draws from the Biblical symbolism of the rainbow representing God's covenant with Man:

My heart leaps up when I behold
A rainbow in the sky:
So was it when my life began;
So is it now I am a man;
So be it when I shall grow old.

The rainbow here is not metaphorical; it's an actual rainbow in the sky, but Wordsworth uses it to symbolise – to stand in for – enduring hope and wellbeing.

Symbolism allows us to add layers of meanings: literal ones that are self-evident, and deeper representative ones. Symbolism gives universality to a piece of literature; characters, objects, places, events can all be given deeper symbolic meanings. Poe's Raven is used to symbolise death and loss, the Albatross in 'The Rime of the Ancient Mariner' is symbolic of the mariner's terrible sin and the burden he must bear:

> Instead of the cross, the Albatross
> About my neck was hung.

The "cross" in Coleridge's poem is one of the most enduring symbols in Western culture: the cross on which Christ was crucified. Like the Albatross, the cross symbolises the crucifixion, but it has a much broader meaning which takes in sacrifice and the entirety of the Christian faith. None of this requires explanation; readers are expected to make the link between the symbol and what it signifies without much thought.

Allegory

One of the best-known examples of allegory is Bunyan's *Pilgrim's Progress*. The symbolism is heavy handed: our hero, Christian, is an Everyman figure representing the ordinary sinner. He leaves the City of Destruction to head for the Celestial City. On his way he is accompanied by

> **ALLEGORY**
>
> Greek: *allegoria*, 'speaking about something else.'
>
> A story containing another symbolic story, often with a moral message. A poem or an entire novel can be allegorical in that the ideas and events described are intended to symbolise something else.

and meets a range of instantly recognisable characters who either help or impede his progress: Faithful, Hypocrisy, Mr.

Worldly Wiseman, Evangelist, Hopeful, Obstinate, Pliable and many more. He travels over the Hill of Difficulty, through the Valley of Humiliation into Vanity Fair and is held prisoner for a while in Doubting Castle. Every character and event is symbolic of the spiritual journey through life before we finally reach our eternal reward or punishment. Bunyan's use of allegory to impart spiritual wisdom follows a venerable tradition. The parables Jesus tells in the Gospels are allegories. The prodigal son, the mustard seed, the faithful servant are all meant to teach us moral lessons that must be inferred from the allegorical stories.

Orwell's *Animal Farm* is a familiar modern example where the actions of the animals in setting up their collective are representative of the overthrow of the Tsar and the Communist Revolution in Russia. The story is not meant to be understood literally and readers are expected to know that the animals on the farm represent different sections of Russian society after the revolution. For instance, the pigs represent the Bolsheviks who came to power following the revolution; the farmer, Mr Jones, represents the overthrown Tsar Nicholas II; while Boxer the horse represents the ordinary working poor. The use of allegory allowed Orwell to take a clear position on the Russian Revolution and expose its evils without discussing the actual people or events involved. Other examples of modern allegorical texts include William Golding's *Lord of the Flies* and C.S. Lewis' *The Lion, the Witch and the Wardrobe*.

Motif

The motif is yet another way to extend metaphors throughout a text. Motifs are often confused with

MOTIF

Medieval Latin: *motivus* 'moving, impelling.'

Recurrent symbol, usually relating to a theme.

themes. We'll discuss themes further in the next chapter, but for now they are underlying abstract ideas that the writer wants to discuss over the unfolding narrative. A motif may represent

> ## THEME
>
> Greek: *thema* 'a proposition, subject.'
>
> Idea that runs through a literary work.

a theme, but it will be distinct from it. Just as decorative motifs may be woven into a textile, literary motifs are woven into texts. So, for instance, disorder is one of the themes of *Macbeth*, but the supernatural is a recurring motif through which we are meant to recognise that all is not as it should be and order is breaking down.

Motifs also get confused with symbols; the basic rule of thumb is that if it's mentioned once or twice it's a symbol, if it repeats throughout a text, it's a motif. For example, in J.D. Salinger's *The Catcher in the Rye*, the carousel in Central Park that Phoebe rides at the end of the novel might be a symbol both of lost innocence and the circular nature of life, whereas Holden's red hunting hat is a motif that pops up at many different points in the novel and is used to represent his alienation from those around him. Holden is acutely self-conscious about his hat and regularly mentions whether and how he's wearing it. The hat mirrors his conflict over whether to fit in or stand out.

Motifs are clues to the reader that a mood is changing; when we notice their presence, they nudge us to pay particular attention to what is being described. In *Romeo and Juliet*, Shakespeare makes frequent reference to the interplay between light and darkness. When Romeo first catches sight of Juliet he exclaims that she teaches "the torches to burn bright." Not only is Juliet "the sun" who can "kill the envious moon," but her eyes are "two of the fairest stars in all the heaven." Both Romeo and Juliet are compared with a light that illuminates the darkness. Juliet "hangs upon the cheek of night as a rich jewel in an Ethiop's ear" and she imagines Romeo "cut out in little stars" that "will make the face of heaven so fine that all the world will be in love with night and pay no worship to the garish sun." Then, as their brief wedding night turns to morning, Romeo says, "More light and light: more dark and dark our woes." This motif reminds us both of the brightness with which their love shines but also of its ephemeral nature.

Motifs can be used to create thematic patterning. For instance, John Steinbeck's novel *Of Mice and Men* is generally considered to explore the theme of loneliness and, to help readers focus on this, each of the characters is lonely in different ways: George is alienated from other works because of his need to care for Lennie but is separated from Lennie due to the disparity in their intellects; Candy is cut off from the other works because he is old and crippled; Crooks because he's the only black worker; Curley's wife because she's the only woman. The actual loneliness experienced by these characters is a motif which binds the larger theme of the novel together.

Metaphor and pragmatics

Pragmatics is the study of the choices we make when we use language, the reasons for these choices, and the effects our choices convey. One area of study is to consider some of the

> ### PRAGMATICS
>
> Greek: *pragmatikos* 'fit for business' from *pragma* 'a deed, act.'
>
> Branch of linguistics dealing with language in context.

effects of using metaphors, how they are understood by others, and what happens when they're not.

Metaphor

Language is an essentially cooperative endeavour. When we write or speak we do so with the expectation that we are understood, and when we read or listen we assume that the speaker or writer is acting in good faith. This simple observation gives rise to the Cooperative Principle, developed by the linguist H.P. Grice. Grice suggested that communication follows a set of conventions, or maxims as he called them:

- Quantity (providing sufficient information)
- Quality (truthfulness)
- Relation (relevance)
- Manner (clarity).

Whenever we read or listen our expectation is that these maxims will be followed and, where they are flouted, we attempt to fill in the gaps and make sense of what we're reading or listening to. This is the essence of pragmatics: we cooperate with our conversational partner to make sense of what is said (or written). Grice saw metaphor as an instance of flouting the maxim of quality which can be expressed as 'Do not say what you believe to be untrue.' The literary critic, Wiliam Empson thought "the essential fact about poetic language" is that "[s]tatements are made as if they were connected, and the reader is forced to consider their relations for himself."[21] If I refer to you as 'the cat's pyjamas' I have said something which is literally false: even if you were a pair of pyjamas it would be ridiculous to assume you could be worn by a cat. The Cooperative Principle means that you will strive to make sense of what I have said and since it's impossible that you can be feline nightwear, I *must* mean something else (in this case that you're rather wonderful).

Metaphor can also breach some of the other maxims. For instance, literary metaphor can either fall short of, or overstep, the maxim of quantity. For instance, when in *The*

Strange Case of Dr Jekyll and Mr Hyde, Utterson shows his concern for his friend, thinking, "Poor Harry Jekyll ... my mind misgives me he is in deep waters!" there is insufficient detail for us to know precisely what is meant. But, operating on the Cooperative Principle, we know 'deep water' is a conventional metaphor for trouble and we extend this to all the trouble Utterson imagines his friend to have become mixed up in.

As an example of the opposite problem, the narrator of Andrew Marvell's 'To His Coy Mistress' is attempting to per-suade a chaste maiden to provide sexual favours, but rather than come out and say what he wants directly, his argument is layered with complex (and at times, disturbing) metaphors. We have to work quite hard – as, we presume, does the object of the narrator's dubious affections – to work out that this is a very long-winded preamble to popping the question he really wants to ask: Will you have sex with me?

Metaphors may also breach the maxim of relation. Consider this exchange between Polonius and Hamlet:

Hamlet:	*O Jephthah, judge of Israel, what a treasure hadst thou!*
Polonius:	*What a treasure had he, my lord?*
Hamlet:	*Why,*
	'One fair daughter and no more, The which he loved passing well.'
Polonius:	*[Aside] Still on my daughter.*
Hamlet:	*Am I not i' the right, old Jephthah?*
Polonius:	*If you call me Jephthah, my lord, I have a daughter that I love passing well.*
Hamlet:	*Nay, that follows not.*

Polonius is desperately trying to make sense of Hamlet's utterances, but is unaware that the brooding Dane is toying with him, deliberately withholding meaning by saying what, to his interlocutor, appears irrelevant. Polonius is bewildered because he believes – or at least, hopes – Hamlet is in love with his daughter, Ophelia. In calling Polonius 'Jephthah,' Hamlet is aware that Polonius will infer this to mean Polonius loves his daughter. However, Hamlet is really implying that Polonius is as ready to sacrifice Ophelia as the Biblical character of Jephthah was willing to sacrifice his own daughter. Therefore, Hamlet denounces Polonius' affirmation that he loves his daughter as a non sequitur. Needless to say, Polonius – and much of the audience – is none the wiser. If we analyse the components of this metaphor, we can set out the relationship like this:

Tenor: *A faithless father*
Vehicle: *Jephthah*
Ground: *Jephthah's sacrifice of his daughter is compared to Polonius trying to marry off Ophelia to Hamlet.*

Hamlet is relying on the fact that his breach of the maxim of relation will be impenetrable to Polonius and it underscores an aspect of Hamlet's character: that he is both cruel and clever.

Teaching metaphor

The best place to start is, I think, with words. Etymology provides an opportunity for vocabulary instruction but also to see the polysemous nature of words as meaning evolves from concrete to abstract. The Online Etymology Dictionary (www.etymonline.com) is a superb repository of stories about where words have come from.

The next step is to demonstrate the ubiquity of metaphor in everyday speech. Encourage students to notice metaphors in 'plain' text and challenge them to speak about abstract ideas without using metaphors. From here, it's a small leap to considering systematic, conceptual metaphor. Introduce them to ideas like argument or medicine = war, love and life = a journey, ideas = food, and so on. Challenge them to notice other systematic metaphors (sensitively done, this provides an excellent opportunity to consider the metaphoric meanings of *black* and *white*) and experiment with overturning some of these established patterns and replacing them with different vehicles. For instance, what happens if we say 'life is an onion,' or 'time is food'?

It should become clear fairly quickly that students need a language to think about the ways in which metaphor works, and so, if you haven't already, this is a good point to introduce the terms tenor, vehicle and ground (or target and source, if you must). Students should practise identifying vehicles and tenors to establish the ground between them. Not only to peer into the conventional metaphors that operate in everyday language but also the rich and strange versions that only exist in literature.

At some point you will probably find it necessary to begin introducing students to the various literary tropes. Similes are, of course, the most straightforward, because the presence of 'like' and 'as' make them easy to identify, but avoid examining only the very simplest, most cliched varieties. Hunt out surprising similes and explore why they have been left with their linguistic skeletons exposed. Can all similes be transformed into metaphors? Yes, but not all metaphors can become similes without ruining them. Why is this? Are similes less sophisticated, or do they offer something that gives them a power more implicit metaphor sometimes lacks?

Personification is also easy to spot and teach. But why is it so popular? The introduction of purpose, agency and animation to what, normally, has none, makes for vivid comparisons and reconceptualisations. Metonymy (and synecdoche) are more subtle tropes; most metonyms are so common we never notice them. The most successful way in is to begin with symbolism. The well-worn homily, 'the pen is mightier than the sword' is one of the most uncomplicated examples of metonymy. On a literal level we know the sword will win every time, but students easily see that there's more at work; that the pen and the sword represent what they are used for. Once students are introduced to this metaphorical aspect of language it can have a powerful effect on their reading and writing as they begin to think about the connections between objects and actions, parts and wholes, symbols and what they represent. By far the most difficult trope for students to get a handle on is irony. Because it relies on tacit understanding, explanations rarely cut it; you're much better off pointing it out when it occurs and discussing how and why the statement or situation is ironic and encouraging students to feel their way forward.

Metaphors are in conversation with each other; new images evoke old ones, and, when they are especially vibrant or delightful they are, in Oakeshott's words, "a sort of truancy, a dream within the dream of life, a wild flower planted among the wheat."[22] The ability to notice, use and appreciate figurative language is a crucial aspect of English disciplinary understanding that invites us to look for patterns and find connections in a world that is tantalisingly open to interpretation. Metaphors also recognise that there are no such things as separate parts in reality, but instead only intimately related phenomena so bound up with each other as to be inseparable. Thinking in this way leads to the possibility of approaching and understanding both ourselves and other people in other times and places. With their potential simultaneously to clarify and make strange, metaphors allow us to explore associative networks of understanding and embrace the shifts and detours of unfolding knowledge, opening the doors to previously hidden analogies.

KEY POINTS

- Metaphor is a form of analogy. We understand new and abstract ideas by comparing them to familiar, concrete ones.
- Metaphor allows us to express ideas for which we have no words and which cannot be directly or easily explained.
- Metaphors can be analysed by considering the tenor (what is being compared) or the vehicle (what the tenor is being compared to).
- Many words either derive from metaphorical roots or can have metaphorical uses.
- It is almost impossible to think or speak without employing metaphors. These 'dead' metaphors usually go unnoticed but often act at a conceptual level, shaping the way we think.
- Literary metaphors – tropes – are more linguistically interesting and original than conceptual metaphors. There's debate about whether the difference is one of kind or degree.
- The 'major tropes' of which students should be aware are metaphor, simile, metonymy and irony. Writers extend metaphors in a variety of different ways. Some of these extended uses of metaphor are allegories, symbolism, conceits and motifs.
- Metaphor can also be analysed in terms of its conformity to the four maxims of the Cooperative Principle (quantity, quality, relation and manner).

Further reading

- As an excellent primer on the subject of metaphor, I can heartily recommend Murray Knowles and Rosamund Moon's *Introducing Metaphor*.
- Anyone interested in the study of metaphor really ought to read George Lakoff and Mark Johnson's seminal *Metaphors We Live By*, although it does get a little repetitive.
- James Geary's *I Is An Other* is also a useful and entertaining read.

6 Story

The novelist E.M. Forster said, "If God could tell the story of the Universe, the Universe would become fictitious."[1] Human beings seem to have a bias towards thinking in narrative. Cognitive psychologist and literary critic Mark Turner says, "Narrative imagining – story – is the fundamental instrument of thought. Rational capacities depend on it. It is our chief means of looking into the future, of predicting, of planning, of explaining."[2] Another psychologist, Daniel Willingham, puts it like this: "The human mind seems exquisitely tuned to understand and remember stories as 'psychologically privileged' meaning they are treated differently in memory than other types of material."[3] Stories exist to make meaning.

In order to simplify the complexity of the world, our ancestors framed their understanding in the form of myths; stories with sequential events, characters and themes. Every culture has generated myths to explain the creation of the world and the cyclical nature of the seasons, whether it's the Greek story of Persephone and Demeter, the ancient Chinese myth of Zhulong the candle dragon, or the Shinto tale of Amaterasu the sun goddess. All stories come from common mythological roots. That's not to say the origins of stories are lost in myth but that myth *is* the origin of story.

Story

'Real life' is full of coincidences, but in stories, everything is connected. T.S. Eliot claimed that poets were,

> ... constantly amalgamating disparate experience; the ordinary man's experience is chaotic, irregular, fragmentary. The latter falls in love, or reads Spinoza, and these two experiences have nothing to do with each other, or with the noise of the typewriter or the smell of cooking; in the mind of the poet these experiences are always forming new wholes.[4]

But it's not just poets, we all strive to find order in chaos. We think in terms of cause and effect, heroes and villains and unifying morals which give meaning to otherwise random events. Every time we recount an incident from our lives, we cast ourselves as the hero and, while our story may well be truthful, it is also, in a very real way, 'made up.' We tend to conform to particular ways of structuring our stories – chronology, climaxes, resolutions – and by doing so we make it easier for those around us to understand our experiences.

Causality

Think about the following pair of words. What connects them?

banana   vomit

Without intending to, you almost certainly told yourself a story in which the consumption of bananas caused you, or someone else, to throw up.[5] This is an automatic response. Whenever we see two or more items placed in proximity we want to create a unifying event to explain their relationship. As long as we can find a connection we will tell a story. Try listening to a ticking clock. The sound is uniform but we seem incapable of not splitting what we hear into tick and tock. Beginning and end. The quietest and simplest of stories. As

Frank Kermode said, "Tick is a humble genesis, tock a feeble apocalypse."[6]

Up a level of complexity, we have sayings, proverbs and maxims: a bad workman always blames his tools; beggars can't be choosers; curiosity killed the cat; every cloud has a silver lining; it's no use crying over spilt milk; lightning never strikes twice; once bitten twice shy; the pen is mightier than the sword; while the cat's away, the mice will play. Each of these conjures a tiny time-worn story that is at once effortlessly familiar and at the same time quietly profound. Depending on how we encounter them, proverbs can seem either specific or abstract. If a teacher walks into a classroom to find children out of their seats 'while the cat's away, the mice will play' takes on one meaning; if describing a marriage, it makes us think of quite another; if we encounter it out of context it can seem like a deep human truth applicable to a huge range of possible scenarios.

Our minds turn the simplest of utterances into surprisingly complex narratives. According to legend, Ernest Hemingway was once bet that he couldn't write a story of only six words. Hemingway took the bet and produced this: "For sale: baby's shoes: never worn." If you're like most people you couldn't help but react with a quiet, 'Oh,' as you imagined the sad story of how those shoes came to be for sale.[7]

The complexity and randomness of reality is just too much for us to bear and so stories provide an illusion of control. As Joan Didion puts it,

> We tell ourselves stories in order to live. We look for the sermon in the suicide, the social or moral lessons in the murder of five. We interpret what we see, select the most workable of multiple choices. We live entirely ... by the imposition of a narrative line upon disparate images, by the 'ideas' with which we have learned to freeze the shifting phantasmagoria, which is our actual experience.[8]

Causation – the idea that every effect follows from a cause – is deeply embedded in the human imagination. Everything we experience is filtered through our perception of antecedents and consequences. We struggle to resist the idea that every-thing happens for a reason, and tend to see every encounter as the product of intentional action.

The stories we study in English evolved from explanations of the 'shifting phantasmagoria' our ancestors saw around them into fully fledged artistic endeavours. *Story* comes from the same root as *history*, the Latin *historia* which, in turn, derives from the Greek *histor*, a form of knowing. Both stories and history have their origins in the same process: the fashioning of narratives to explain the world. Interestingly, it's only from the 16th century onwards that the two words begin to be used to describe distinctly different ideas. Until then, 'historie' and 'storie' had been used interchangeably. But, just as historians might feel a little embarrassed to learn that their subject is merely an adjunct of English, so we need to focus on the more disciplinary aspects of story and how it can unlock understanding in English.

Telling it slant

The act of storytelling is, to paraphrase Emily Dickinson, telling the truth but telling it slant. A story is not the literal truth of an event. Sometimes this is clear and sometimes it's concealed from us. The story of Jesus feeding the five thou-sand is intended to be understood as a literal truth (and for centuries that's how it *would* have been understood) while the parable of the prodigal son is meant to furnish us with a moral truth. We're not expected to believe the events actually took place. One story is presented as historical fact, the other is symbolic. More sophisticated stories use a range of devices to make themselves distinct from our everyday experience of reality. The *Odyssey* flits about across several different time periods and settings in a way the audience knows is artificial. Indeed, much of the epic poem is focussed on Odysseus retelling his own story (and we suspect he may not be an entirely reliable narrator). This process of 'making strange' or 'telling it slant' is the literary frame that tips us off that we're in the presence of a story rather than a retelling of 'real' events.

The story of storytelling and how it can be structured and framed helps us understand where literature comes from: the customs of epic, tragedy, comedy; the various forms in which stories are told: poems, plays, novels; the genres, or types, of story with which we've become familiar (detective stories, romances, quests) and their associated conventions; the way in which narrative is constructed (first and third person, past or present tense) and the way stories build on and interpret one another (intertextuality) are all ideas which students need to be explicitly introduced to.

How stories are made

Stories can seem a little like dead metaphors; if we're not trained to notice how they work, we mistake artifice for nature. All the components of stories we now see as entirely unexceptional were, at one time, new and surprising. Greek drama grew from epic poetry and Dionysian ritual into a brand-new way of telling stories. Originally, actors took the stage one at a time and declaimed their part of the narrative, but then the dramatist Aeschylus came up with the idea of introducing a second actor to the stage and thus dialogue

> **DIALOGUE**
>
> Greek: *dialogos*, 'conversation,' from *dia*, 'across, between' + *legein* 'speak.'
>
> Verbal exchanges between characters.

was born. A bit later Sophocles experimented with a *third* actor on stage and gave us action. Today we take dialogue and action utterly for granted, but once they were startling and fresh. According to broadcaster and classicist, Natalie Haynes, the writers of *EastEnders* routinely and deliberately recycle the plots of the Greek tragedies within the context of Albert Square – the characters and setting are new but the plots are taken straight from *Medea* or *Antigone*.[9]

Within the concept of narrative nests a host of other literary concepts: character, setting, plot, action, theme, motif, perspective, and within these nest many more. For instance, the category 'character' contains the category of 'hero' within which we find 'epic heroes,' 'antiheroes,' 'heroic flaws,' etc. By introducing students to these smaller components as well as their relationship to the broader concept of story, the study of literature is opened up, and the possibility of telling more satisfyingly constructed stories of our own is born. Understanding the underlying structures of stories helps us to better understand the texts we read.

The structure of the epic is probably the oldest form of *literary* story, the evolution of myth into literature is one marker on the boundary between recorded history and our legendary past. Like myths, epics were spoken or sung. Later, some came to be written down but we now only have fragments of many epics. The stories of Gilgamesh, Achilles and Beowulf, although separated by thousands of years, share certain unifying features. Epics chronicle the birth of nations. *The Epic of Gilgamesh* tells the story of the founding of Uruk and good government; Gilgamesh begins as a tyrannical despot but through friendship and loss becomes a better and wiser ruler. Homer's epics mark the emergence of Greece on to the world stage. The *Iliad* tells of the victory of the rival power of Troy, while the *Odyssey* ends with the establishment of the rule of law as Odysseus and the families of the slain suitors set aside the cycle of revenge. Beowulf charts the story of the slaying of monsters to ensure a safe, orderly society. Although the events take place in Scandinavia, the story was imported to Britain with the Anglo-Saxon migration and became a template for the establishment of a new state.

Just as epics share their roots so do tragedies. Although the conventions are altered over time, *Oedipus, Hamlet, Hedda Gabler* and *Death of a Salesman* stem from a common set of narrative components. Aristotle noted that epic poetry and tragedy have much in common, but the fact that tragedies were, at that time, staged rather than sung made for some important differences in their narrative structures. Epic has a wider scope: it extends beyond a single day and can depict multiple simultaneous events, whereas the plot of a tragedy ought, according to Aristotle, to unfold in the same time it takes to view the events on stage. Although epic poetry can contain longer scenes, and more of them, Aristotle asserts that the plot at its heart ought to be easily summarised. He illustrates his point with a brief summary of the *Odyssey*, omitting most of the hero's entanglements to emphasise his initial misfortune and ultimate triumph:

> A certain man is absent from home for many years; he is jealously watched by Poseidon, and left desolate. Meanwhile his home is in a wretched plight – suitors are wasting his substance and plotting against his son. At length, tempest-tossed, he himself arrives; he makes certain persons acquainted with him; he attacks the suitors with his own hand, and is himself preserved while he destroys them.[10]

"This is the essence of the plot," Aristotle explains, "the rest is episode."

Plot

Aristotle saw plot as the most important aspect of story-telling. If story is *what* is told, plot is *how* it is told. The events of a story are not its plot. The novelist Philip Pullman uses the image of a path through the woods in Robert Frost's poem, 'The Road Not Taken' to make an apt analogy:

> The wood, or the forest if you like, is a wild space. It's an unstructured space ... a space where anything can happen. ... There are monsters in the wood. The path, on the other hand, is a structure. And it has a function: it leads from A to B. It's extremely linear; even when it doubles back and crosses itself it does so with an air of purpose. ... It was made.[11]

The wood is the story; plot is the path we take through the wood. As Rob Pope puts it, "Plot is what motivates and organises the raw material."[12]

Unity

The concept of *unity* guides much of Aristotle's thought about plot. He explains that you can test the unity of a work by removing a section of, or reordering, the plot. If the plot's meaning and sense survive, the work is not unified; it has superfluous parts. In a good plot, every event should result from a previous occurrence. Every portion is crucial to the plot's development. Incompleteness is no better than excess, but if a plot has a beginning, middle and end, it is whole. This sounds like a relatively low standard, but Aristotle has specific definitions of beginning and end. They must be at opposite ends of the cause-and-effect chain that form the substance of the plot. A beginning has no cause; an ending has no effect.

Aristotle also divides the concept of 'plot' into the smaller concepts of 'complication,' 'turning point' and 'denouement.' The turning point is a change of fortune, either from bad to good or

DENOUEMENT

French: *dénouer,* 'untie' or 'unravel.'

The resolution of a plot.

from good to bad. Naturally, the latter is most appropriate in a tragedy. Aristotle adds that a tragic plot has the greatest emotional impact if it takes place within a single day. 'Complication' covers all the events that lead up to the turning point, and 'denouement,' or unravelling, is everything that follows it.

Based on his standard of causal relationships – that each element of a plot must arise from preceding elements – Aristotle frowned on the use of *deus ex machina* (divine intervention) within the action of a story. It may precede the play – for example, a character may recount a prophecy – but otherwise it disrupts the integrity of a plot. For example, the "and it was all a dream" ending that plagues many children's attempts at creative writing. This sort of naïve plot device gets (over)used because children cannot think what to do next and default to stock ideas they've encountered previously. This may have worked for Lewis Carroll, but for professional writers this is now considered bad form and disrespectful of readers. Plots can take fantastical twists and introduce fabulously unlikely elements as long as they're internally coherent. You have to mention your miracle early on. If time travel is allowed, say so at the start. Rewards have to be balanced with risks; benefits must be paid for with costs, otherwise we end up not caring.

All plots entail a change of fortune, but Aristotle argued that the best stories are complex. For a plot to be complex, changes must arise from the internal structure of the plot. Two ways in which this might occur are for a writer to use 'reversal' or 'recognition.' With reversal, intended occurrences fail to happen, and the opposite occurs instead. Aristotle cites Sophocles' *Oedipus the King* as an example. In it, the messenger who intends to reassure Oedipus that he avoided his prophesied fate ends up horrifying Oedipus by revealing the reverse. This moment also works as an example of recognition: Oedipus has already killed his father and married his mother when the messenger arrives; his fortune changes when he recognises this situation, in what Aristotle called the "change from ignorance to knowledge."[13]

So, according to Aristotle, a good plot will contain the following five ingredients:

1. Beginning – an inciting moment which sets in motion all the following events
2. Complication – events leading up to the turning point
3. Middle – the turning point; a reversal of fortune from good to bad (tragedy) or bad to good (comedy)
4. Denouement or unravelling of the plot to a single strand; complications are undone
5. End – the moment of final surprise.

Tragedy

According to Aristotle, tragedy involves a protagonist who is 'better than we' falling from prosperity to misery through a series of reversals and discoveries as a result of *hamartia* (roughly translatable as

---

TRAGEDY

Greek: *tragodia* 'goat song,' from *tragos* 'goat' + *ōidē* 'song.'

Plot moving from order to disorder and disaster.

'an error of judgement'). Aside from this initial mistake, the protagonist is basically a good person; the downfall of an evil protagonist is not tragic so, for instance, *Macbeth* would not meet Aristotle's standard. The action in a tragedy includes reversal and recognition which leads, inevitably, to disaster and, typically, the death of the protagonist. Tragedy must evoke 'pity and fear' in the audience, leading to *catharsis*, the purgation of these passions.

PROTAGONIST

Greek: *prōtagōnistēs* 'actor who plays the chief or first part,' from *prōtos* 'first' + *agōnistēs* 'competitor.'

Main character in a literary text.

By the time Chaucer was writing, tragedy still concerned the fall of a great man but, in tragic tales such as 'The Monk's Tale,' the downfall of the protagonist comes not from a tragic flaw but as a result of random ill fortune as Fate spins her wheel. The Renaissance saw the rediscovery of Aristotle's ideas through Latin translations, and writers like Shakespeare would have been aware of some of the Greek classics through the versions written by Seneca. Tragic heroes once again became responsible for their downfall due their own frailties and errors.

Setting aside Aristotle's five-part structure, the Shakespeare scholar A.C. Bradley divided tragedy into three parts: *exposition* which sets out the state of affairs before events get underway, *conflict* which charts the growth and progress of events, leading to the *catastrophe* of the tragic outcome. In Bradley's view it was crucial for the catastrophe to be brought about by the actions or omissions of the tragic hero, and that they should in some sense deserve their fate. He said, "This is always so with Shakespeare. The idea of the tragic hero as a being destroyed simply and solely by external forces is quite alien to him; and not less so is the idea of the hero as contributing to his destruction only by acts in which we see no flaw."[14] However, this is not always entirely true. For instance, although there's little doubt that Lear is responsible for setting in motion the events that led to his destruction, does Cordelia deserve to die? And, for that matter, does Lear deserve the punishments he suffers?

The literary critic, Northrop Frye distinguished tragedy into five stages of action which he called *encroachment* (where the protagonist makes their fatal mistake); *complication* (where the effects of the protagonist's mistake begin to sink in); *reversal* (the point at which it becomes clear that the hero's fate will be the reverse of what had been hoped); *catastrophe* (where everything goes to hell in a hand cart and the bodies start to pile up); and, finally, *recognition* (where the audience – if not the protagonist – confronts the full consequences of the action set in motion at the start of the story). These events must come about as a result of a 'tragic flaw' in the hero's character which sets in motion an inevitable series of consequences: "Just as comedy often sets up an arbitrary law and then organizes the action to break or evade it, so tragedy presents the reverse theme of narrowing a comparatively free life into a process of causation."[15] Cutting across all of this, Terry Eagleton argues, "The truth is that no definition of tragedy more elaborate than 'very sad' has ever worked."[16]

Comedy

However tragic plots are conceived, the one constant is that their protagonists come to a sticky end. This might be fine for purging us of fear and pity, but sometimes we're after a happier ending. And it's no

> **COMEDY**
>
> Greek: *kōmōidia* 'amusing spectacle,' from *kōmos*, 'revel, festival' + *aoidos* 'singer, poet.'
>
> A plot moving from disorder to order.

surprise to find that comedy has been around at least as long as tragedy.

Story theorist Christopher Booker explains that comedy is a special kind of plot, not merely a story that happens to be amusing. For Aristotle, the key difference between tragedy and comedy is that "comedy aims at representing men as worse, tragedy as better than in actual life."[17] A tragic hero must be admirable for us to experience the pity and horror of their descent; a comic character must be foolish enough for us to laugh at their exploits. Aristotle is fairly dismissive of comedy seeing it as something of a Johnny-come-lately, without the good breeding of epic and tragedy. But the plays of Aristophanes and other ancient Greek comic writers are merely the first step of comedy's historical development.

Only by the time we get to Shakespeare do all the elements of comedy begin to fully emerge. Booker argues that the key to what makes the plot of comedies unique is the way in which the process of recognition – the 'change from ignorance to knowledge' – plays out. He identifies four important plot components:

1. At the start of a comedy, characters will be in a state of confusion and division. Characters who are trapped in some negative state must either come to recognise their faults and become a new person or be punished in some way.
2. Some characters may have their true identities concealed and these will need to be brought to light before the plot can be resolved.
3. Characters must recognise their other half or true love in order to be fully themselves.
4. Wherever there has been separation, loss or confusion it will be resolved. Families and lovers will be reunited, lost objects found and order re-established.[18]

Story

Understanding how these elements relate to the texts students are expected to read helps demystify the process of studying literature. As students come to recognise that stories are carefully crafted, often following organising principles laid down thousands of years ago, they can begin to perceive the difference between the everyday narratives we construct for ourselves and those deliberately created to entertain or educate us.

For instance, reading (or teaching) *Romeo and Juliet* as a tragedy is deeply unsatisfing; the actions of the characters do not justify their fates, and there's this weird, seemingly tacked on resolution at the end. The tragedy that unfolds seems more down to bad luck and ill will than due to any particular flaw in the characters of the protagonists. If only Friar Lawrence's letter got to Romeo in time all would have been well. If only Tybalt hadn't been such a macho fool all would have been well. If only Capulet had been a little more interested in his daughter's happiness all would have been well. We feel the unfairness that Romeo and Juliet should feel forced to act as they do, and end up railing in frustration against their youthful foolishness. But if we understand the play as a comedy, everything makes more sense.

Admittedly, it's not often very funny – especially at the end – but this is to misunderstand comedy. The defining feature of comedy is not that it's amusing, but that it neatly resolves an imbalance between chaos and order. For a comedy to work there must be some factor that is causing social disorder and forcing the characters into conflict. In *Romeo and Juliet* this is the "ancient grudge" between Montagues and Capulets. The role of the "star-crossed lovers" is not to fall in love and live happily ever after but to "bury their parents' strife." In this they are successful. Capulet and Montague take each other's hands and praise the virtues of each other's children, acknowledging them as "Poor sacrifices of our enmity." Prince Escalus

158

wraps up the play in a sombre mood saying simply, "go hence, to have more talk of these sad things." Sure, the play's a sad one (as Escalus himself says, "never was a story of more woe than this of Juliet and her Romeo") but it ends with hope for a better future where, despite the spilling of civil blood, civil hands might, one day, be clean. This is not a modern story of 'rugged individualism' where the young lovers cast off their parents' outdated social mores to ride off happily into the sunset, but is instead a tale of its time in which the few must be sacrificed for the needs of the many; where society trumps family and family trumps the individual. From a modern perspective, we tend to see the play as tragic because of our myopic focus on the wasted lives of the young instead of stepping back to see what really matters, or at least, what mattered for the Elizabethan play-going public.[19]

Seen in this light, the great novels *Middlemarch* and *War and Peace* are also comedies. At its heart, Tolstoy's novel is about the bringing together of two couples – Natasha and Pierre, and Nikolai and Maria – against the backdrop of the French invasion of Russia with all the carnage and tragedy involved in such a conflict. George Eliot's novel is about the unification of Dorothea and Will Ladislaw against the backdrop of the repressive social mores of a provincial Victorian town. In both novels there is a malign figure separating our lovers. In *Middlemarch* the dark shadow is cast by Dorothea's tedious first husband, Casaubon; in *War and Peace* it is the Emperor Napoleon.

Although Napoleon is responsible for forces that act to separate the lovers, he is also presented as something of a farcical character. At one point during Napoleon's invasion of Russia, there's an incident where his army reaches the river Niemen but is unable to cross. He gets out his maps and telescope to work out what to do and then sends off an aide-de-camp to tell a regiment of Polish Uhlans to find a suitable ford to cross the river. In an effort to find favour with the Emperor, the Uhlans plunge gallantly into the river and many of them are drowned. At this point the aide-de-camp points out the drowning Poles to Napoleon:

> He began pacing up and down the bank with him, giving him instructions and occasionally glancing disapprovingly at the drowning Uhlans who distracted his attention.

> For him it was no new conviction that his presence in any part of the world, from Africa to the steppes of Muscovy alike, was enough to dumfound people and impel them to insane self-oblivion. He called for his horse and rode to his quarters.

While this moment is far from representative of the novel taken as a whole, it does help to illustrate its essentially comedic nature. Far from being the existential threat we might imagine him to be, Bonaparte is dismissed as "the little man in the grey overcoat." Clearly, reducing such a rich novel to its barest bones detracts from the beauty of its language and the complexity of its plot, but from this skeletal foundation readers are better able to perceive the writers' intentions.

The basic plot structures

Christopher Booker argues there are seven plot structures to which an emotionally satisfying narrative can conform. In addition to tragedy and comedy there are also:

- *Overcoming the Monster*: in which the hero must venture to the lair of a monster threatening the community, destroy it, and escape. *Beowulf* is a classic example, as is *Dracula*.
- *Rags to Riches*: in which someone who seems quite commonplace or downtrodden but has the potential for

greatness manages to fulfil that potential. See, for instance, Dickens' *Great Expectations* or Charlotte Brontë's *Jane Eyre*.

- *The Quest*: in which the hero embarks on a journey to obtain a great prize that is located far away. Examples include *The Hobbit* or *Treasure Island*.
- *Voyage and Return*: in which the hero journeys to a strange world that at first is enchanting and then so threatening the hero finds he/she must escape and return home to safety. The *Odyssey* or *Gulliver's Travels* are examples.
- *Rebirth*: in which a dark power or villain traps the hero in a living death until he/she is freed by another character's loving act. *A Christmas Carol* or *Pride and Prejudice* provide excellent examples.

Despite their distinctive features, Booker echoes Aristotle in describing these plots in terms of five stages:

1. *Anticipation*: in which the initial setting is established and the reader is introduced to the hero/heroine, who is somehow constricted or unfulfilled.
2. *Dream*: in which the hero embarks on the road towards a possible resolution and experiences some initial success.
3. *Frustration*: in which the hero's limitations and the strength of the forces against him/her become more obvious, which makes attaining the resolution seem increasingly difficult.
4. *Nightmare*: in which a final ordeal takes place that determines the resolution.
5. *Miraculous Escape/Redemption/Achievement of the Prize* or (in the case of Tragedy) the *Hero's Destruction*. Booker uses various terms for this stage, depending on the basic plot, but in each case a resolution is achieved.

Other theorists have proposed various refinements to Aristotle's ideas on narrative structure. The structuralist literary critic Tzvetan Todorov saw narrative structure as cyclical, with stories beginning in a state of equilibrium which is disrupted by outside events until, finally, a new equilibrium is restored. The anthropologist Claude Lévi-Strauss viewed the formality of this sort of structure as excessively rigid and proposed that mythic stories could be boiled down to a narrative structure as simple and as open as: elements oppose or contradict each other, then other elements resolve or mediate the conflict.

Narrative structure

If there's a distinction between plot and narrative structure it's a subtle one. Figure 6.1 provides a model to picture the interactions between writer and reader.

The story is written by the *actual writer*, a real, living, breathing human being like, say, Robert Louis Stevenson, Emily Brontë or Toni Morrison who, for whatever reason, has set pen to paper (or fingers to keyboard). The *'external' narrator* is the self that the actual writer projects into the text; how they wish to be perceived by the reader. T.S. Eliot argued that the separation between a writer and her persona should be as great as possible saying, "the more perfect the artist, the more completely separate in him will be the man who suffers and the mind which creates; the more perfectly will the mind digest and transmute the passions which are its material."[20] Modern writers may tend to ignore this injunction against

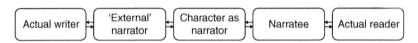

Figure 6.1   The interactions between writer and reader

Source: This model is adapted from Rob Pope, *The English Studies Book*, p. 218.

emotional investment but stop well short of the authorial intrusion of 'dear reader.'

Many novels have omniscient narrators, disembodied voices who tell us what is happening. This third person narration is located outside the narrative and is the voice of authorial authority. What they say goes. If we're told, "Marley was dead," we accept it. If we're later told that Marley is up and about wrapped in chains and looking a little transparent we don't, as Scrooge does, start doubting what we're told, we just go along with it.

The character as narrator is a particular construction who acts as the mouthpiece for the writer's words but also takes part in the action. In *Dr Jekyll and Mr Hyde,* the *character as narrator* is Utterson. *Wuthering Heights* has many narrators, but the story is mostly told by Lockwood who retells the story told to him by Nelly Dean. In *Beloved,* the *character as narrator* switches between the perspectives of Sethe, Denver and Beloved. When we have characters as narrators we sometimes suspect they're not altogether reliable. One of the joys of *Wuthering Heights* is that the actions of Cathy and Heathcliff are filtered through two removes. Lockwood is far from the brightest bulb in the box and Nelly has got it in for Heathcliff. Maybe, we suspect as we read, we're not being told the truth entire?

In each of these examples, the *narratee* is the writer's construction of a reader; who they imagine is reading and responding to their words. *You* are my *narratee* and I have imagined you as a fresh-faced, enthusiastic young English teacher anxious to win over the hearts and minds of your pupils. This can be made explicit (as I just did) but is usually not. And then finally we have the *actual reader.* Maybe you're an old and embittered English teacher. Maybe you're not an English teacher at all. Maybe you're only reading this book to pick apart and mock my ideas. *Actual readers* impose their own needs and decide whether they will cooperate with the writer. The two-way arrows stand for the ways in which we reach backwards and forwards as readers and writers and suggests something of the dialogue between us.

Character

Just as stories must have plots, a plot needs characters. F. Scott Fitzgerald went so far as to say, "Character *is* action." One point that students need to have made early and often is that characters are not real. Of course, they exist at some philosophical level but they have no existence beyond the texts they inhabit. It makes little sense to speculate about what George gets up to after shooting Lennie, or whether Beatrice and Benedick live happily ever after: there is no after. But lots of people, even those who should know better, do ask these questions. L.C. Knight's wonderfully titled essay 'How Many Children had Lady Macbeth?' pokes fun at A.C. Bradley's tendency to pry non-existent details out of the backgrounds of characters.[21] Despite this, the heroes and villains of the stories we tell can take on a vivid reality for the duration of their brief fictional lives.

As we've seen, Aristotle described characters as 'higher' or 'lower' types. His higher types are heroes. Sebastian Faulks argues that applying 'hero' to the central character of a story is "at best a misnomer and at worst a category error."[22] Hero, like so many other words, has changed its meaning over time. Today we think of a hero as somebody who puts themselves at risk to help somebody else, or as someone we can admire and look up to, but that definition doesn't always work when considering the concept of story. First and foremost, the hero is the principal character – the protagonist – around whom the plot revolves, but certain types of story work best with certain types of hero.

For instance, the heroes of Greek epics rarely fit modern ideals of heroism; for the most part they were a pretty selfish bunch and often behaved badly. For instance, Achilles sulks in his tent for weeks on end as his allies are slaughtered. In the end, only the death of his closest friend, Patroclus, gets him back in the fray. An epic hero was usually of divine ancestry (the Greek word *hērōs* in fact meant 'demi-god') and was endowed with great courage and strength, celebrated for his bold exploits, and favoured by the gods. But epic heroes like Achilles, Gilgamesh, Beowulf are all rather one dimensional. They represent an ideal and cannot deviate from it, bound as they are by their destinies and situations. At once these characters are complete, whole, admirable, but – from a modern perspective – rather wooden. Odysseus is perhaps a deviation from the epic ideal in that he vacillates between weakness and strength, action and observation, but even Odysseus cannot be said to learn much or grow in any meaningful way as a result of his circuitous route home.

The heroes of tragedies are a little more complex. Although they must also be of noble bearing – usually a man of wealth and status – they must also possess a flaw which will lead to their downfall. For Oedipus it is hubris – his belief he can outwit the gods; for Othello it's jealousy; Macbeth, ambition; Lear, arrogance; and for Hamlet, that most tragic of tragic heroes? Well, the traditional view is that he's undone by procrastination – an inability to act – but this isn't really right. When he feels he knows what to do he acts with alacrity (think of his killing of Polonius and his savage rejection of Ophelia) but when it comes to the crunch he's crippled with doubt, not dithering. In the matter of exacting revenge on Claudius for his father's murder, he fears that his father's ghost may be a sending of the Devil trying to trick him into evil. If you genuinely don't know what to do, inaction is a virtue.[23] Maybe Hamlet is not so much flawed as unable to shoulder an impossible burden?

Modern heroes are much more in the mould of Hamlet: a bit of this, a bit of that; some good, some bad. According to Mikhail Bakhtin, heroes of novels differ from the heroes of other literary forms in two respects. First, "the hero of a novel should not be 'heroic' in either the epic or the tragic sense of the word: he should combine in himself negative as

> **MIKHAIL BAKHTIN**
> **1895–1975**
>
> Russian philosopher, literary critic and scholar who worked on literary theory, ethics and the philosophy of language.

well as positive features, low as well as lofty, ridiculous as well as serious," and second, "the hero should not be portrayed as an already completed and unchanging person but as one who is evolving and developing, a person who learns from life."[24] As a result, we can identify with the heroes of novels in a way we cannot with the heroes of epic and tragedy.

From Bakhtin's prescriptions, it's a short step from hero to antihero. Antiheroes abound in literature from Thackery's exquisitely self-centred creation Becky Sharp; to Graham Greene's viciously vulnerable Pinkie Brown; to the flamboyantly lonely and solipsistic outsider Jay Gatsby; to that template of schoolboy angst, Holden Caulfield. We like them despite themselves, despite their weaknesses and poor decisions; we care about their plights even if they are all their own fault.

Characterisation

One of the naïve misconceptions that leaks into students' observations about characters is that they are, in some way, real: with their own agency and an existence beyond their stories. This is as likely to be true for obviously unreal characters

(Charlotte in *Charlotte's Web*, Napoleon in *Animal Farm*, Ariel in *The Tempest*) as it is for more plausibly realistic creations. One of the most important distinctions for students to learn to make is that between *character* and *characterisation*. If a character can be defined as a fictional figure constructed from words, characterisation is the literary, linguistic and cultural processes through which that construction takes place.

Whatever texts students study, they will encounter a multiplicity of characters but all these emerge from the same processes of character creation. Characters tend to be of particular *types*. We've already thought about heroes (or protagonists) as a type of character, and a story will also often have a villain (antagonist) but there are many other stock characters. One of Aristotle's students, Theophrastus, was the first to attempt a systematic catalogue of the different types. He listed over thirty distinct types such as 'the flatterer,' 'the boor,' 'the coward' and 'the lover of bad company.' More recently stock characters as 'the wise old guardian,' 'the temptress' and 'the mad woman' are all endlessly recycled in the stories we tell.

Beyond types of character, characters can be conceived of in all sorts of other ways. The novelist E.M. Forster saw characters as being either 'rounded' or 'flat' and felt that both were necessary. A rounded character has a rich interior life, is psychologically complex and will develop as her story progresses. A flat character is only known through external appearances and behaviour, and is more likely to descend into caricature. Flat characters may be easy for readers to recognise and remember. Forster reckoned that Dickens' characters "are nearly all flat," and "can be summed up in a single sentence," but still manage to produce "a wonderful feeling of human depth."[25] By, contrast, he saw all Jane Austen's characters as rounded. Comparing her to Dickens he says, "her characters, though smaller than his, are more highly organized."[26] Whether or not characters are well rounded, what's most important is that they have life and vitality, or as Sebastian Faulks puts it, "the highest virtue a fictional character can possess is *interest*."[27]

The boundaries between character and narrative device are often blurred: Orwell brutally sacrifices Winston Smith to make his point about the inhumanity of totalitarianism; Fielding too frequently provides a deus-ex-machina to pull Tom Jones out of his various scrapes; Hardy's characters (with the exception of Tess with whom he seemed to have been in love) are firmly bound upon the wheel of fate and have little chance to develop; and Dickens' pointless and indiscriminate insistence on the 'Jewishness' of Fagin sits uncomfortably for modern readers.

Characters can either be narrators or actors. A character-narrator provides the frame through which the story is viewed; actors are merely encountered and described. Some characters act as narrative manifestations of the author, a means for the author's ideas and perspectives to intrude into a story. This can be done clumsily as in Priestley's use of Inspector Goole as a proxy for his socialist ideology; cruelly as in Thackery's constant mocking of his characters' weaknesses to demonstrate 'all is vanity'; or elegantly as with Austen's subtle judgements of the rude and depressive Mr Darcy.

What stops characters from becoming dull and formulaic is the process of characterisation and the interaction of character and plot. The most well-known of these interactions has come to be called the hero's journey in which a character goes on an adventure, triumphs in some pivotal crisis and returns transformed. Joseph Campbell, who popularised the notion in his book, *The Hero with a Thousand Faces*, described the hero's journey like this:

> A hero ventures forth from the world of common day into a region of supernatural wonder: fabulous forces are there

encountered and a decisive victory is won: the hero comes back from this mysterious adventure with the power to bestow boons on his fellow man.[28]

Campbell saw this journey as 'the monomyth' – a term he lifted from *Finnegans Wake* – as the ultimate narrative archetype to which all characters' arcs conform; the story behind all stories.

Various theorists have suggested the hero's journey follows predictable patterns. For instance, Vladimir Propp analysed the structure of folk tales and identified 31 distinct structural elements, or 'functions,' that would occur in a predictable order. Campbell boiled this down to seventeen stages which could be further clumped into three broad 'acts': departure, initiation and return.

Flaw and façade

These grand, mythic schemes are all very well, but perhaps what happens inside a character's head is as, if not more, important than their progress through plot. John Yorke sees characters as possessing both a flaw and a façade. The façade is how they present themselves to the world, the parts of themselves they believe to be honourable and worthwhile but which, as the story progresses, are revealed as that which will stand in their way or even destroy them. Conversely, the traits a character believes to be flaws, those aspects of themselves they conceal, are revealed as strengths and the source of their redemption. Characters wear masks to hide the things they fear, as do we all.[29]

In *A Christmas Carol*, Scrooge's perceived flaw of generosity and cheerfulness is carefully hidden away under layers of misanthropy. He "carried his own low temperature always about with him." His façade is encapsulated by his wish to be left alone. But the ghost of Christmas past shows him his younger self; lonely and self-contained. He pities the flaws of this younger version of himself and we see the seeds of his bitter façade take root. The spirit tells him,

> You fear the world too much. ... All your other hopes have merged into the hope of being beyond the chance of its sordid reproach. I have seen your nobler aspirations fall off one by one, until the master passion, Gain, engrosses you.

When the second spirit appears, Scrooge, now submissive says, "if you have aught to teach me, let me profit by it." By the time the third spirit arrives, Scrooge's heartless façade has been torn down and the 'flaw' of his compassion is revealed. He is reborn: "I'm quite a baby. Never mind. I don't care. I'd rather be a baby."

Or, in more tragic plots, the reverse sequence occurs. In *Macbeth*, our hero's façade as "valiant cousin" and "worthy gentleman" wins him admiration and reward, but when he realises he might be "king hereafter" his "vaulting ambition" drives him to murder his way to throne. But his façade stands in his way. His wife worries he is "too full o' the milk of human kindness." He is indecisive and worries about losing the "golden opinions" he has won. When he does act he's wracked with guilt and fear. But fear leads to further bloodshed. One by one, he murders his friends and his allies desert him. He is increasingly "steeped in blood" until, beheaded by Macduff, the façade is completely stripped away and he is vilified as a "dead butcher."

As Figure 6.2 shows, at different points in a story, different aspects of character are foregrounded as flaw and façade are integrated and rebalanced.

John Yorke expresses the process like this:

> What appear to be random quirks of individual characterization are in fact intimately linked to a pattern, one built on the war of opposites, and seeking perfect symmetry.[30]

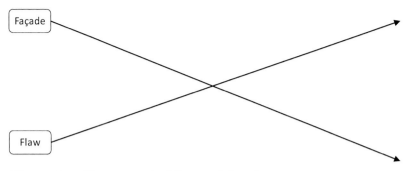

Figure 6.2 The reversal of flaw and façade

In this way, character, characterisation and plot are inextricably connected. The fascination is that such seemingly simple structures can manifest in such an infinite variety of characters and stories.

Thought: speech

An essential aspect of storytelling is how characters are revealed and plot is developed through thought. When Aristotle named this as an important part of narrative he had in mind only the forms of story available to him: epic sung poems and drama. Whilst it might have been perfectly possible to relate the internal thoughts of the characters in epic, in practice this innovation would have to wait until more modern times. In both epic and drama, characters' thoughts must be voiced. I mentioned earlier that the dramatist Aeschylus is credited with the invention of dialogue as an on-stage representation of real conversation. This now seems so natural and unremarkable that we struggle to see it as an invention, but a little thought demonstrates that the speech we see in plays and in books is very different from spoken exchanges in the real world that stories seek to imitate.

171

Story

If you've not seen transcripts of actual conversations before they can come as a bit of shock. The following is a transcript of a conversation between Mike and his friends Jimmy and Rob:

> J *yeah (.) cheers Mike*
>
> R *getting ol. married /ən/ stuff*
>
> M *this is what I've got in my head (1) I want to incorp-orate a* **wrestling** *show (.) into the wedding (1) I want /ləʊdzə/ action between with fire-breathi:::ng (1) /ən/ all* _{accel} *sorts I want ring girls with ca:::rds I want it to be a* **big** *spectacle a* **huge** *show*
>
> R *you've got some good plans you've got some good* **plans**
>
> J *you've* **thought** *about (1) it which is the main // thing*
>
> M *// yeah**

Here's another example, this time between the footballer John Barnes and his mother:

> M *my favourite picture of your father is that one on the wall (1) ⬀*
>   *yes*
>
> J *what was that?*
>
> M *that was taken (1) 1988 (2)* **we** *went to Up Park Camp when you were a couple of months old in about (.) '64 you had some* **good** *times there didn't // you*
>
> J *// I had (1) (accel)* <u>well all times</u>
>
> M *you had a good place /kɒz/ you // could run up and down*
>
> J *//* **all** *good times*
>
> J *and the football field right opposite where we lived we had & eighty mango trees in th. (1) in the garden*

---

*   The inverted e symbol 'ə' represents the schwa sound. See page 221 for details.

M   *yes (.) and you used to (.) play a lot of football there
that was **all** you used to do*[31]

Without trying to explain all the technicalities of transcribing
spoken language, we can see that it's disappointingly different
from the crisp dialogue we expect to see in literature. We talk
over each other, we lose the thread of what we're saying, we
pause for no clear reason and we're *really boring.*

When we consider dialogue as the fictional representation of
conversation, we tend to make judgements about whether it's
natural or authentic, but as you can see from these transcripts,
naturalness and authenticity are *not* what we really want. For
the most part, storytellers are content to conform to highly
conventional expectations of how people speak.

The most important function of dialogue is that it is a
key part of the process of characterisation; we learn about
characters through their speech, both in terms of what they
say and how they say it. Here is an example of a conversation
from chapter two of *The Catcher in the Rye* between Holden
Caulfield and his teacher, Mr Spencer:

"What did Dr. Thurmer say to you, boy? I understand you
had quite a little chat."

"Yes, we did. We really did. I was in his office for around
two hours, I guess."

"What'd he say to you?"

"Oh ... well, about Life being a game and all. And how
you should play it according to the rules. He was pretty
nice about it. I mean he didn't hit the ceiling or anything.
He just kept talking about Life being a game and all.
You know."

"Life is a game, boy. Life is a game that one plays according to the rules."

"Yes, sir, I know it is. I know it."

Throughout the text, Caulfield lies to and tries to manipulate the adults he encounters. In this extract we get a glimpse of Caulfield's true character as we watch him try to convince Mr Spencer that he cares about school.

In the following extract from *Wuthering Heights*, Heathcliff has broken into Catherine's room to confront her on her death bed while her husband is at church. The love they felt as children has become twisted up with hate and resentment. Although Heathcliff feels betrayed, he has just discovered she is dying:

"You teach me now how cruel you've been – cruel and false. *Why* did you despise me? *Why* did you betray your own heart, Cathy? I have not one word of comfort. You deserve this. You have killed yourself. Yes, you may kiss me, and cry; and wring out my kisses and tears: they'll blight you – they'll damn you. You loved me – then what *right* had you to leave me? What right – answer me – for the poor fancy you felt for Linton? Because misery and degradation, and death, and nothing that God or Satan could inflict would have parted us, *you*, of your own will, did it. I have not broken your heart – *you* have broken it; and in breaking it, you have broken mine. So much the worse for me that I am strong. Do I want to live? What kind of living will it be when you – oh, God! would *you* like to live with your soul in the grave?"

"Let me alone. Let me alone," sobbed Catherine. "If I've done wrong, I'm dying for it. It is enough! You left me too: but I won't upbraid you! I forgive you. Forgive me!"

"It is hard to forgive, and to look at those eyes, and feel those wasted hands," he answered. "Kiss me again; and don't let me see your eyes! I forgive what you have done to me. I love *my* murderer – but *yours*! How can I?"

Brontë's dialogue captures the melodrama of their relation-ship, alternating between violent cruelty and anguished passion. Not only the words, but the punctuation is put to use to help us hear Heathcliff's torment. When he cries, "I love *my* murderer – but *yours*! How can I?" the italics denote anguished emotion; the dash simulates a stutter as he searches for words and the exclamation point suggests impassioned shouting as he refuses Catherine the forgiveness she craves.

Sometimes dialogue reveals as much in what it doesn't say as in what it does. The following extract from the first chapter of *Pride and Prejudice* is a case in point:

"My dear Mr. Bennet," said his lady to him one day, "have you heard that Netherfield Park is let at last?"

Mr. Bennet replied that he had not.

"But it is," returned she; "for Mrs. Long has just been here, and she told me all about it."

Mr. Bennet made no answer.

"Do not you want to know who has taken it?" cried his wife impatiently.

"You want to tell me, and I have no objection to hearing it."

This was invitation enough.

To Mrs Bennet's first question we have her husband's answer in the form of reported speech, we don't actually hear his reply. To her next statement he returns only silence. Mr Bennet's only line of direct speech is almost unnecessary except it shows him toying with his wife and making his lack of interest plain. This sketched relationship between a giddily excited wife and an aloof, indifferent husband hardly needs Austen's exposition a few pages later.

Internal thought

Some thought is internal. In drama, internal thought is often shown in the form of a soliloquy, where a character speaks her thoughts aloud. In a novel a character's thoughts are revealed through first person narration or passages of stream of consciousness.

> ### SOLILOQUY
>
> Latin: *soliloquium* 'talking to oneself,' from *solus* 'alone' + *loqui* 'to speak.'
>
> Character's thoughts spoken aloud for the benefit of an audience.

Stream of consciousness became popular in the 20th century with writers such as James Joyce and Virginia Woolf. Here's an example from Woolf's novel, *Mrs Dalloway*:

> What a lark! What a plunge! For so it always seemed to me when, with a little squeak of the hinges, which I can hear now, I burst open the French windows and plunged at Bourton into the open air. How fresh, how calm, stiller than this of course, the air was in the early morning; like the flap of a wave; the kiss of a wave; chill and sharp and yet (for a girl of eighteen as I then was) solemn, feeling as I did, standing there at the open window, that something awful was about to happen ...

Here, Woolf gives her character the freedom to travel back and forth in time. As Mrs Dalloway goes through the mundane act of buying flowers, her thoughts move through the past and present, allowing us an insight into the complex nature of her character.

Some of Shakespeare's finest dramatic moments come when a character delivers a soliloquy, revealing their innermost thoughts and feelings. Just after Macbeth learns of his wife's death he reflects on the futility of all that he has done:

> To-morrow, and to-morrow, and to-morrow,
> Creeps in this petty pace from day to day
> To the last syllable of recorded time,
> And all our yesterdays have lighted fools
> The way to dusty death. Out, out, brief candle!
> Life's but a walking shadow, a poor player
> That struts and frets his hour upon the stage
> And then is heard no more: it is a tale
> Told by an idiot, full of sound and fury,
> Signifying nothing

The plodding melancholy of "to-morrow, and to-morrow, and to-morrow" suggests Macbeth's despair at how hopeless and pathetic life now seems. He begins to build himself up into a rage as he rails that his life's a "walking shadow," that for all its noise and activity it might as well be the mumblings of a halfwit ... and here Macbeth seems to run out of steam, ending with the anti-climactic observation that life has no meaning. From sorrow, to bitter rage to numb acceptance in ten lines, and never once do we doubt the sincerity of Macbeth's words, spoken, as they are, just to us.

In poetry, the dramatic monologue – a form perfected by Robert Browning – provides the same sort of opportunity to reveal character. In 'My Last Duchess' the Duke of Ferrara negotiates his marriage to the daughter of a neighbouring Count and, in conversation with the Count's emissary he shows him the painting of his previous wife.

The Duke reveals – inadvertently or otherwise – that he ordered his wife's murder for the inexcusable crime of being a little overly friendly. We get glimpses of his coldly psychotic nature in phrases such as, "if they durst" and, "the faint half-flush that dies along her throat." Browning's use of strict iambic pentameter blends effortlessly with disorientating enjambment and sudden caesura to give the Duke both a stateliness and a staccato lack of assurance to his narration that marks him out as both believing himself above his unheard interlocutor and confused by the attitudes and emotions of other people.

Thought – whether alone and internal or in dialogue with others – is one of the most effective tools for revealing character, progressing plot and telling a story.

Theme

Theme is a rather slippery, hard-to-define concept that students often find difficult to grasp. As mentioned in the previous chapter, a theme is an abstract idea that the writer wants to discuss over an unfolding narrative. Themes are woven throughout the plot of a story; they are evident in the actions of characters and expressed in their thoughts. Themes are typically universal human problems that can never be resolved, just better understood. The sorts of themes dealt with in the stories students are likely to encounter in English might include various different kinds of power, coming of age, disillusionment and dreams, injustice, loss of innocence, identity, loyalty, jealousy, revenge, ambition, loneliness and many more. Once students learn that although there may be an infinite variety of stories there is a much more limited number of themes to be explored, this can give them a way in to better understanding the texts they will explore.

A theme should unify every element of plot and character, should run through a story like the writing in a stick of rock, or a golden thread. In Greek mythology, the lives of both mortals and immortals were controlled by the three Fates as they spun the threads of each individual life into the tapestry of reality. In Dickens' novel *A Tale of Two Cities*, fate is represented by two characters: Madame Defarge is the pitiless embodiment of the French Revolution, stitching the names of her enemies into her knitting, condemning them to death; and Lucie Manette, who has the power to recall her father back to life after his long imprisonment. Where Madame Defarge is the brooding figure of evil, Lucie is the representation of goodness who weaves the "golden thread" that knits together both the characters and the themes of sacrifice and redemption.

The metaphor of the golden thread is a useful way to think about theme; it is not a separate element like character or plot but a relationship between them and us, the reader. Another way to think about theme is as a perspective, or frame, from which and through which we view stories. Perhaps theme is best understood as a relationship between what is being looked at and from where it is being viewed. The more complex a story, the more frames of references it offers from which we are able to observe. For instance, *Macbeth* can be viewed as a warning of the dangers of "vaulting ambition." Every choice and event lends itself to being viewed in this way: the witches play on an inherent flaw in Macbeth's character; once the seed is planted in his mind Macbeth obsesses about becoming "king hereafter"; once Lady Macbeth hears the news she is concerned that although her husband is "not without ambition" he lacks "the illness should attend it" and determines to push him forward despite himself; once the Macbeths have achieved their ambition their thoughts move to being "safely thus," and so the play unfolds to its inevitable end.

But if we follow a different thread, the play can be viewed from a different perspective. In *The Imperial Theme*, the critic G. Wilson Knight chooses to follow the threads of fear and courage. Macbeth begins the play in heroic mode as "brave," "noble" and "valour's minion." He is rewarded for his courage in battle, but all is spoiled when Duncan names his son, Malcolm, as his heir. Immediately, Macbeth is frightened of what he might do:

> The eye wink at the hand; yet let that be
> Which the eye fears, when it is done, to see.

When Lady Macbeth seeks to sway her doubting husband she appeals to his "valour" and, despite the claim that he "dare[s] do all that may become a man," in actual fact he gives in to his fear of appearing weak. As Wilson puts it, "Macbeth really gives way all along from fear: from fear of fear."[32] Right from the start he has been tormented: his "present fears are less than horrible imaginings." He can be brave in battle but is unmanned by the supernatural. Again, this thread is stitched throughout the play until, at last, Macbeth can "refuse to play the Roman fool" and face up to the entirely human threat of Macduff.

Whenever we read, whether it's a play, a novel or a poem, we should be alert for these golden threads. Whenever we notice one we should tug. *Where else have we noticed this theme? What analogies can we make?* If it comes loose then it was probably a false perspective from which to view, but if we can follow it throughout the story, we will have a powerful tool for making meaning.

Teaching story

When introducing the concept of story, it makes sense to start with myth. Show how different cultures have reached for explanations of the same natural phenomena by exploring creation myths alongside William Tyndale's translation of Genesis and Milton's Biblical epic, *Paradise Lost*. Show how modern myths arise to serve the same purposes; why are superheroes so popular? Why did people believe in UFOs until very recently? And other, more mundane myths, such as the 'rags-to-riches' stories told by reality TV.

From there, you could introduce Aristotle's five-part plot structure: beginning; complication; the turning point; denouement; and resolution, and show how these elements can be traced in all stories, from the familiar tales of childhood, to those of popular culture, to those studied in English. Once students grasp that the underlying essence of stories can be similar despite their different surface features they can use it to build analogies between what they are reading now and all the other stories they know. Then, use Christopher Booker's notion of the 'seven basic plots' to show how story structures are different as well as similar; students can try to work out which plots best fit the stories they know and then try to work out whether there are stories that don't fit, and why that might be.

I suggest focussing on tragedy and comedy as, arguably, the two most enduring and important of the archetypal plots and learning to see how they are reflections of each other – from order to disorder or the reverse – and how these directions can be hidden away in stories which might not otherwise fit our assumptions of tragedy and comedy.

As students come to understand that the stories have recognisable structures and tend to follow well-trodden paths they become better able to notice the artifice in the stories they encounter. Here are some questions we can usefully ask about plot:

- Does the story we're reading conform to a particular structure?
- Are there any points of departure where a writer bends the 'rules' of a particular genre?
- Are there recognisable complications, turning points and denouements?

Story

- What are the moments of recognition or reversal?
- Is there a 'deep structure' to the plot which runs counter to the mood of the story?

Students need to distinguish between real people and characters; no matter how complex or satisfying a character may be it has no life beyond their text and is conjured into a vivid half-life simply through words. This process of character creation – characterisation – is one that needs to be taught for students to recognise the craft of writers and experiment with it in their own writing.

I suggest starting with Forster's idea of rounded and flat characters and then using John Yorke's scheme of flaw and façade to trace the development of characters. Students should be guided to a range of examples of writers' techniques for depicting character: narration, description and speech.

Just as characters are not real people, so speech in stories is very different to speech in the real world. It's fun to get students to transcribe their own speech as well as looking at transcripts like the ones on pages 172–3 and comparing to speech in plays, poems and novels.

Some questions to discuss might include:

- If there are different types of characters, what types are there in the stories we have studied?
- How does the writer guide our response to their characters?
- How do we know if the protagonist of the story is heroic?
- How have characters changed over time? Are our expectations different?
- Can we identify hidden flaws and unhelpful façades?
- How do writers use speech to present and distinguish their characters?

Then, once plot and character are well understood, introduce the idea of theme as a 'golden thread' running through a text, uniting character and action in underlying, universal concerns. Make connections with motifs and other forms of metaphor to explore how themes are embedded and brought to the surface.

Again, here are some questions to discuss:

- Are actions or incidents repeated or reversed?
- Do characters embody particular traits?
- Are we drawn to notice particular objects or ideas?
- What might they symbolise?

KEY POINTS

- We seem to have an instinct for constructing narratives to help us understand the world; we automatically create causal links between potentially unrelated events.
- All stories fit a fairly narrow set of structures but different types of story tend to follow different conventions. Students should be particularly alert for the structures of tragedy and comedy.
- Recognition (where either characters or readers understand the consequences of an action) and reversal (where expected events fail to turn out as we expect) make a plot complex and emotionally satisfying.
- Noticing the balance of characters' façades and flaws helps us understand how characters are made vivid and interesting.

> - Depending on the form literature takes, writers have a range of techniques available to reveal their characters' inner workings. Students should be guided to notice how these different approaches achieve their aims.
> - Students need help to understand how a theme forms a 'golden thread' that runs throughout a text and can be manifested in a variety of different ways.

It might be said that a story is a form of argument. Certainly, some of the most memorable stories seek to persuade us that a particular course of action is either good or bad. If a story is successful we will be convinced by it, at least for the duration of our reading. In the next chapter we turn to argument as a complementary, but distinct mode of making meaning in English.

Further reading

- By far the most thorough and wide-ranging text on storytelling I've read is Christopher Booker's *The Seven Basic Plots.*
- Aristotle's *Poetics* is very readable, very short and still very influential.
- John Yorke's *Into The Woods* is a wonderful book on narrative from a screenwriting perspective.
- Anyone wanting a deeper psychological account of story would be well advised to track down a copy of Mark Turner's *The Literary Mind.* For a more accessible introduction I'd also recommend Will Storr's *The Science of Storytelling.*

7 | Argument

Argument, as a way of making meaning, extends far beyond bickering and negation. Remember the Monty Python sketch? Graham Chapman's character pays to have an argument with the character played by John Cleese but after several minutes of fruitless back and forth, Chapman, exasperated, says, "this isn't an argument ... it's just contradiction." After another series of contradictions, Chapman insists that an argument is "a connected series of statements intended to establish a proposition."[1] Predictably, he continues to be contradicted. Chapman was right: this is not an argument.

The basis of any argument is that we advance an opinion for which supporting evidence is supplied. An argument should offer a clear, logical, convincing progression of thought. Comedy sketches aside, this is inherent in thought and language. Stephen Fry says,

> From the thesis, antithesis, synthesis of the earliest logicians, the propositions, suppositions and proofs of Euclid and the strophe, antistrophe and epode of Greek performance and poetic ode to our own parliaments and senate chambers, boardrooms, courtrooms and committee rooms, this structure of proposal, counterproposal and vote, prosecution, defence and verdict is deep within us. It

is how we seem best to frame the contrary flows of thought and feeling that would otherwise freeze us into inaction or propel us into civil war or schizophrenic uncertainty.[2]

Language is essentially transactional; we speak – or write – because we want something, some response, from a listener or reader. That said, we tend not to put much conscious thought into what that response should be, or into the language tools they will employ to secure it. If students are to make meaning, they must learn the knowledge needed to participate in the long tradition of rational argument and debate.

The purpose of argument is persuasion. Persuasion exists with a context which includes a speaker, an audience, a point of contention, the argument itself and a common body of knowledge. By identifying and understanding the roles of each of these components we can learn to notice how arguments work. Here are some questions to ask about each of these five ingredients:

1. The speaker: What is known of their character and experience? Are they knowledgeable and trustworthy? Do we like or dislike what we know about them?
2. The audience: What is known about their biases and preferences? What is their mood? Has anything happened recently to make them more or less predisposed to a particular argument?
3. The point of contention: What is at stake? How serious is the dispute? Is it emotionally loaded?
4. The argument: What is the 'premise' (what Aristotle called the 'formal cause') for disagreement? What reasons will be advanced and what tactics employed to make these reasons persuasive?
5. Common body of knowledge: These 'commonplaces' might be established facts or values that we can assume the speaker

and the audience share. Does the speaker know what these are? Are these commonplaces explicit or implicit? How do we *know* these facts or values are shared? (The consequences for misjudgement can be severe.) Are opinions being falsely presented as facts? Are we being browbeaten into accepting something as true which may not be?

Imagine a very trivial piece of persuasion: I want you to look up the endnote at the end of this paragraph. In this case, the speaker is me, the author of the book you're reading. As I wrote it, I know more about the book than you do (at least until you've finished). I know little about the audience – you – except that you've chosen to read the book and so must be at least somewhat interested in following my reasoning. The point of contention is that you have not yet finished the current page and are, one assumes, unwilling to turn to the end just yet. The argument, such as it is, is that there's a treat and a surprise waiting for you when you turn to the back. Our common body of knowledge consists of how books work, the subject matter of this particular book and a shared interest in teaching children English.[3]

Needless to say, most acts of persuasion are a lot more involved and sophisticated than this. So, if we want to inspire, frighten, cajole or chasten our audience, it's worth learning a set of tools to help you make your reasoning effective and your arguments count. This set of tools was first thought out by the ancient Greeks and goes by the name *rhetoric*.

Rhetoric

Originally rhetoric was the art of public speaking; the act of making speeches. A speech, even though it is spoken, is not like most spoken language. It is carefully planned and executed (indeed we know that in the ancient world speeches were often written down both in the planning stage and to be enjoyed afterwards) and shares more in common with written language than it does with everyday speech.

In antiquity, teachers identified three branches of rhetoric: judicial (relating

> ## RHETORIC
>
> Greek: *rhētorike tekhnē* 'art of an orator,' from *rhetor*, 'speaker' + *techne*, 'art,' or 'skill.'
>
> The art of persuasive argument.

to matters of proof in the law courts), deliberative (arguing what is most beneficial in a meeting) and demonstrative (the act of praising or blaming). Although there is a wide range of activities considered vital for budding rhetoricians, we'll restrict ourselves here to the most immediately useful in the English classroom: *invention* and *arrangement*.

Invention

Aristotle distinguished two distinct means of persuasion. The first, *non-artistic proofs*, are those that do not have to be invented: witness statements, written documents and so on. The second, *artistic proofs*, were those a speaker must invent. Aristotle identified three artistic proofs or appeals: *ethos* (appeal to character), *pathos* (appeal to emotion) and *logos* (appeal to reason). Working out what you want to argue benefits from a sound understanding of these three rhetorical appeals.

- Ethos is the image we present to those we are attempting to persuade and the attempt to win over an audience by portraying ourselves as ethical: 'You should believe my argument because you believe *me*,' or perhaps '... believe *in* me.'

- Logos is the Greek for 'word' and refers to the use of logic and reason to prove an argument true. This can take the form of using evidence, facts and statistics, citing examples of our proposals that have worked elsewhere, drawing parallels between *this* situation or person and another. The appeal to reason gives us credibility, makes our arguments seem obvious and paints alternatives as illogical.
- Pathos is the emotional influence of the speaker on the audience. Its goal is to create a favourable emotional response and play on our audience's fears and weaknesses, as well as exciting them to compassion and, of course, making 'em laugh.

We should encourage students to notice the interplay of these appeals in examples of speeches from life or literature. Act 3 scene 2 of *Julius Caesar* provides an excellent opportunity to see rhetoric at work. Mark Antony begins his oration at Caesar's funeral with the famous line, "Friends, Romans and Countrymen, lend me your ears." Instead of boasting about himself, Antony is showing the crowd that he is one of them. He is first appealing to his audience on a human level as friends, establishing a feeling of fellowship. He reminds them they are all Romans, with the privileges and responsibilities which come with being a citizen. Finally, in referring to them as countrymen he uses a term that suggests both friendship and civic responsibility. To be a countryman is to share a bond of loyalty and tradition. Then, rather than command silence he asks the crowd to, "lend me your ears." He's asking for the people to trust him with a loan. All of this begins to change the way the crowd feels about Antony. At first, they're suspicious but as he continues to speak they are reassured by his appeal to character.

Antony appeals to reason by providing logical arguments to show that Caesar did not deserve to be murdered: he made

Rome richer; he cried along with the poor; he refused a crown, etc. Antony is careful to avoid coming out and simply saying that Caesar's killers are the baddies, instead he allows the crowd to come to this conclusion themselves as they weigh Antony's evidence and decide that maybe Caesar has been a bit hard done by and that Brutus and the other conspirators must all be selfish liars.

Finally, Antony appeals to the crowd's emotions when he shows the crowd Caesar's murdered body. He pretends to choke up saying, "Bear with me, my heart is in the coffin there with Caesar." The crowd sees his tears and begins to warm to Antony and interpret everything he says in a more favourable light. Is this cheating? Well, maybe, but feeling – and fellow feeling – is the basis for pretty much everything that most people regard as important. Feelings may not be logical but they often change the way we think and act.

John Milton's epic poem *Paradise Lost* offers us another chance to admire one of the great masters of rhetoric. Formerly the most beautiful of all angels and God's right hand, Lucifer – now Satan – was unwilling to accept God's authority and led a rebellion in Heaven. Following its failure, he has been cast out from Heaven and condemned, with all the demons who followed him, to Hell. Utterly defeated, Satan needs to convince Beelzebub and the other demons that they're in this together and that losing the war with God was merely a setback. He claims he isn't really to blame for their current predicament as surely no one could have anticipated the power of God's 'dire Arms':

> ... so much the stronger proved
> He with his Thunder: and till then who knew
> The force of those dire Arms? yet not for those
> Nor what the Potent Victor in his rage
> Can else inflict do I repent or change,

Though changed in outward lustre; that fixed mind
And high disdain, from sense of injured merit,
That with the mightiest raised me to contend,
And to the fierce contention brought along
Innumerable force of Spirits arm'd
That durst dislike his reign, and me preferring,
His utmost power with adverse power opposed
In dubious battle on the Plains of Heaven,
And shook his throne.

Satan urges his followers back to the fight arguing, with an appeal to reason, that his rule would be preferable to the "Tyranny of Heaven." Having, one presumes, suitably inspired Beelzebub and the others, Satan turns his attention to the future, arguing that their defeat wasn't really a defeat at all. Even though their eternal lives are blighted, at least God couldn't break their spirits:

All is not lost; the unconquerable Will,
And study of revenge, immortal hate,
And courage never to submit or yield:
And what is else not to be overcome?
That Glory never shall his wrath or might
Extort from me. To bow and sue for grace
With suppliant knee, and defile his power
Who from the terror of this Arm so late
Doubted his Empire, that were low indeed,
That were an ignominy and shame beneath
This downfall; since by Fate the strength of Gods
And this imperial substance cannot fail,
Since through experience of this great event
In Arms not worse, in foresight much advanced,
We may with more successful hope resolve
To wage by force or guile eternal war

Argument

> Irreconcilable, to our grand Foe,
> Who now triumphs, and in the excess of joy
> Sole reigning holds the Tyranny of Heav'n.

Defeat, Satan argues, has been a valuable lesson. He launches into a rousing appeal to emotion by claiming they are now much better prepared to launch a counterattack against Heaven. Surely, next time the forces of Hell will triumph against the "grand Foe"! What could possibly go wrong?

Arrangement

Once you have come up with the appeals you want to make, you need to arrange your ideas into their most effective form. The Roman orator Cicero, one of the most important figures in the development of rhetoric, published his first work on the subject while he was still a teenager. Later, after an eventful career in which he managed a stint as consul (the highest office of the Roman republic), he wrote a second text on rhetoric. Cicero's writing had a tremendous influence on rhetoric throughout the Middle Ages and into the Renaissance. The result is probably the best-known and widely used six-part rhetorical arrangement:[4]

> **MARCUS TULLIUS CICERO – 106–43 BC**
>
> Roman statesman, lawyer and philosopher who played an important role in the politics of the late Republic. Assassinated because of his opposition to Mark Antony. He wrote two influential works on rhetoric: *On Invention* and *On the Ideal Orator*.

1. *Exordium* – An introduction, establishing credibility, grabbing attention
2. *Narration* – Setting out the facts as agreed on

3. *Division* – Setting out differences
4. *Proof* – Supporting arguments
5. *Refutation* – Refuting opponents' arguments
6. *Peroration* – A conclusion, reiteration of main points, final flourish

Exordium – Cicero advised that "every exordium ought either to convey an intimation of the whole matter in hand, or some introduction and support to the cause, or something of ornament and dignity."[5] Quintilian, another Roman rhetorician, adds that "the sole purpose of the exordium is to prepare our audience in such a way that they will be disposed to lend a ready ear to the rest of our speech."[6] As long as your audience is in the right frame of mind to pay attention and has some of idea of what to expect, all should be well.

Milton not only wrote enduringly powerful epic poetry, he also provides us with a masterclass by writing an exordium about writing exordiums:

> The noblest masters of rhetoric have left behind them in various screeds a maxim which can hardly have escaped you, my academic friends, and which says that in every type of speech – demonstrative, deliberative, or judicial – the opening should be designed to win the goodwill of the audience. On those terms only can the minds of the auditors be made responsive and the cause that the speaker has at heart be won. If this be true (and – not to disguise the truth – I know that it is a principle established by the vote of the entire learned world), how unlucky I am! What a plight I am in today! In the very first words of my speech, I am afraid that I am going to say something unbecoming to a speaker, and that I shall be obliged to neglect the first and most important duty of an orator. And in fact, what good will can I expect from you when in as great an

assembly as this I recognize almost every face within eye-
shot as unfriendly to me? I seem to have come to play an
orator's part before an utterly unsympathetic audience.[7]

Clearly, young Milton was a bit of a show-off and – as he himself acknowledges – this is possibly not the best way to get your
audience on side. Probably something a little simpler would
be a better bet. Cicero observes that the best time to decide on
your exordium is after you've finished writing the rest of your
argument; only then do you know what will best suit the rest
of the speech. He warns that whenever he attempted to write
the exordium first, "nothing occurs to me but what is jejune,
or nugatory, or vulgar and ordinary."[8] And no one wants that.

Narration – A narration should, as you might have guessed,
tell a story. In particular, the story behind the argument
you intend to make. According to Cicero, a good narration
should have three qualities: brevity, clarity and plausibility.
Quintilian expanded the definition, explaining that narration
is "the persuasive exposition of that which either has been
done, or is supposed to have been done."[9] Here's an apt
example from a speech William Wilberforce made in 1789 to
convince the House of Commons that the slave trade should
be abolished. His narration is a passionate pathos appeal
asking listeners to imagine the horrors of the trade:

I must speak of the transit of the slaves in the West Indies.
This I confess, in my own opinion, is the most wretched
part of the whole subject. So much misery condensed in
so little room, is more than the human imagination had
ever before conceived. I will not accuse the Liverpool
merchants: I will allow them, nay, I will believe them to
be men of humanity; and I will therefore believe, if it were
not for the enormous magnitude and extent of the evil
which distracts their attention from individual cases, and

makes them think generally, and therefore less feelingly on the subject, they would never have persisted in the trade. I verily believe therefore, if the wretchedness of any one of the many hundred Negroes stowed in each ship could be brought before their view, and remain within the sight of the African Merchant, that there is no one among them whose heart would bear it. Let anyone imagine to himself 6 or 700 of these wretches chained two and two, surrounded with every object that is nauseous and disgusting, diseased, and struggling under every kind of wretchedness! How can we bear to think of such a scene as this?[10]

Although this first attempt to introduce a bill abolishing the trade failed, Wilberforce's 'impassioned exposition' succeeded in swaying the hearts and minds of many of his contemporaries, until the weight of public opinion shifted and the Slave Trade Act was finally passed into law in 1807.

Division – Here's where you set out what divides you and your opponents, what you agree and disagree on. In Richard Nixon's infamous 'Chequers Speech' – given that he was being accused of misusing election expenses – he accepted that he'd received money from his supporters and set out where and how this could be said to be 'morally wrong':

I say that it is morally wrong if any of that $18,000 went to Senator Nixon for my personal use. I say that was morally wrong if it was secretly given and secretly handled. And I say that it was morally wrong if any of the contributors got special favours for the contributions they made.[11]

He then went on to show that as none of these three things had occurred he was a blameless, persecuted innocent.

Proof – This is where you set out the arguments supporting your case. Now logos comes to the fore. If the law is on your side, say so. If you have witnesses and supporters who agree with you, point to them. If you can draw on common sense, tradition and authority, do so. If promises were made that have been broken, explain what they were.

As an example, consider Mark Antony's cynical use of Caesar's will in order to prove how much Caesar had loved the people of Rome. The crowd are already incensed, and about to embark on burning Brutus' house, but Antony calls them back to hear him read the document. Whether it's a real document (non-technical proof) or one he's made up on the spot (technical proof) is not made clear, although, by this point, we can believe Antony capable of any depths of cunning:

> Here is the will, and under Caesar's seal.
> To every Roman citizen he gives,
> To every several man, seventy-five drachmas
> ...
> Moreover, he hath left you all his walks,
> His private arbours and new-planted orchards,
> On this side Tiber; he hath left them you,
> And to your heirs for ever, common pleasures,
> To walk abroad, and recreate yourselves.
> Here was a Caesar! when comes such another?

The rascal! We can well imagine Antony rubbing his hands in malicious glee as the crowd rampage off and he says, "Now let it work. Mischief, thou art afoot, / Take thou what course thou wilt!"

Refutation – This is, as the name suggests, the part of an argument where you refute your opponent's position and, if possible, smash it into tiny bits. This can sometimes get a bit nasty. You might try to paint your opponent as having a ridiculous view, or to interpret what they say in the least charitable way possible. It can be far easier to ridicule someone else's arguments than to come up with good ones yourself. By refuting another's position, it can be easier to articulate what we propose. Here's an example from Martin Luther King rebutting the arguments of fellow clergymen who wanted him to draw a halt to his protest movement in Birmingham, Alabama:

> You deplore the demonstrations taking place in Birmingham. But your statement, I am sorry to say, fails to express a similar concern for the conditions that brought about the demonstrations. I am sure that none of you would want to rest content with the superficial kind of social analysis that deals merely with effects and does not grapple with underlying causes. It is unfortunate that demonstrations are taking place in Birmingham, but it is even more unfortunate that the city's white power structure left the Negro community with no alternative. In any nonviolent campaign there are four basic steps: collection of the facts to determine whether injustices exist; negotiation; self-purification; and direct action. We have gone through all these steps in Birmingham. There can be no gainsaying the fact that racial injustice engulfs this community. Birmingham is probably the most thoroughly segregated city in the United States. Its ugly record of brutality is widely known. Negroes have experienced grossly unjust treatment in the courts. There have been more unsolved bombings of Negro homes and churches in Birmingham than in any other city in the nation. These are the hard, brutal facts of the case. On the basis of these conditions, Negro leaders sought to negotiate with the city fathers. But the latter consistently refused to engage in good faith negotiation.[12]

Hard to argue with that. Just as you set out your legal arguments, witnesses, supporters and promises, so will your

Argument

opponent. A good refutation will show how your opponents have misunderstood the law, will discredit their witnesses, pour scorn on their supporters and demonstrate that their promises are not worth a copper farthing.

Peroration – The peroration is an opportunity to weave the threads of your argument together, sum up the points you've made and end with a memorable conclusion. The ideal speech will end with a bang, not a whimper, and this is where you should aim to let off all your verbal fireworks in an unforgettable virtuoso display.

One of the most powerful examples of the peroration was uttered by Frederick Douglass. Douglass had been born into slavery in the American South but escaped to the North where he campaigned to end slavery. He ended a fundraising speech to a group of wealthy, well-intentioned white Americans on Independence Day, the 4th of July, by piling on the pathos:

> What, to the American slave, is your 4th of July? I answer: a day that reveals to him, more than all other days in the year, the gross injustice and cruelty to which he is the constant victim. To him, your celebration is a sham; your boasted liberty, an unholy license; your national greatness, swelling vanity; your sounds of rejoicing are empty and heartless; your denunciations of tyrants, brass fronted impudence; your shouts of liberty and equality, hollow mockery; your prayers and hymns, your sermons and thanksgivings, with all your religious parade, and solemnity, are, to him, mere bombast, fraud, deception, impiety, and hypocrisy – a thin veil to cover up crimes which would disgrace a nation of savages. There is not a nation on the earth guilty of practices, more shocking and bloody, than are the people of these United States, at this very hour.[13]

An unforgettably pungent end to a speech!

This six-part structure is pretty much how students have been taught to write essays for hundreds of years. It's a skeleton onto which you can add all sorts of twists and permutations and, as long as you don't mess with the basic structure, it'll work for almost any argument.

Decorum

Decorum shapes our choice of how to address an audience; it is an ethos appeal working at the level of the language itself. As a rhetorical concept, decorum includes what the Greeks called *kairos*: timeliness, tone, how the speaker stands and moves, and the references she makes; basically, everything to do with how well a speech is suited to its purpose and audience. If you're writing a letter of application for a job, it is decorum that lets you know that text speak and emojis are not appropriate.

> ### DECORUM
>
> Latin: *decorum* 'that which is seemly,' from *decor* 'beauty, elegance, ornament.'
>
> The suitability of a rhetorical style.

There are generally agreed to be three main stylistic approaches: high or grand style, low or plain style, and the middle style. Plain style values clarity, brevity and honesty over anything that seems overtly manipulative. Mark Antony uses the plain, informal style very deliberately when he tries to contrast himself to Brutus:

> I am no orator, as Brutus is,
> But, as you know me all, a plain blunt man
> That love my friend.

The more 'rhetorical' it sounds, the more metaphors, rhetorical figures and fussy words, the grander the style. Despite calling himself a "plain, blunt man," Antony sometimes slips into the grand style. Here he is describing the death of Caesar:

> O, what a fall was there, my countrymen!
> Then I, and you, and all of us fell down,
> Whilst bloody treason flourish'd over us.

Middle style, as the name suggests, is a midpoint between flowery and direct language.

A good orator should have a command of all three – and will be capable of mixing them up in a single speech, just as Mark Antony does. The narration might call for the clarity of the plain style whereas the peroration – where you typically seek to stir up your audience – provides an opportunity for a higher style.

One reliable method for speaking the language of your audience is to make them laugh. Aristotle quotes the philosopher Gorgias' recommendation that, "one must destroy the seriousness of the other with laughter, and their laughter with seriousness."[14] Laughter is an important part of an appeal to pathos not just because it can change the mood of an audience but because it is based on a common set of values and assumptions: a joke is only funny if you get it. As Cicero pointed out, stand-up comedians aside, "we should not fancy ourselves obliged to utter a jest whenever one may be uttered ... moderation and forbearance in jesting, and a limitation in the number of jokes, will distinguish the orator from the buffoon."[15] If your witticisms are not adding to your argument, they're probably best avoided.

This way of thinking about how to communicate is the backbone of effective argument. It's important to know that *everyone* uses rhetoric. Even those who profess disdain for the sleights of hand and trickery of flowery speech are using rhetoric: the denial of this mode of expression is just another appeal to character. But although everyone uses rhetoric, not everyone uses it knowingly or well.

Dialogue, dialectic and debate

Dialectic is a close cousin of rhetoric. Whereas rhetoric is the art of public speaking, dialectic is the art of conversation. To be in dialogue is to take part in a discourse, to exchange ideas, to debate. The dialectic method is a means of arriving at truth through reasoned argument.

> **DIALECTIC**
>
> Greek: *dialektos* 'discourse, conversation.'
>
> The process of investigating truth through discussion.

A position is advanced, countered, and a new, better position is established. This approach to argument is synonymous with the figure of Socrates. In Plato's *Dialogues*, Socrates does not so much advance arguments as ask questions. He is presented as a simple man who confesses that he knows nothing. By asking questions he manages to demonstrate the inconsistency of his conversational partner's views in whatever domain is being discussed. In this way Socrates points the way to wisdom.

For the German philosopher, Hegel, dialectic was a process of resolving or merging contradictions to attain higher truths. Others took on Hegel's ideas proposing a model of dialectic in which a thesis is expounded and then tested against an opposing, but equally logical, antithesis. Although these opposites ought to be incompatible, Hegel saw truth as emerging from a synthesis of contraries. This synthesis would then be challenged by a new antithesis, and so on until ultimate truth is arrived at.

The notion of ideas in constant struggle with the new emerging from the ashes of the old is as much at work in a discipline like English as in any other. Neo-classicism gives way to Romanticism, structuralism to post-structuralism, modernism to post-modernism. Whether we get any closer to 'truth' is a different matter. A more useful conception of dialectic might be to imagine the old in conversation, rather than competition, with the new. F.R. Leavis saw the ideal critical exchange as the posing of the question, "This is so, is it not?" followed by the response, "Yes, but ...". One conversational partner makes a judgement, invites discussion and the other responds with a clarification or refinement.[16]

Bakhtin, who we met earlier, is probably best known for his 'dialogic principle.' He claimed, "'To be' means to communicate dialogically."[17] To be alive is to be connected in ceaseless conversation. We cannot speak or think without using someone else's words or ideas and that, "these words are a site of struggle,"[18] where our voice contends with that of others. Our thoughts project across space to our contemporaries as well as backwards through time to all those who've gone before, and forwards in anticipation of those who will respond. Dialectic in the Hegelian sense seeks agreement, but for Bakhtin listening to and empathising with contradictory thoughts is inherently worthwhile. Dialectic doesn't have to lead to agreement; simply exchanging ideas is worthwhile in itself.

In literary terms, Harold Bloom saw this ongoing conversation as a "struggle between texts" from which "aesthetic value emanates."[19] We are enriched by being challenged and considering contrary points of view, but rather than being obliged to accept them we can agree to differ. This is similar to Oakeshott's conception of conversation: "It is with conversation as it is with gambling, its significance lies neither in winning nor in losing, but in wagering."[20] Oakeshott argued that views are formed and expertise is developed in conversation with others, living and dead in an "unrehearsed intellectual adventure."[21] Our beliefs and ideas are just one side of an argument and, by engaging with these contrasting opinions our arguments become more compelling.

Conversation

Gerald Graff and Cathy Birkenstein contend that the rhetorical structure underlying all arguments is 'They say / I say.'
In responding to what 'they say' we can more clearly articulate what it is that we think. For instance, one of the central
arguments in this book can be boiled down like this:

> *They say* English is a skills-based subject and that it
> doesn't matter what texts students study, but *I say*, mas-
> tery of English requires both substantive and discip-
> linary knowledge and that students' ability to think about
> English is only as good as what they know about language
> and literature.

Graff and Birkenstein claim this structure can be seen,
implicitly or explicitly, in all arguments. Here's an example
from Saul Bellow:

> The fact that there are so many weak, poor and boring
> stories and novels written and published in America has
> been ascribed by our rebels to the horrible squareness of
> our institutions, the idiocy of power, the debasement of
> sexual instincts, and the failure of writers to be alienated
> enough. The poems and novels of these same rebellious
> spirits, and their theoretical statements, are grimy and
> gritty and very boring too, besides being nonsensical,
> and it is evident by now that polymorphous sexuality
> and vehement declarations of alienation are not going to
> produce great works of art either.[22]

Bellow's argument can be configured as,

- *They say*: "there are so many weak, poor and boring stories
  and novels written and published in America" due to
  "the horrible squareness of our institutions, the idiocy of

power, the debasement of sexual instincts, and the failure of writers to be alienated enough."

- *I say*: "The poems and novels of these same rebellious spirits, and their theoretical statements, are grimy and gritty and very boring too, besides being nonsensical, and it is evident by now that polymorphous sexuality and vehement declarations of alienation are not going to produce great works of art either."

It even seems to hold true in arguments where the structure is implicit. Here's another Nobel prize winner, Joseph Brodsky, discussing what happens when a poem is 'finished':

> For the poet the credo or doctrine is not the point of arrival but is, on the contrary, the point of departure for the meta-physical journey.[23]

- *They say*: the credo is the point of arrival.
- *I say*: it is the point of departure.

By taking part in this conversational back and forth, we not only get better at formulating our own opinions, we get better at spotting the structures used by other writers. If all arguments are, at some level, in dialogue with other arguments then students' ability to master English depends, in part, on recognising what views the writers they study are responding to.[24]

Students can learn to 'listen' to the writers of the texts they study by viewing texts as conversations. By summarising a writer's point of view, we are more likely to notice the nuance of their arguments. And, by extracting more, we will better develop our own responses and interpretations, both at the level of literature (Shakespeare says / but I say) and at the level of criticism (Eagleton says / but I say). By 'arguing' with the writers they study, by thinking about what they read and responding, students embark on the path to mastery of the discipline of English.

Argument and poetry

Whilst it would be foolish to make some grand claim about the role of argument in poetry, it is none the less true that a great many poems do strive to encapsulate a debate. The sonnet, especially in its Shakespearean form, does an excellent job of moving from an initial observation or statement and, at the *volta*, performing a turn in which ideas are refined, reconsidered or refuted before, in the final couplet, they are resolved. Marvell's 'To His Coy Mistress' overtly positions itself as an argument moving as it does from "Had we …" (if) in its first stanza, to "But …" at the start of its second, and then to "Now," as it makes its closing arguments in the third and final stanza.

But the role of argument transcends the form and content of individual poems; it is our principal means for discovering what poems are about and whether we think they are successful. Whatever else it is, poetry is a form of communication. Once students have begun to wrestle with some interpretations, they can start shaping their personal response. It helps to see a poem as a conversation *and* as a puzzle to be figured out. There are plenty of educators who will gasp at this conception of poetry, but it seems to me that poetry takes work to appreciate and understand. It's rare that I fall into a poem on first reading. More often the words seem to bounce off me and the rhythm goes unnoticed until I slow my attention and weigh each phrase and line with care and deliberation. Poems really *are* puzzles. Of course, they're not like crossword puzzles with only one right answer, rather they're delightfully puzzling. And sometimes, as Oakeshott observes, "images in contemplation are merely present; they provoke neither speculation nor inquiry about the occasion of their appearing but only delight in their having appeared."[25] Many poems are deliberately dense, carefully wrought and reward contemplative reading. Sometimes I don't 'get it' even after a couple of readings. What makes poems – and indeed any literary texts – different from crossword puzzles is you don't have to 'get it.' T.S. Eliot reflected that appreciating poetry was an "inexact formula."[26] Not getting it is, perhaps, sometimes the point.

Precision, clarity and economy

As well as responding to the ideas of others, a writer has to consider the response of a variety of readers who she will probably never meet. This is as true for the writers students will study as it is for their own writing. Magazine editor Dick Mack points out that "verbiage, obscurity, and imprecision ... hamper communication."[27] This matters because we want our thoughts both to serve some sort of purpose and to be read and remembered. And what's memorable is "... clear, brief, and forceful. No one would willingly consign his work to obscurity, but we do so with imprecise, ambiguous, and verbose manuscripts."[28]

The grammarian, Ernest Gowers saw that the problem with poorly constructed argument is its inefficiency:

> It wastes time: the time of the readers because they have to puzzle over what should be plain, and the time of the writers because they may have to write again to explain their meaning. A job that needed to be done only once has had to be done twice because it was bungled the first time.[29]

Making a clear argument is challenging because expressing complex ideas in straightforward language demands time and practice. In order to be clear, precise and economical you need to know your subject matter inside out. If an argument is 'a connected series of statements intended to establish a proposition,' clarity may not be sufficient, but it's certainly necessary if an argument is to be effective.

Why do so many arguments employ obfuscation? Filip Buekens and Maarten Boudry suggest the motivation for obscuring meaning is to "set up a game of verbal smoke and mirrors to suggest depth and insight where none exists."[30] That which Harry Frankfurt calls "bullshit" by any other name would smell as sweet:

> What bullshit essentially misrepresents is neither the state of affairs to which it refers nor the beliefs of the speaker concerning that state of affairs. Those are what lies misrepresent, by virtue of being false. Since bullshit need not be false, it differs from lies in its misrepresentational intent. The bullshitter may not deceive us, or even intend to do so, either about the facts or about what he takes the facts to be. *What he does necessarily attempt to deceive us about is his enterprise.* His only indispensably distinctive characteristic is that in a certain way he misrepresents what he is up to.[31]
>
> [emphasis added]

If you want to bullshit a reader then using lots of technical sounding bobbins and unwieldy syntax is definitely the way to go. Consider this confection:

> The move from a structuralist account in which capital is understood to structure social relations in relatively homologous ways to a view of hegemony in which power relations are subject to repetition, convergence, and rearticulation brought the question of temporality into the thinking of structure, and marked a shift from a form

of Althusserian theory that takes structural totalities as theoretical objects to one in which the insights into the contingent possibility of structure inaugurate a renewed conception of hegemony as bound up with the contingent sites and strategies of the rearticulation of power.[32]

It's difficult to believe that, at least at some level, the writer is not engaged in a 'game of smoke and mirrors.'

Teaching argument

How best can we help students to organise their thoughts and marshal their arguments to avoid vagueness, imprecision and obscurantism? To begin with students often need help to fit the structure of their argument to the task at hand.

The thesis statement

Most essays are written in response to a question, and so answering the question is of paramount importance. Here are two examples:

'Cordelia's death is the shocking climax of cruelty in Shakespeare's exploration of evil.' To what extent do you agree with this view?

'Tragedies leave readers and audiences with a final sense of emptiness and disillusion.' To what extent do you agree with this view in relation to two texts you have studied?[33]

Test designers deliberately make questions as open as possible to allow for as broad a range of responses as conceivable, but attempting an answer can seem overwhelming precisely because there are so many possibilities. The trick is to narrow the range of options by constructing a tightly focussed thesis statement which sets out the terrain to be explored. A good thesis statement should present an idea which can 'tested' against different interpretations and aspects of the text.

In the case of the question on *King Lear* we might come up with something like this:

> Cordelia's death, whilst shocking, has more to do with the redemption of her father than as an inevitable consequence of evil.

For the question on tragedy we might construct a statement such as this one:

> As both *Richard II* and *Death of a Salesman* demonstrate, the aim of tragedy has always been to leave audiences with a sense of catharsis.

Both statements can be tested, both offer students a clear way *into* an essay, both usefully narrow the field of possible interpretations to a more manageable pool, and both demonstrate to a reader exactly what the essay sets out to argue right from the outset.

Not everyone agrees, however. Some argue the imposition of a thesis statement closes down exploration of ideas within an argument. English professor, David Bartholomae talks about "the tyranny of the thesis [which] invalidates the very act of analysis we hope to invoke."[34] This is, I suspect, more a criticism of the simplistic writing frames used to hurry students from introduction to conclusion than a general condemnation of articulating a forceful line of argument.

Marking discourse

Once begun, where next? Metaphors are helpful for visualising the process of essay writing. In the same way that a skier slaloms between the poles set out on a downhill ski slope, so too should students follow a line of argument; not directly, but weaving in and out between the points they make, always progressing to a predetermined finishing line. Similarly, when a ship sails against the wind, it needs to tack in a zigzag pattern to make headway. These metaphors help students to see that the points we want to make can be approached directly or indirectly, but the indirect approach is more artful and elegant.

A line of argument should flow naturally from a well-designed thesis statement. Consider the example from *King Lear* earlier: *Cordelia's death, whilst shocking, has more to do with the redemption of her father than as an inevitable consequence of evil.* What is the finish line? Such an essay begs for a conclusion in which death is seen in a larger context than evil, perhaps even with the sort of rhetorical flourish which links the death of Cordelia to the death of Christ, thus redeeming Lear and, by extension, the audience. But rather than setting off to stride from A to B, the path between our thesis statement and this conclusion is tacked towards indirectly.

While there's no substitute for a thorough knowledge of texts and contexts, the use of discourse markers – words and phrases that signpost our discourse – can be a real boon both in the construction of an essay and in the ease with which it can be read. Not only should we select textual references, we should also select language that allows us to position critical perspectives and follow a course. Here's a handy collection of such markers:

- Adding: *and, also, as well as, moreover, too*
- Cause and effect: *because, so, therefore, thus, consequently*
- Sequencing: *next, then, first, finally, meanwhile, before, after*
- Qualifying: *however, although, unless, except, if, as long as, apart from, yet*
- Emphasising: *above all, in particular, especially, significantly, indeed, notably*

- Illustrating: *for example, such as, for instance, as revealed by, in the case of*
- Comparing: *equally, in the same way, similarly, likewise, as with, like*
- Contrasting: *whereas, instead of, alternatively, otherwise, unlike, on the other hand*

A note of caution: it's perfectly possible to include these types of marker in an essay and make it less readable. The key is to be clear about the connection between each phrase and its intended purpose. Some, like the markers for sequencing, adding and cause and effect, make writing more direct. Qualifying and contrasting discourse markers, on the other hand, allow us to tack in unexpected directions. And the illustrative and emphasising markers allow for useful slaloms. Discourse markers act as buoys around which we must navigate, always conscious of the conclusion to which we're building. Sometimes we need to explain away or argue against an irritatingly awkward piece of information, but that's all part of the game in a subject like literature. It's not true to say that style is valued over substance, you still need to know your texts inside out, but the point is not to arrive at a universal and eternal truth, it is to be both erudite and stylish in the construction of your argument.

Nominalisation

And on that point, nominalisation is one such way students can appear more erudite and take on that all-important critical style. Nominalisation is simply the act of creating nouns from other words, usually verbs:

- *To judge* becomes a *judgement*
- *To develop* becomes a *development*

Argument

- *To admire* becomes *admiration*
- *To react* becomes a *reaction*
- *To swim* becomes *swimming*
- *Careless* becomes *carelessness*
- *Intense* becomes *intensity*

Informal communication tends to be active and depends on verbs to give a sense of immediacy and action. Academic writing is abstract and depends on nouns to convey densely packed concepts or ideas. Turning an action into a concept is to nominalise it. This is sometimes the difference between a good essay and a poor one: essays which are nominalised tend to exude confidence and authority, essays which aren't can suffer from sounding a bit vague.

Consider these brief examples:

1. Because Cordelia **dies** at the end of the play, many people decide that King Lear is a play about the consequences of the evil things people do. Before she dies Cordelia is ready to **forgive** her father and because they are **reunited** we think the play will end happily. This is also suggested by the fact that she dies off-stage and that we only learn about it when Lear enters carrying her body and howling. When he says "She's dead as earth. Lend me a looking-glass; If that her breath will mist or stain the stone" he seems pathetic and feeble; his **grieving** is undignified. This could suggest not so much that evil has **triumphed** but that Lear has to lose the last shreds of his dignity and authority in order to be truly **humbled**.

2. Cordelia's **death** at the end of the play is often seen as evidence that the consequences of evil are inescapable. Before her death, Cordelia's **reunion** with, and **forgiveness** of, her father is suggestive of a happy ending. The arbitrary nature of her sudden death provides further evidence of

the inevitability of evil, but a different **interpretation** of the lines "She's dead as earth. Lend me a looking-glass; If that her breath will mist or stain the stone" might lead to the **conclusion** that his **grief** and the pathetic desperation with which Lear clings to the possibility that she yet lives are proof not of the **triumph** of evil but of the need for the king to lose the last shreds of royal **dignity** and authority before he can truly experience **humility**.

Although both say pretty much the same thing, is one better than the other? Or, more to the point, which better demonstrates "informed, personal and creative responses to literary texts, using associated concepts and terminology, and coherent, accurate written expression?"[35]

Nominalisation sometimes gets a bit of bad press and Stephen Pinker demonises it as the 'zombification of language' with the passive lurch of an awkward noun replacing the graceful leap of verbs.[36] Ironically, I find 'zombification' a rather elegant example of the beauty and flexibility of language. Clearly nominalisation can be overdone (see the example on pages 207–8) and equally obviously, nominalisation alone is not enough to elevate an essay, but teaching students about *how* to nominalise concepts provides them with a straightforward, easy to implement strategy to shift style from the clunkily informal to the confidently academic. Nominalisation is a useful jumping-off point. It is an easily grasped concept which, once explained, allows students to see at a glance where their prose style can be spruced up. A simple *N* in the margin of an essay can be sufficient to prompt an elevation in their critical perspective.

Once students learn to analyse the ways arguments are structured and made persuasive, they can start to take part in shaping their world in a much more deliberate way. Not only do they become better able to notice and understand the currents that have shaped their own patterns of thought, they can start to ask what would happen if the levers of argument were placed elsewhere and pressure applied in another direction.

Most importantly, perhaps, students should be given the opportunity to speak persuasively, to debate, discuss, present and probe. Of course, students will be examined on their ability to write fluently, but the habit of regular and formal speech is often more useful preparation – for life as well as exams – than is most anaemic writing practice.

KEY POINTS

- The purpose of argument is persuasion; if an argument is not persuasive it is a poor argument.
- Understanding the speaker, the audience, the knowledge they share and the points of contention between them allows us to analyse arguments effectively.
- Knowledge of ethos (appeal to character), pathos (appeal to emotions) and logos (appeal to reason) allows us to make more persuasive arguments.
- The six-part arrangement attributed to Cicero provides a useful framework for constructing arguments.
- When conceived as dialectic, argument can enrich our own understanding as well as persuading others.
- If essays are framed as conversations we not only become more familiar with opposing views but also make stronger arguments ourselves.
- Arguments should always be expressed with 'clarity, precision and economy.'

> - There is a range of strategies that can be learned and practised to improve essay writing (thesis statements, nominalisation, tacking with discourse markers, etc.).
> - If students are attuned to the structures and textures or argument they will find it easier to spot and understand in literature as well as more obviously persuasive texts.

By examining examples of arguments in different times and places we can better understand who we are as well as being better equipped to choose to be someone else. The ability to think logically and analytically relies on an understanding of sequencing ideas and to build a way of seeing, point by careful point. This notion that there is an underlying pattern to all the ways we think is explored more thoroughly in the next chapter.

Further reading

- James M. May's beautifully edited and selected translation of Cicero's works on rhetoric, intercut with extracts from his speeches, is a great way in for anyone wanting to get to grips with Cicero.
- Sam Leith's *You Talking to Me?* was an invaluable source for the section on rhetoric.
- I can also recommend Jay Heinrichs' very practical guide, *Thank you for Arguing.*

8 Pattern

Human beings are natural pattern seekers. Our minds are alert for repeating patterns and disruptions: What's new? What's the same? What's important? What does that remind me of? Out of these patterns we make sense of our surroundings; pattern recognition is one of our primary mechanisms of making meaning. This allows us to recognise family members, pick up the patterns of sound in language and avoid danger. It also causes us to see faces in wallpaper and creatures in clouds:

> *Hamlet:*   *Do you see yonder cloud that's almost in shape of a camel?*
> *Polonius:*   *By the mass, and 'tis like a camel, indeed.*
> *Hamlet:*   *Methinks it is like a weasel.*
> *Polonius:*   *It is backed like a weasel.*
> *Hamlet:*   *Or like a whale?*
> *Polonius:*   *Very like a whale.*

Our minds are shaped by an ability to make rapid judgements using minimal data and, while this can sometimes lead us astray, it means we can be incredibly efficient at communicating ideas from mind to mind.

The quality of noticing is crucial to getting a feel for the effects of the patterns we encounter in language and literature. What patterns do you notice about the examples of text that follow?

1. gunna meet dave at 10 cu there

2. deeds cannot dream what dreams can do—time is a tree (this life one leaf)

3. The mains voltage in the house must be the same as that of the appliance, which is specified on data plate at the bottom of the cleaner.

4. "Hold your noise!" cried a terrible voice, as a man started up from among the graves at the side of the church porch. "Keep still, you little devil, or I'll cut your throat!"

I'm guessing you 'just knew' what sort of texts these different extracts belong to without having to think much at all. You may have matched the patterns so rapidly that you're unsure why you are able to categorise each text. The way pattern recognition works is that we instantaneously compare what we're looking at with all the other examples of texts we've ever seen and, if we've seen enough similar examples, we come up with a match. Obviously, if I showed you something for which you had no match you would have been stumped. For instance, it'll be impossible for most readers to say much of interest about the patterns in this sentence: A Noyes lány egy réges-régi rigmusba rejtette a kitalálandó személyt.*

Pattern-spotting is automatic but 'noticing' is more than automatic categorisation; it requires us to read more deliberately and to think about the effects of features picked out by our pattern-matching engines. The first example is easy: the

---

* This Magyar sentence means "The Noyes girl was busy building a camouflaged image with an old poem." You're none the wiser, are you?

lack of punctuation and capitalisation, the informal contraction "gunna" along with the abbreviation "cu" are all features of text messages. The second one is a little trickier but the repetition of "dream" and the presence of alliteration

> **ALLITERATION**
>
> Latin: *alliterare* 'to begin with the same letter,' *ad* 'to'+ *littera* 'letter, script.'
>
> The repetition of consonant sounds.

are suggestive of techniques we see in poetry. The brackets are unusual, but you know enough about how they're used to know that what is inside the brackets "this life one leaf" relates to what is outside "time is a tree." This time/life = parts of a tree metaphor again makes us think of poetry. (If you're familiar with e e cummings' oeuvre, you will have got there far faster.*) Text 3 is a fairly standard looking formal sentence but "mains voltage" and "appliance" suggest this is technical writing. The reference to a "data plate at the bottom of the cleaner" suggests the reader has access to the cleaner and so we quickly alight on the fact that this is product information for an electrical cleaning device, probably a vacuum cleaner.[†] The final extract contains both direct speech and the use of, strictly speaking, surplus adjectives. Where might we find sentences like this? Why, in novels or short stories. The addition of detail such as "graves" and "church porch" make it clear where the action is taking place. Whether or not you were able to pinpoint precisely where this comes from probably depends on how well you know *Great Expectations*.[‡]

---

[*] The lines come from Cummings' poem [freedom is a breakfastfood].

[†] Yep – the sentence is taken from here: http://download.beko.com/Download.UsageManualsBeko/IQ/en_US_BKS_9316_EN.pdf

[‡] It's from chapter 1. The speaker is Magwitch and the "little devil" is, of course, Pip.

Much pleasure can be had by rattling quickly through a novel, but the sort of reading we need to engage in to become attuned to patterns is of a different kind. Students need to learn the kind of reading that's more typical of poetry, where words and phrases are weighed and savoured. This strand of the epistemology of English seeks to explore the various ways structure is used to impose meaning on texts. At its broadest level, texts are structured into books, chapters, sections and paragraphs; plays into acts and scenes; poems into lines and stanzas. But it wasn't always thus.

When we speak we tend not to notice the way our speech is patterned. It comes as something of a surprise to discover that English is an accentuated, stress-timed language in which we place emphasis on some syllables and not on others in a consistent and predictable pattern. (Contrast this with, for instance, French, where every syllable is equally stressed.) Speakers almost never consider the rhythm of their speech and rarely think about grammar, or word order. It's even unusual – at least today – to spend much time deliberating on the patterns of the words we say when considered as a whole. Written text is a different matter because it is necessarily artificial. When we speak we tend to have an audience ready to hand, but writing is intended to be read out of the context in which it was first conceived and communicated.

Written texts use all sorts of patterns to help establish meaning. Assonance, alliteration, rhythm, rhyme, careful word placement and sentence structure are all patterns that can and do exist in spoken language but are crucial in shaping the way we interpret and understand writing. This is most obvious in the

> ## ASSONANCE
>
> Latin: *assonantem*, 'to resound, respond.'
>
> The repetition of vowel sounds.

carefully crafted combination of language and form that is poetry.

Noticing sound

We seem to have an instinct for acquiring and making meaning out of patterns of sound. The first linguistic pattern we learn is that of the sounds we hear uttered around us. Long before we have any conception of language, we learn to differentiate the phonetic sounds that make up speech. At six months, our ears are so well attuned that we can hear all of the different sounds that make up human language, but over the next three months we learn to home in on the distinctive sounds featured in the languages that make up our environment. By the time we reach our first birthday, we have learned to ignore sounds not present in our native language and lose the ability to tell them apart. For instance, Japanese speakers struggle to hear the difference between /r/ and /l/, while to an English speaker the distinction is obvious. As Patricia Kuhl puts it, our "language experience warps perception."[1]

English is made up of 44 sounds, or phonemes.* According to David Crystal, Rotokas (spoken in New Guinea) and Pirahã (spoken by an Amazonian hunter gather people) have only eleven phonemes whereas !Xũzn (a dialect of !Kung spoken in West Africa) has as many as 141![2] Whilst we have only

> **PHONEME**
>
> Greek: *phōnēma* 'a sound made, voice.'
>
> The smallest unit of sound.

---

* We also have over 170 graphemes which can be used to represent these sounds in writing, which is one of the reasons spelling in English is such a minefield.

five official vowels (seven if you include *y* and *w*) there are twenty different vowel *sounds* in English (twelve pure sounds and eight diphthongs). This can get very technical but for our purposes, vowel sounds are either long (d<u>ay</u>, f<u>ee</u>t, fl<u>y</u>, b<u>ow</u>l, m<u>u</u>sic) or short (c<u>a</u>t, p<u>e</u>t, p<u>i</u>p, d<u>o</u>g, b<u>u</u>g).* Vowels carry most of the emotion in speech;

> # DIPHTHONG
>
> Greek: *diphthongos*, 'having two sounds,' from *di-* 'double' + *phthongos* 'sound, voice.'
>
> Sound formed by the combination of two vowels in a single syllable, in which the sound begins as one vowel and moves towards another, e.g. *coin, loud* and *side.*

it's often possible to work out the emotional tenor of a conversation even if you can't make out individual words. The emphasis we place on the vowel sounds of simple phrases like, say, 'I love you,' can result in an abundance of different possible meanings.

Consonants, by contrast, allow us to distinguish between the semantic content of these emotional contexts. The 21 English consonants produce 24 different sounds. Consonants have friction when they are spoken, mostly using the position of the tongue against the lips, teeth and roof of the mouth. These sounds can either be voiced (produced with vibrations from the larynx) or unvoiced (made without vibrations). The 24 consonant sounds can be divided up as follows:

---

*   In addition to these twenty vowel sounds, there's also s*chwa* – the most common sound in English – represented by the symbol ə. This is the unvoiced, unstressed sound in 'this presənt is fə my brothə,' or 'to səvive thə cold weathə you have tə make thorə prepərati əns.'

Pattern

	Voiced	Unvoiced
Plosives	/b/ /d/ /g/	/p/ /t/ /k/
Fricatives	/v/ /TH/ (as in them)	/f/ /th/ (as in myth)
Sibilants	/z/	/s/ /sh/
Glottal	/h/	
Affricates	/j/	/ch/
Nasal	/m/ /n/ /ng/	
Glides	/w/ /wh/ /y/	
Liquids	/l/ /r/	

How, you might be wondering, might we use all this information to make meaning? The point is that different sounds produce different effects. We can say exactly the same thing using different words, but those words will *feel* different. For instance, what's the difference between these?

- Hush
- Be quiet
- Shut up

Every child implicitly understands that each phrase is suitable for some contexts and inappropriate for others, but why? Part of the reason is the sounds made by the words. The combination of the glottal /h/, the short /u/ and the unvoiced /sh/ produce a calming effect; the hardness of the plosive /b/ sound gets attention but is quelled by the long /ee/ and the clipped /t/ at the end of quiet signals that there will be no discussion; the abruptness of the plosives /t/ and /p/ in 'shut up' are unsoftened by the short vowels and the final explosions of their respective words make it clear the speaker is irritated.

If we look at the first stanza of Robert Frost's 'Stopping on a Snowy Evening' we can examine the sounds used and see what we are able to notice about their effects:

Whose woods these are I think I know.
His house is in the village though;
He will not see me stopping here
To watch his woods fill up with snow.

The combination of sounds – the glides in "woods," "know," "though," "watch" and "snow," the unvoiced /th/ of "think," "though," the liquids of "will," "fill" and "village," the heaviness of the vowels and the softness of the consonants ending words – encourage it to be read slowly, quietly, perhaps in a whisper. The only hard consonant – in "think" – is softened and absorbed by the long vowel of "I" that follows it.

What changes in the second stanza?

My little horse must think it queer
To stop without a farmhouse near
Between the woods and frozen lake
The darkest evening of the year.

The whispering intonation continues with the rustling sound of "little horse must" but then the /k/ of think followed immediately by the short vowel in "it" is a snap of the fingers, a click of attention, as we're directed to consider the nervous horse. The plosive at the end of "stop" does indeed cause us to pause momentarily before we glide over the rest of the line and most of the next until the sharp /k/ of "lake" repeated in "darkness" like two breaking twigs, barely heard but hinting at another presence.

The tone changes again in the third stanza:

He gives his harness bells a shake
To ask if there is some mistake.
The only other sound's the sweep
Of easy wind and downy flake.

Where before any guttural consonants were absorbed by softer sounds, now they leap to attention and make themselves felt: the /g/ of "give" is almost lost in the repeated aspiration of "his harness" but felt again in the /b/ of "bells" and amplified further by "shake." The sharp cracks of "ask" and "mistake" sound a rising tone of alarm; in fact, each line in the stanza ends with another crack except the sudden thud of the plosive in "sweep" at the end of line 3. Not only the words of the poem but its very sounds contribute to the sense that something is stirring.

Expectations are thus raised for the final stanza:

> The woods are lovely, dark and deep,
> But I have promises to keep,
> And miles to go before I sleep,
> And miles to go before I sleep.

But it's an anti-climax. Nothing happens. The sounds – the glide of "woods," the long liquidity of "lovely" – return us to the peace of the first stanza, and the alliteration in "dark and deep" is somehow reassuring. The plosives of "But" claim our attention but the mellifluousness of "promises to keep" is calm, heavy and soft. And then that repeated final line with the soothing feel of the voiced plosive /d/ in "And" lulling us into the long vowels of "miles" and "sleep" to that final empathic /p/. But are we soothed? Or is the music of the woods a siren's song? We'll return to the poem later in the chapter.

Meaning in sound

In Plato's *Dialogues*, Socrates argues that the essence of meaning is made by syllables, but this has tended to be dismissed by modern linguistics. There's a tradition going back to Ferdinand de Saussure, the father of structuralism, that the relationship between the sounds words make (signs) and their meaning (signifiers) is arbitrary, onomatopoeia aside. But as every poet –

> **ONOMATOPOEIA**
>
> Greek: *onoma* 'word, name' + *poiein* 'compose, make.'
>
> The naming of something by a reproduction of the sound made by or associated with it, e.g. *buzz, drip.*

and every serious student of literature – knows (and as corpus studies of language is beginning to catch up with[3]) the sounds words make is far from random. At one level we feel that some words, once we learn their meaning, 'sound wrong.' For instance, no one would guess at the meaning of 'pulchritude' from its sounds.

As Margaret Magnus has pointed out, phonemes do seem to carry inherent meaning; words beginning with the voiced plosive /b/ often involve bulging, blocking, booming and bursting. Similarly, words that start with /gl/ are disproportionately related to vision (glance, glare, glazed, glimpse, glint, glower) or reflection (glare, gleam, glimmer, glint, glisten, glitter, gloaming, glow, glass, glacier, gloss). So, while a word has a clear referential meaning – its dictionary definition – it will also have an inherent meaning or '*Is-ness.*' Magnus argues that, "Inherent meaning is a word's identity, and reference merely its resumé, where it has gone and what it has done, an itemisation of its contexts." Where, "'Is-ness' is unifying ... reference is divisive." Inherent meaning "gives all those multifarious senses the power to become a single word."[4]

Some writers are more attuned to these 'multifarious senses' than others. For a wonderful example of a writer really paying attention to sound patterns, look at this short passage from Vladimir Nabokov's novel *Lolita*:

> Lolita, light of my life, fire of my loins. My sin, my soul. Lo-lee-ta: the tip of the tongue taking a trip of three steps down the palate to tap, at three, on the teeth. Lo. Lee. Ta.

I defy anyone to read this without hearing the language sing in their mind's ear.

Anaphora

Patterns of similarity and difference are the lifeblood of language. Various linguistic schemes draw on our thirst for repetition in various ways, but we only notice what's repeated

> **ANAPHORA**
>
> Greek: 'to carry back' from *ana* 'back,' + *pherein*, 'to carry.'
>
> The repetition of words and phrases.

because it stands out from what isn't. The final lines of the Frost poem we looked at earlier are one of the most celebrated instances of anaphora in English literature:

> And miles to go before I sleep.
> And miles to go before I sleep.

Although the repetition lulls us, it's also odd, out of place. There's something not quite right in an otherwise perfectly constructed poem. It raises the hairs on my neck and makes me think of haunted woods, grim fairy tales and the creeping suspicion that the narrator is slowly freezing to death in the snowbound woods. What could otherwise be a beautiful but unremarkable poem is made strange and dangerous by this considered use of repetition.

Look at another example in the final paragraph of James Joyce's short story, 'The Dead':

> [The snow] was falling softly upon the Bog of Allen and, further westwards, softly falling into the dark mutinous Shannon waves. It was falling too upon every part of the lonely churchyard where Michael Furey lay buried. It lay thickly drifted on the crooked crosses and headstones, on the spears of the little gate, on the barren thorns. His soul swooned slowly as he heard the snow falling faintly through the universe and faintly falling, like the descent of their last end, upon all the living and the dead.

"Falling" is repeated five times in four sentences. Pay particular attention to the last sentence. Not only do we have the repeated sibilants and assonant long /ow/ of "<u>s</u>ou<u>l</u> <u>s</u>w<u>oo</u>ned <u>sl</u>ow<u>l</u>y" as well as the unvoiced fricatives preceding the repeated /ay/ in "<u>f</u>alling <u>f</u>aintly," but the "falling faintly" is repeated – and reversed – as "faintly falling." Why would Joyce do that? Students, unattuned to power of pattern, might assume this repetition was a careless oversight, but anyone practised in noticing patterns of sound might pick out the unvoiced fricatives and make a link to the softness and deadening effect of heavy snowfall; its repetition and reversal brings to mind a shaken snow globe, with the world being gently obliterated by spinning snowflakes as the distinctions between the living and the dead are buried under pristine white drifts.

Alliteration

Alliteration is one of the oldest and most popular patterns in English. Before there was rhyme or regular metre in English verse there was alliteration. The poetry of the Anglo-Saxons was patterned according to accentual rules and relied heavily on alliteration for its effects. *Beowulf*, the oldest known work of literature in English, was patterned in this way, as were later works like *Sir Gawain and the Green Knight*, written in Middle English at some point in the 14th century by an unknown poet. Here's a taste from Simon Armitage's recent translation:

> After Britain was built by this founding father
> a bold race bred there, battle-happy men
> causing trouble and torment in turbulent times.

Although the rhythm isn't metrical, the alliterated syllables show us where to place stress and bring the words to life.

Alliteration is everywhere in English today – busy bee, dead as a doornail, give up the ghost, good as gold, home sweet home, last laugh, leave in the lurch, make a mountain out of a molehill, pleased as punch, right as rain, ride roughshod, short, sharp shock, tittle-tattle, world wide web, zigzag – but is, surprisingly, far less common in other European languages. Not only is alliteration a routine feature of newspaper headlines and advertising copy, it crops up regularly in literature too.

One of the most famous examples of alliteration and assonance comes from Dylan Thomas's radio play, *Under Milk Wood*. The repeated /b/ in the first line, "To begin at the beginning," provides a rhythmic sense, almost a formulaic feel with the short vowel /e/ restraining the plosive consonant. But as they repeat into the next paragraph they build and swell. "Bible black" feels ancient and threatening and then the weaving, wending feel of alternating sibilants and plosives and glides in "sloe black, slow, black, crow black, fishing boat-bobbing sea," is gorgeously hypnotic, lulling us into the assonance of the "dumbf<u>ou</u>nd t<u>ow</u>n."

In contrast, see how subtle alliteration can be in this sentence from Maya Angelou's *I Know Why The Caged Bird Sings*:

Up the aisle, the moans and screams merged with the sickening smell of woollen black clothes worn in summer weather and green leaves wilting over yellow flowers.

Although "sickening smell" stands out the alliterated words are not always placed next to each other: "moans and screams merged"; "woollen black clothes worn in summer weather and green leaves wilting." Our attention isn't so much drawn to an individual word or phrase, but the repeated sounds produce a sense of disquiet: we know something is going on, even if it's hard to point to precisely. The words and the sounds they make are full of queasiness and uneasiness as young Maya makes her way through church to gaze upon the body of Mrs Taylor.

These schemes of repetition – anaphora, alliteration and assonance – not only add music to words, they focus our attention; we *notice* them.

Noticing rhyme

One of the first linguistic patterns of which children become aware is rhyme. We delight in finding, making and reading rhyme. In pre-literate times, rhyme provided a convenient aide memoir for bards and skalds to remember the lines of sung epics and sagas. As Seamus Heaney put it, "It's difficult to learn poems off by heart that don't rhyme."[5] Leaving aside the vexed question about whether poetry *should* rhyme, it is worth noting that it often does. Poetry seems to produce the expectation of rhyme; when it comes on cue it can cement meaning in a way that is deeply satisfying.

The most obvious rhymes come at the ends of lines. End-stopped rhyme adds to metrical effects, emphasising the rhythm and music in verse. In Blake's poem 'The Tyger' you can almost hear the beat of jungle drums as the tiger prowls through the shadows and the crash of the rhyme as the beast emerges, briefly, into the light:

> Tyger, tyger burning bright
> In the forests of the night.

But sometimes end-stopping can feel a little too mannered, a little too pernickety and precise. I always baulk a little, for instance, at the regularity of the rhyme in John McCrae's 'In Flanders Fields':

> In Flanders fields the poppies blow
> Between the crosses, row on row,
> That mark our place; and in the sky
> The larks, still bravely singing, fly.
> Scarce heard amid the guns below.

There's nothing *wrong* with it, but it feels a bit too ordered to fit with the hammering of "guns below." That said, maybe the regular end-stopping could be said to pleasingly echo the neat lines of crosses. There's no right or wrong to these things, just what we notice, the analogies brought to mind and the meaning we make.

Some of the most successful poetry uses end stopped rhyme where it fits but doesn't insist on slavishly mangling the sense to fit a regular scheme. Look again at the first stanza of 'Stopping by Woods on a Snowy Evening':

> Whose woods these are I think I know,
> His house is in the village, though;
> He will not see me stopping here
> To watch his woods fill up with snow

There's no attempt to make the third line fit the rhyme scheme. This could have been done relatively simply. "He will not see me stopping, no" might have worked, or "He will not see me stop and go." But although the rhyme would have been retained, what might be lost? The use of the unrhyming "here" not only makes more sense, it peeps out of the poem; it waves, hesitantly. It's cautiously visible in a way that captures something of the nervous narrator's decision to loiter in woods owned by someone else.

One of my favourite poems using end stopped rhyme is Edna St. Vincent Millay's sonnet 'I shall forget you presently, my dear.' The final couplet elegantly captures the poem's spirit of love turned to cruel indifference:

> Whether or not we find what we are seeking
> Is idle, biologically speaking.

Rhyme schemes

Most rhyming poems follow deliberate schemes. The previous example is a couplet, sometimes denoted as AA, whereas three consecutive rhyming lines would be a triplet and labelled AAA as in this slightly lecherous example from Robert Herricks' 'Upon Julia's Clothes':

> Whenas in silks my Julia goes,
> Then, then, methinks, how sweetly flows
> The liquefaction of her clothes.
>
> Next, when I cast mine eyes, and see
> That brave vibration, each way free,
> O, how that glittering taketh me!

Pattern

The final exclamation point should leave in little doubt of what's happened as the poem reaches its climax. As I said, lecherous.

Next up is the quatrain, and here things become more varied and interesting. A quatrain made up of two couplets is AABB, and an alternately rhyming quatrain is ABAB:

I wandered lonely as a cloud (A)
That floats on high o'er vales and hills, (B)
When all at once I saw a crowd, (A)
A host, of golden daffodils (B)

This is also sometimes called cross-rhyme. An envelope rhyme envelops a couplet inside two rhyming arms and brings to mind a Swedish pop group as it's labelled ABBA. Here's one from Tennyson's 'In Memoriam':

So word by word, and line by line, (A)
The dead man touch'd me from the past, (B)
And all at once it seem'd at last (B)
The living soul was flash'd on mine. (A)

End-stopping

Shakespeare's plays are, for the most part, written in blank, unrhymed verse, but some of his most memorable lines are those that use end stopped rhyme. End-stopping is most noticeable at the end of scenes and provides punctuation to let us know one incident is over and a new one will begin.* After the ghost of Hamlet's father has made his son swear to exact revenge on Claudius, Hamlet seals his pact with these lines:

* Apparently, of the 821 scenes in Shakespeare's plays, 379 end in rhyming couplets.

232

> The time is out of joint. O cursèd spite,
> That ever I was born to set it right!

You can almost imagine the actor stamping his foot and giving a little flourish as the curtain closes.

Then there are speeches such as Lady Capulet's in Act 1 scene 3 of *Romeo and Juliet* where she seeks to entice her daughter to agree to marry Paris by singing his praises in rhyming couplets:

> Examine every married lineament
> And see how one another lends content,
> And what obscured in this fair volume lies
> Find written in the margin of his eyes.
> This precious book of love, this unbound lover,
> To beautify him only lacks a cover.
> The fish lives in the sea, and 'tis much pride
> For fair without the fair within to hide.
> That book in many's eyes doth share the glory
> That in gold clasps locks in the golden story.
> So shall you share all that he doth possess
> By having him, making yourself no less.

The rhyming here underlines the flowery nature of Lady Capulet's sugared words but ends up undermining them. Rhyme helps the speech feel forced and false; an act of transparent persuasion. Especially when contrasted with Romeo's reaction to first seeing Juliet later on in the same scene where the rhyme adds depth to his awed emotion:

> Oh, she doth teach the torches to burn bright!
> It seems she hangs upon the cheek of night
> Like a rich jewel in an Ethiope's ear,
> Beauty too rich for use, for earth too dear.
> So shows a snowy dove trooping with crows

> As yonder lady o'er her fellows shows.
> The measure done, I'll watch her place of stand,
> And, touching hers, make blessèd my rude hand.
> Did my heart love till now? Forswear it, sight!
> For I ne'er saw true beauty till this night.

These lines represent some of the most breathlessly beautiful love poetry in the language. But even here, are we meant to see Romeo as callow and insincere? After all, only moments ago he had "a soul of lead" and was sinking under "love's heavy burden" as he mooned away for Rosaline.

Fascinatingly, Shakespeare's use of rhyme varies according to character. In *The Two Gentlemen of Verona* the womanising Proteus speaks in rhyme, whereas the dull but virtuous Valentine speaks in blank verse. In *Richard II*, Bolingbroke only begins to use rhyme after he's become king, using it most consistently in his final conciliatory speech:

> Come, mourn with me for that I do lament,
> And put on sullen black incontinent:
> I'll make a voyage to the Holy Land,
> To wash this blood off from my guilty hand:
> March sadly after; grace my mournings here;
> In weeping after this untimely bier.

And in *Twelfth Night*, Olivia speaks in prose until Viola appears on the scene: the rhymes increase as she falls more desperately in love. Here are her closing lines from the end of Act 1 scene 5 where they first meet:

> I do I know not what, and fear to find
> Mine eye too great a flatterer for my mind.
> Fate, show thy force: ourselves we do not owe;
> What is decreed must be, and be this so.

In *Othello*, Iago speaks in rhyme when at his most persuasive and most villainous. His attempts to poison Othello against Desdemona use rhyme to punctuate the progress of the argument. He pretends to be hurt that Othello challenges his motives:

> I thank you for this profit, and from hence
> I'll love no friend, since love breeds such offence.

And as his plot reaches fruition his rhymed aside to the audience makes us complicit in his scheming:

> Will you go on, I pray? This is the night
> That either makes me, or fordoes me quite.

Internal rhyme

So much for end-stopping but there's much more to rhyme than that. Rhyme can also be internal in that it occurs in the middle of lines. There's a variety of different internal rhymes, many of which are show cased in Edgar Allan Poe's poem 'The Raven':

> Once upon a midnight dreary, while I pondered, weak
> and weary,
> While I nodded, nearly napping, suddenly there came a
> tapping,
> As of someone gently rapping, rapping at my
> chamber door.
> "Tis some visitor," I muttered, "tapping at my
> chamber door ..."

Pattern

On display we have examples of internal rhymes where the words rhyme in the same lines, in separate lines and in the proceeding lines.

Internal rhymes can have a range of effects. It sometimes feels defter and more fleeting than an end-stopped rhyme, such as this line from Elizabeth Barrett Browning's 'Sonnet 43':

I love thee to the depth and breadth and height.

It can also be employed to add a comic note as this example from Kipling's 'Pink Dominoes' demonstrates:

Jenny would go in a domino—
Pretty and pink but warm;
While I attended, clad in a splendid
Austrian uniform.

And sometimes internal rhyme can add emphasis to a poem's rhythm, as in Coleridge's 'The Rime of the Ancient Mariner,' or Edgar Allen Poe's poems 'The Raven' and 'Annabel Lee.'

Slant rhyme

Poets also employ half rhymes, sometimes called slant rhymes. These imperfect rhymes get away from the sing-song effect often produced by full, end-stopped rhyme. Slant rhymes rely on either *assonance* (in vowel sounds such as unp<u>a</u>ck and det<u>a</u>ch) or *consonance* (consonant

CONSONANCE

Latin: *consonantia,* 'harmony, agreement,' from *consonantem,* 'agreeing in sound.'

The recurrence of similar sounding consonants.

236

sounds, e.g. pa<u>ct</u> and sli<u>cked</u>) for their effects. In 'Ozymandias,' Shelley alternates full and slant rhyme:

> I met a traveller from an antique land,
> Who said: Two vast and trunkless legs of stone
> Stand in the desert. Near them, on the sand,
> Half sunk, a shattered visage lies, whose frown ...

Philip Larkin also used consonant slant rhymes in 'Toads,' rhyming "work" with "pitchfork" and "life" with "off."

Slant rhyme can have a subtler, cohesive effect and can surprise readers by shifting away from more obvious full rhymes, such as in Dylan Thomas' 'The Force that Through the Green Fuse Drives the Flower,' or in Carol Ann Duffy's 'Text,' where the slant rhyme 'chord' deliberately and jarringly breaks the otherwise careful rhyme scheme.

Eye rhyme

Poems can also be patterned with *eye rhyme* – 'rhyme' which only works visually and relies on words looking alike on the page: prove/love, warp/sharp, etc. There's some speculation that Shakespeare may have been a keen proponent of eye rhyme as seen in his couplet from Act 3 scene 2 of *Hamlet*:

> The great man down, you mark his favourite flies;
> The poor advanced makes friends of enemies

But the more likely explanation is that these words were full rhymes when Shakespeare penned them. There's considerable evidence that English underwent a 'Great Vowel Shift' between 1400 and 1700 where the long vowels of Middle English became shorter or completely unpronounced. This is the main reason why so many English spellings – which became standardised during the 15th and 16th centuries – no longer correspond with their pronunciations. The linguist David Crystal has done much to advocate for 'Original Pronunciation' performances of Shakespeare's plays so audiences can hear them as they were originally intended.[6]

While rhyme is a common feature of poetry it's rare in prose. It might crop up in comic prose, but if the subject matter is serious, rhyme jars. Intentional rhyme tends to resonate pleasantly; unwitting rhyme sets up a jarringly poetic cadence rendering the sense either silly or overly solemn.

Noticing metre

There's a word for noticing the metre in a line of verse: *scansion*. If we want students to be able to make meaning with metre we need

> **METRE**
>
> Greek: *metron* 'to measure.'
>
> The basic rhythmic structure of a poem.

to teach them something about scansion, but to do that, there's some essential information students need to know first. Metre is, arguably, the least well taught aspect of English (although grammar gives it a run for its money). Whilst everyone knows more or less what it is, the specifics too often remain opaque.

The poet and literary critic J.V. Cunningham once said, "Poetry ... is metrical composition"[7] and Robert Frost famously dismissed free verse – poetry without metre – as 'playing tennis with the net down.'[8] However, the claim that poetry should be metrical is widely contested; today metre is disastrously out of fashion and often considered fussily artificial. But, as I.A. Richards pointed out, "Through its very appearance of artificiality metre produces in the highest degree the frame effect, isolating the poetic experience from the accidents and irrelevancies of everyday existence."[9] Whatever your view of the merits of metre, it's certainly true to say that poetry (and in that I'm including dramatic verse) is where we're most likely to find metrical composition.

Metre adds a layer of estrangement between students and poetry. It's like a gilded frame around a painting, drawing attention both to itself and the artwork it frames. Reading poetry as if it's prose kills it. To bring it to life we need to hear and feel it sing inside us, and for that to happen you need to listen to it being read aloud by someone with an educated ear. When introducing students to metre the following approaches are invaluable:

1. Expose students to as much metrical poetry as possible and practise finding the stresses in rhythmically regular lines of poetry.
2. Get students to prepare readings, ideally ask them to learn some lines by heart.
3. Embody different metres by getting students to write (and perform) their own metrical poems.

If time is spent on building up metrical understanding it really pays off when students have to analyse unseen poems later on. The point is not to learn the names of metrical features in order to feature spot but to have a vocabulary to better think – and write – about the meanings we unearth.

Iambic pentameter

The basic building block of metre is the foot – a unit of stressed and unstressed syllables. The two most common feet in English poetry are the *iamb* (eye-YAM) and the *trochee* (TRO key). Both are made up of

> **IAMB**
>
> Greek: *iaptein* 'to send forth' or, to attack.'
>
> Metrical foot consisting of one unstressed and one stressed syllable.

just two syllables. The iamb is an unstressed followed by a stressed syllable (di-dum) whereas the trochee is the reverse (dum-di). The most common arrangement of lines of poetry in English is five iambs, from which we get the term *iambic pentameter*.

> ## TROCHEE
>
> Greek: *trokhaios* 'running.'
>
> Metrical foot consisting of a stressed and an unstressed syllable.

Iambic pentameter is everywhere: from Chaucer to Shakespeare, to Milton, to Dryden, Pope, Keats, Byron, Wordsworth, Owen, Yeats to modern stalwarts of poetry anthologies like Carol Ann Duffy and Simon Armitage. Here are a few fine examples:

> Whan that aprill with his shoures soote
> The droghte of March hath perced to the roote*
> Chaucer, General Prologue to *The Canterbury Tales*

> For I have sworn thee fair and thought thee bright,
> Who art as black as hell, as dark as night.
> Shakespeare, 'Sonnet 147'

> The mind is its own place, and in itself
> Can make a Heaven of Hell, a Hell of Heaven.
> John Milton, *Paradise Lost*, Book I

> My heart aches, and a drowsy numbness pains
> My sense, as though of hemlock I had drunk
> John Keats, 'Ode to a Nightingale'

* *When April with his sweet showers / Has pierced the drought of March to the root.* It can be hard for readers of modern English to scan Chaucer's metre because stress patterns were different in Middle English. If in doubt, assume each vowel is pronounced separately.

That's my last Duchess painted on the wall,
Looking as if she were alive. I call
Robert Browning, 'My Last Duchess'

But T. S. Eliot, I am sad to find,
Damns you with: 'an uninteresting mind'.
W.H. Auden, 'Letter to Lord Byron', III

If in some smothering dreams, you too could pace
Behind the wagon that we flung him in
Wilfred Owen, 'Dulce Et Decorum Est'

Miss J. Hunter Dunn, Miss J. Hunter Dunn,
Furnish'd and burnish'd by Aldershot sun
John Betjeman, 'A Subaltern's Love Song'

That all the lovely canfuls smelt of rot.
Each year I hoped they'd keep, knew they would not.
Seamus Heaney, 'Blackberry Picking'

Here's how they rated him when they looked back:
Sometimes he did this, sometimes he did that.
Simon Armitage, 'Poem'

For too long he has suffered, with no friends
Sea all around him, sea on every side.
Emily Wilson, from her translation of the *Odyssey**

* It might interest you to know that the *Odyssey*, like all classical epics, was actually composed in dactylic hexameter (a dactyl is a stressed syllable followed by two unstressed ones; hexameter is made up of six feet) but that Emily Wilson deliberately chose to use iambic pentameter because "it is the conventional metre for regular English narrative verse" (*Odyssey*, p. 82).

Pattern

In each of these examples you can hear the regular, unique, metrical heartbeat of English verse:

di-dum – di-dum – di-dum – di-dum – di-dum.

But in that simple rhythm you can hear a multitude of tones and voices: serious, comic, wistful, imperious, formal and matter-of-fact. The cadence is different in each example – some zip along, some tread slowly and carefully – and together they showcase the range of effects possible using such a flexible metre. Poet and critic, Clive James once noted that, "The iambic pentameter is always being called tum-ti-tum by people who couldn't write even the tum-ti-tum version if their lives depended on it."[10]

Enjambment and caesura

The metrical patterns in Shakespeare's plays can, at first reading, obscure meaning as students may be tricked into placing stress and emphasis unnaturally, but when they compare the patterns of lines on a page with a skilled performance they can begin to perceive both the pattern and where it breaks. We often – wrongly – tell students that Shakespeare's plays are written in iambic pentameter. In fact, though, all of his plays make use of pentameter – we usually call it blank (i.e. unrhymed) verse – not all of it is iambic. To get one's head around this requires some knowledge of *enjambment* and *caesura*. Consider this passage from *Macbeth*:

> The <u>prince</u> of <u>Cumberland</u>! <u>That</u> is a <u>step</u>
> On <u>which</u> I <u>must</u> fall <u>down</u>, or <u>else</u> o'er<u>leap</u>,
> For <u>in</u> my <u>way</u> it <u>lies</u>. <u>Stars</u>, hide your <u>fires</u>;
> Let <u>not</u> light <u>see</u> my <u>black</u> and <u>deep</u> de<u>sires</u>.

What is the punctuation doing? The exclamation point in the first line breaks the sense being communicated quite

242

dramatically, as does the full stop in the third line. Both are examples of caesura which interrupt the flow of the line. Now look at the ends of lines 2 and 3: the sense being communicated

CAESURA

Latin: *caedere* 'to cut down.'

A pause or break in the rhythm of a line of poetry.

spills from one line to the next. This is enjambment and it serves to prevent us from resting at the end of the line, forcing our attention on to the next line. But something else happens with these caesuras and enjambments. In the first line, the rhythm changes with the caesura: "The Prince of Cumberland" is iambic, but "That is" is a trochee. The caesura doesn't just disrupt the meaning, it disrupts the metre. It's almost as if Shakespeare wants us to notice the jerkiness of Macbeth's thoughts. Something similar happens in line 3: "For in my way it lies" is iambic, but then the stress shifts straight from "lies" to "Stars." "Stars hide" is another trochee, but what's

going on in the final foot of line 3? It looks a bit like an iamb except it seems to trail off with the extra, unloved syllable of "fires."

In Heaney's 'Storm on the Island,' caesura and enjambment echo the poem's meaning:

ENJAMBMENT

French: *enjamber*, 'to stride over,' or 'to straddle.'

Where the syntax of a phrase runs over two or more lines of poetry.

> Blast: you know what I mean – leaves and branches
> Can raise a tragic chorus in a gale

The strict iambic pentameter is disrupted, one imagines, by the gathering and swelling of the wind. "Blast: you," a spondee amongst iambs, makes us hear and feel the invisible force of the storm.

What's the stress?

When we look closely at a line from a Shakespeare play we expect to see the regular stress patterns of iambic pentameter, but for the passage from *Macbeth* on page 242, which begins "The prince of Cumberland!", this is what we see:

> **SPONDEE**
>
> Greek: *spondeios*, the name of the metre originally used in chants accompanying libations, from *spondē*, 'libation.'
>
> Metrical foot consisting of two stressed syllables, e.g. *hard luck*.

```
di-dum – di-dum – di-dum – dum-di – di-dum
di-dum – di-dum – di-dum – di-dum – di-dum
di-dum – di-dum – di-dum – dum-di – di-dum-di
di-dum – di-dum – di-dum – dum-di – di-dum-di
```

As well as the trochaic substitutions already mentioned, the last two lines have an eleventh, unstressed syllable. This is sometimes called a feminine ending (or a weak ending) with lines ending on the stressed syllable being masculine or strong endings. This might look sloppy at first glance but it's an important aspect of using iambic pentameter. In English we have some polysyllabic nouns which end on the stressed syllable (ma*chine*, ciga*rette*) as well as most polysyllabic verbs (pre*sent*, ex*port*, de*cide*, be*gin*) but in most polysyllabic words emphasis is placed on the first syllable. If iambic pentameter forbade weak line endings then we'd be excluding an awful lot of words from our metric toolkit.

Getting a feel for scansion can be very revealing. Often, patterns of weak and strong line endings are used to create a feeling of call-and-response, or question and answer: weak endings have the rising intonation of a question, strong endings the emphatic thud of a reply. We can see the questioning nature of the unstressed final syllable in Shakespeare's most famous line: "To be, or not to be: that is the question."

Of course, iambic (or trochaic) pentameter is just one of the very many metric patterns a poet might employ. We have *spondees* – a foot with two stressed syllables, for example 'hard luck' and 'fat chance' – and the *pyrrhic foot*, which has two unstressed syllables (usually two consecutive grammatical words such as 'in the' or 'by a'). Feet can also be more than two syllables: *anapests* and *dactyls* are both composed of three syllables (*ternary feet*). The ana-

pest (ditty-dum) is, like the iamb, a rising foot with the stress going from weak to strong, whereas the dactyl is its reverse (dum-ditty) and, like the trochee, goes from strong to weak.

> **ANAPEST**
>
> Greek: *anapaistos*, 'struck back, rebounding.'
>
> A foot consisting of two unstressed followed by a stressed syllable.

Anapests

Clement Clarke Moore's seasonal favourite provides a fine example of anapestic tetrameter:

'Twas the night before Christmas, when all through the house
Not a creature was stirring, not even a mouse;
The stockings were hung by the chimney with care
In hopes that St Nicholas soon would be there.

Strictly speaking, it's not *entirely* composed of anapestic feet: the first feet of lines 3 and 4 are iambs. The effect of this metre is for the lines to race along, evoking perhaps the nervous excitement young children typically feel on Christmas Eve.

Now, look at this second example of a poem employing the anapest:

> I sprang to the stirrup and Joris and he
> I galloped, Dirk galloped, we galloped all three.
> (Stevenson, 'How They Brought the Good News from Ghent to Aix')

Again, Stevenson has chosen to lop off the head of the first anapests in each line, replacing them with iambs. He could easily have started the lines, "Then I sprang," and "And I galloped," retaining the anapestic feet, but in refusing to do so, we hear a more forceful rhythm, more readily redolent of horse hooves beating the earth as they race along.

Dactyls

So much for anapests, what about the aforementioned dactyl? Many common English words and names are dactyls: difficult, mockingbird, alphabet, trivial. And counterintuitive is a nice example of a double

DACTYL

Greek: *daktylos*, 'finger breadth' (the three joints of a finger).

A metrical foot consisting of one stressed followed by two unstressed syllables.

dactyl. We can also hear dactyls at work in nursery rhymes such as 'Hickory, dickory dock.' Even poetry itself is a dactyl. The erstwhile leader of the Labour party, Jeremy Corbyn, enjoyed a brief moment of popular appeal when it was noticed that his name fit the pattern of a dactyl followed by a trochee, and could be sung to the tune of The White Stripes' hit 'Seven Nation Army': *Ohhh Jeremy Corbyn!*

The dactyl was the basic building block of ancient Greek epic and both the *Iliad* and the *Odyssey* are wrought from dactylic hexameter. They're less common in English verse, but have still been used to great effect as in Tennyson's thunderous, 'The Charge of the Light Brigade':

<u>Half</u> a league, <u>half</u> a league,
<u>Half</u> a league <u>on</u>ward,
<u>All</u> in the <u>val</u>ley of <u>Death</u>
Rode the <u>six</u> hundred.
"<u>For</u>ward, the <u>Light</u> Brigade!
<u>Charge</u> for the <u>guns</u>!" he said.
<u>In</u>to the <u>val</u>ley of <u>Death</u>
Rode the <u>six</u> hundred.

The first line is a dactylic dimeter, the second line is a dactyl followed by a trochee, the third line is two dactyls with either an extra beat added on "Death" followed by a single stress followed by a trochee in line 4, or maybe "Death / Rode the" is a dactyl employing enjambment. It doesn't really matter. Read it to yourself to decide which you think works best.

Just as Stevenson employed anapests to echo the galloping feet of horses, Tennyson uses dactyls to create a similar effect, except having the stress on the first syllable maybe suggests a more urgent, more concerted surge forward that we might imagine if six hundred horsemen all charged together into the Valley of Death.

Robert Browning achieved something similar in 'The Lost Leader,' his rant against Wordsworth who, Browning felt, betrayed the poetic community by accepting the office of Poet Laureate. You can't please everyone.

<u>Just</u> for a <u>hand</u>ful of <u>silver</u> he <u>left</u> us,
<u>Just</u> for a <u>rib</u>and to <u>stick</u> in his <u>coat</u>—

Pattern

> <u>Found</u> the one <u>gift</u> of which <u>for</u>tune be<u>reft</u> us,
> <u>Lost</u> all the <u>oth</u>ers she <u>lets</u> us de<u>vote</u>;
> <u>They</u>, with the <u>gold</u> to give, <u>doled</u> him out <u>sil</u>ver,
> <u>So</u> much was <u>theirs</u> who so <u>lit</u>tle all<u>owed</u>:
> <u>How</u> all our <u>cop</u>per had <u>gone</u> for his <u>ser</u>vice!
> <u>Rags</u>—were they <u>pur</u>ple, his <u>heart</u> had been <u>proud</u>!

The poem alternates between lines of dactylic trimeter and lines that end with either a trochee or a single stressed beat. The rhythm created is urgent, angry, spitting forth its arguments and accusations against poor old Wordsworth.

The proliferation of all these technical terms might excite you or fill you with dread, but it's important to know that metre is a powerful frame for meaning. Knowing the names of some of its most common features can help students better articulate what they notice. The point is not that students should be instructed to spot trochees and anapests in the poems they study, but that they can talk about their effects more efficiently. What I really think matters is that students learn to see and hear the metre in poetry and begin to notice its effects, especially when broken or altered.

Form

Before moving on from poetry, we should consider one more important aspect of patterns within and between texts: *form*. The word comes to us from the Latin *forma* meaning 'beauty.' This might be important; literature – especially poetry – that has form is perhaps more beautiful than that which is formless. There's a lot of confusion and debate about what, precisely, the difference is between form, genre and structure. The definition I favour is that writing which has form operates within a tradition. It makes meaning by experimenting with the conventions, not by brushing them aside. Form provides constraints which allow for more, not less creative freedom. Form prevents meaning from descending into slop. But it should be fairly clear that sit-coms and chat shows are two different forms of television show; concerto and opera are different musical forms; ballet and street are different dance forms.

For our purposes the major literary forms are prose fiction, non-fiction prose, poetry and drama. These days, most, but not all, fictional prose takes the form of the novel. A novel might be romantic, historical, epistolary or 'literary.'* These are genres, or types. There is a wide array of niche poetic forms but almost everyone will have heard of a few: haikus, limericks, ballads and sonnets. Poetic forms have rules or conventions, as does any form. The extent to which these rules are followed, broken or subverted tells us something about what a writer is trying to achieve. For instance, we know a limerick has five lines which have to scan: they are made up of anapests and have a regular AABBA rhyme scheme, like so:

Ditty-dum – ditty-dum – ditty-dum (A)
Ditty-dum – ditty-dum – ditty-dum (A)
Ditty-dum – ditty-dum (B)
Ditty-dum – ditty-dum (B)
Ditty-dum – ditty-dum – ditty-dum (A)

If you didn't follow this pattern you might have written something wonderful, but it wouldn't be a limerick. But this isn't all: a limerick must be amusing:

There was a young man of Peru
Who was hard up for something to do.
So he took out a carrot

* Either pretentiously unreadable or unjustly unread.

And buggared his parrot,
And sent the results to the Zoo.

There was a young Royal Marine
Who tried to fart "God Save the Queen".
When he reached the soprano
Out came the guano,
And his breeches weren't fit to be seen.[11]

Of course, you could bend the rules. Some of the lines don't quite scan in the examples earlier, but they're close enough for us not to mind. Sometimes limericks work precisely *because* the rhymes are refused. Here's a fabulous example from W.S. Gilbert:

There was an old man of St Bees
Who was horribly stung by a wasp
When they said: 'Does it hurt?'
He replied: 'No it doesn't–
It's a good job it wasn't a hornet.

Is this a limerick? Yes. No. Does it matter? A limerick is still a limerick; the point is that by playing with the rules, Gilbert was using the expectations of form to surprise and delight his readers.

Before we continue picking apart poetic form, we should briefly consider the stanza. Just as the basic building block of meaning in prose is the paragraph, in poetry it is the *stanza* (from the Italian for 'standing place,' or room). This presents us with the satisfying image of a poem as a house divided into different rooms. Stanzas can be any length, from a single line to a couplet, to tercets, quatrains, cinquains, sestets, octaves and so on. Some poems have stanzas of varying line lengths as do some forms: a sonnet can be either a single stanza of fourteen lines; an octave and a sestet; three quatrains and a couplet; or any other variation that appeals.

The sonnet

Sonnets have a long and rich history. Invented sometime in the 13th century by, we think, Giacomo da Lentini, the sonnet quickly became all the rage in Holy Roman Emperor Frederick II's court in Palermo, Sicily.

SONNET

Italian: *sonetto*, 'little song,' from Latin *sonus* 'sound.'

Fourteen-line poem, usually composed with regular metre and rhyme scheme.

There are, sadly, no surviving copies of Lentini's sonnets, but the form took off. Dante wrote a number of sonnets as did the painter Michelangelo, but it was Petrarch who made the sonnet his own, penning over three hundred specimens. What we today call the Petrarchan Sonnet consists of fourteen lines of iambic pentameter divided into an octave (eight lines) with two envelope rhymes: ABBA ABBA, and a sestet (six lines) which followed the pattern CDE CDE or CDC CDC. The ninth line would, typically, be the *volta* (from the Italian for turn) – the point at which the poem pivots between one perspective or line of argument and another.

FRANCESCO PETRARCHA 'PETRARCH' – 1304–1374

Italian scholar and poet during the early Italian Renaissance who was one of the earliest humanists. Petrarch's rediscovery of Cicero's letters is often credited with initiating the 14th-century Italian Renaissance.

Pattern

Here's a Petrarchan sonnet written by John Milton in the 1600s:

> When I consider how my light is spent,
> Ere half my days in this dark world and wide,
> And that one talent which is death to hide
> Lodged with me useless, though my soul more bent
> To serve therewith my Maker, and present
> My true account, lest He returning chide;
> "Doth God exact day-labour, light denied?"
> I fondly ask. But Patience, to prevent
> That murmur, soon replies, "God doth not need
> Either man's work or His own gifts. Who best
> Bear His mild yoke, they serve Him best. His state
> Is kingly: thousands at His bidding speed,
> And post o'er land and ocean without rest;
> They also serve who only stand and wait."

Can you see where the volta comes? Milton helpfully marks it with a caesura: "But Patience ... replies."

Although Chaucer was aware of Petrarch and would certainly have read his sonnets, he never, as far as we know, wrote any of his own. According to Stephen Fry, the sonnet was a step too far for the medieval English mindset: "their humanism, their promotion of personal feeling and open enquiry, the vigour and self-assertion of their individual voice would have made any attempt on his part to write such works ... a kind of heresy or treason."[12] It took the coming of the Renaissance and Reformation for the sonnet to worm its way into the English consciousness.

Sir Thomas Wyatt, a diplomat in the court of Henry VIII, is widely credited with first importing the sonnet to English shores. Wyatt translated a number of Petrarch's sonnets and wrote a few of his own. These went down well with King

Henry and this opened the way for others to try their hand. Henry Howard, Earl of Surrey, built on Wyatt's modifications by changing the ABBA ABBA rhyme scheme to one that was more manageable in rhyme-poor English: ABBA CDDC.

The English form of the sonnet eventually became known as the Shakespearean sonnet due to Shakespeare's virtuosity. By the time Shakespeare's sonnets were published in 1609, the conventions of love sonnets were firmly established: four quatrains rhymed ABAB CDCD EFEF and a final rhyming couplet. In the accompanying online resource on the sonnet form I've included Sir Philip Sidney's 'Astrophel and Stella' that uses iambic hexameter, and 'Amoretti LXVI' by Edmund Spenser written in more typical pentameter.

Shakespeare's innovation was not to alter the form of the sonnet, but its scope. Instead of limiting himself to love, he introduced philosophical issues, perplexing ironies and clever parodies. We've already seen 'Sonnet 130' (on pages 98–9) – here are three more examples of Shakespeare's mastery of the form:

Sonnet 29
When, in disgrace with fortune and men's eyes,
I all alone beweep my outcast state,
And trouble deaf heaven with my bootless cries,
And look upon myself and curse my fate,
Wishing me like to one more rich in hope,
Featured like him, like him with friends possessed,
Desiring this man's art and that man's scope,
With what I most enjoy contented least;
Yet in these thoughts myself almost despising,
Haply I think on thee, and then my state,
(Like to the lark at break of day arising
From sullen earth) sings hymns at heaven's gate;
    For thy sweet love remembered such wealth brings
    That then I scorn to change my state with kings.

Pattern

If you look at the punctuation you might notice the sonnet is one long sentence, hinging on the phrase "Haply I think of thee." The solace offered by "thee" soothes all pain, rights all wrong and allows the poet to be content with his place in the world. This is not romantic love, but it may be an ideal to which most of us would aspire.

> Sonnet 116
> Let me not to the marriage of true minds
> Admit impediments. Love is not love
> Which alters when it alteration finds,
> Or bends with the remover to remove.
> O no! it is an ever-fixed mark
> That looks on tempests and is never shaken;
> It is the star to every wand'ring bark,
> Whose worth's unknown, although his height be taken.
> Love's not Time's fool, though rosy lips and cheeks
> Within his bending sickle's compass come;
> Love alters not with his brief hours and weeks,
> But bears it out even to the edge of doom.
> If this be error and upon me prov'd,
> I never writ, nor no man ever lov'd.

One of the advantages of the Shakespearean version is that the pattern of three quatrains and a final couplet lent itself to the development of a train of thought. 'Sonnet 116' is much more clearly demarcated with the punctuation revealing the skeleton of its form. The first quatrain makes a statement (love is unchanging), the second develops the theme with a series of images (love = a star that sailors can rely on for navigation), the third moves to a general point on the natures of love and time, and the final couplet seals the deal with an empathetic, 'I'm right, so there!'

Finally, in Act 1 scene 5 of *Romeo and Juliet*, Shakespeare has the lovers share a sonnet when they first meet. The first quatrain is spoken by Romeo and plays on the idea that to kiss Juliet's hand is an act of pilgrimage and religious awe. In the second quatrain, she takes up the image and accepts his homage as her due. The third quatrain is shared; continuing the imagery of prayer and devotion, Romeo introduces the idea that they should kiss and then, in the final couplet, she agrees. This combination of dialogue, metre, rhyme and imagery transcends form. The lovers sharing lines from a love sonnet make this both a carefully judged character study and a dramatic engine driving the emotional intensity of the scene.

The sonnet continued in popularity after Shakespeare's death with Donne and Milton both writing excellent examples, but the energy of the form seemed to fizzle out. After Milton, the sonnet disappeared for over one hundred years until Wordsworth revived it in the 1820s. The sonnet took up a central place in the estimation of the Romantics and featured heavily in the work of Keats, Coleridge and Shelley, but it was Wordsworth who best loved the sonnet form, writing 523 of them. He even wrote a sonnet about sonnets, chastising those who looked down on the fourteen-line wonder, 'Scorn not the Sonnet ...'

From there, the sonnet has gone from strength to strength, remaining surprisingly popular even today. When modern poets such as Heaney, Duffy and Armitage use sonnets, we ought to ask why. They have the whole poetic world open to them, why choose the humble sonnet? There are a number of possible reasons. One is that writing a sonnet is entering into a conversation with poets from earlier ages. Duffy does this very deliberately in her sonnet 'Anne Hathaway' where she imagines the relationship between Shakespeare and his wife. It's also a test, a proving ground. If you can master this fourteen-line form then you can really call yourself a poet. You can see Armitage doing this in one of his early collections, *Book of Matches*, which includes a number of excellent sonnets. And Heaney's masterfully constructed sonnets in *The Haw Lantern* consciously build on a venerable tradition, rooting themselves in this fertile poetic soil. All of the poets who choose the sonnet form play with its structure, bend its flexible rules and use it to create something distinctively their own.

Form in fiction

Thinking about form and structure in poetry is one thing, but it can feel even more daunting in prose, where pattern is equally important, if less immediately apparent. When reading longer texts, structure has to be temporal in that it has to hold our reading together from moment to moment. Peter Elbow suggests that the problem of structure in narrative is "the problem of how to bind time." Patterns like metre, rhyme and alliteration can successfully bind poems, but for longer texts something else is required. This something else could, according to Elbow, include "the experience of anticipation or tension which builds to some resolution or satisfaction. In well-structured discourse [there should be] a pattern of alternating dissonance-and-consonance or itching and scratching."[13] This back and forth, question and answer is present in all good prose.

When reading novels, short stories, extracts or articles we should be alert for these "itch and scratch" sequences a writer has chosen to present her ideas in. The two major strands to follow are story and argument. Is the writer recounting a narrative, or ordering a set of points with a particular objective? Superficially, it's obvious that all fiction tells stories and all non-fiction makes arguments, but this is too simplistic. Many works of fiction make arguments – either over the whole text (think of Orwell's *Animal Farm* for instance) or at certain points within the text (much of Mary Shelley's *Frankenstein* consists of explaining the arguments about natural education Rousseau made in *Emile*). Likewise, many writers of non-fiction weave wonderful narratives. You only have to open a book by Michael Lewis or Annie Dillard to be gripped by the stories that unfold.

Here are some reminders of the distinctive patterns stories and arguments can take: Are narratives unfolded chronologically or episodically? Is there evidence of the kinds of narrative structures we considered in chapter 6? If students are reading an extract from a longer work, the opening of a passage presents rich opportunities to identify and comment on, for instance, the disruption of equilibrium. How does exposition occur? This could be through conflict, a character's internal thoughts, a stream of consciousness, dialogue, the ways in which characters are introduced, background details and descriptions, and references to other texts like letters or newspaper clippings. How does the story or argument cohere? Does the writer connect ideas through cause and effect or problem and solution, or some other pattern? And, most crucially, what is the *effect* of these different structural choices?

Students can learn to notice the structural devices used to move the action on within stories and think about how they alter meaning. Writers can make sudden shifts in place, narrative perspective, or time. There might be patterns like narrative summaries, flashbacks to events that happened prior to the action of the story and flashes forward to incidents in the future. All writers manipulate incidents and ideas using patterns within their texts, and all readers can more fully appreciate the choices writers make when they become attuned to these patterns.

Teaching pattern

I would suggest that phonemes make the best starting point. Students will be familiar with the vowels but might not have previously explored the effects of long and short vowel sounds. Some extracts from Sylvia Plath's 'Daddy' provide a great example of the stabbing, staccato rhythm produced by short vowels (although the whole poem may not be appropriate for younger students) and the opening of Dylan Thomas' *Under Milk Wood* showcases the mellow fruitfulness of long vowels. To demonstrate how emotion is mainly conveyed with vowels, remove the consonants from sentences and ask students to guess the tone or mood of the speaker. Then, I think it's worth spending some time on the different consonants and their effects. Students often learn about sibilants and plosives but little else. Students should not only learn the names of the various voiced and unvoiced consonant sounds and experience how they feel, but notice which part of the mouth is involved in making them.

It's a short hop from here to the literary schemes, alliteration and assonance, and then onto rhyme. These are everywhere in modern life: popular songs, adverts, brand names all make liberal use of them. Why? As always, focus on the significance of these techniques. Experiment with and without: what changes as a result? Why do we like rhyme? Read the W.S. Gilbert 'limerick' on page 250 and ask students what they think – why is it (or, isn't it) successful? For gloriously crashing alliteration, read some of Gerald Manley Hopkins' poems – don't worry so much about meaning but concentrate on the sounds they make and the feelings they evoke. A poem that exemplifies all these uses of sound is Walt Whitman's 'Beat! Beat! Drums!' It has it all: alliteration, assonance, consonance, internal rhyme, and it nails the pulse of war like little else.

Next, introduce students to the stress patterns of speech. Showing how stresses change between word classes can be a useful exercise: com**bat** (v), **com**bat (n), **di**rect (adj), di**rect** (v), per**mit** (v), **per**mit (n). Once they recognise how stresses naturally fall, it's time to introduce them to scansion by marking up lines of poetry to expose the stress patterns. I'd definitely recommend starting with iambic pentameter because it's the most common poetic metre and because it's relatively easy to hear. Use the examples on pages 240–1 if you're stuck for inspiration. Write up a line and separate the feet, and underline where emphasis should be placed, as follows:

You <u>blocks</u>!ǀYou <u>stones</u>!ǀYou <u>worse</u> ǀthan <u>sense</u> ǀless <u>things</u>!

This line from *Julius Caesar* is as obvious an example of iambic pentameter as you're likely to find, and students will have no trouble hearing where the stresses fall. Next, give students lines where the stress patterns are more ambiguous, such as these from Marlowe's *Doctor Faustus*:

Settle thy studies, Faustus, and begin
To sound the depth of that thou will profess.

Get students to argue over where the stresses fall. Obviously, you can read those lines in a sing-song di-dum, di-dum, but students should quickly see that's not how the first line should be read. 'Settle,' for instance, is pronounced with the emphasis placed on the first syllable (a trochee). After students have argued this back and forth, let them know that there's no right or easy answer. Marlowe's great innovation was to avoid sticking to strict metre and to use what has become known as 'the mighty line,' a flexible construction capable of capturing the natural rhythms of English speech. And it's at this point that you need to make sure they can distinguish rhythm from metre.

Pattern

If metre is the pattern of feet in which lines are composed, rhythm is the *effect* of the metre. Metre is the way a poem is written; rhythm is how it is *read*. Rhythm can also be created through repetition (see Whitman's 'O Captain, My Captain'), alliteration (almost anything by Gerald Manley Hopkins), line length (Matthew Arnold's 'Dover Beach') or through end-stopping, caesura and enjambment. Once students know what iambic pentametre feels like introduce them to different line lengths: tetrameter (Marvell's 'To His Coy Mistress'), trimeter ('The Rime of the Ancient Mariner') and hexameter (Byron's 'There's Pleasure in these Pathless Woods'). It's worth exploring why these variations are less popular than pentameter. Get students to discuss what these different line lengths feel like and how they might add to or detract from meaning.

I advise making students familiar with iambs, trochees, spondees, anapests and dactyls so that they can recognise them and consider their effects, particularly if they notice rhythm being disrupted. (The pyrrhic foot comes up so rarely that it's perfectly possible to omit but I'd want to include it for completeness.) Of these additional feet the trochee is the most important and, as trochaic substitution is so commonly associated with caesura, it's worth teaching them together. Where you find one the other will probably be present, and, especially in Shakespeare's plays, the substitution of an iamb for a trochee adds to the meaning conveyed in the words themselves. And, of course, you can't teach caesura without covering enjambment.

Obviously, most of these patterns are bound up with poetry. It's important to make the point that prose depends on different structural techniques for its form and shape. The patterns made by sentences are addressed in the next chapter, but students should also think about the patterns made with theme, motif, character and the echoes created by the various different schemes of repetition.

260

Pattern presents potentially difficult, abstract ideas which, when students first have their attention drawn to them, can seem impossibly distant from their naïve perspective of how literature and language work. What is an obvious and beautiful pattern to an expert is just random noise to them. It takes time for students to become familiar and comfortable enough to discuss assonance and enjambment with the same fluency with which they pull apart metaphor because there's less to grip on to. It takes training to understand that structure makes meaning just as much as words do. If students are inducted into these ways of perceiving and creating meaning they will not only be able to note and interpret their use, but become better able to deploy them in their own writing.

KEY POINTS

- Pattern-seeking is automatic (we match everything we know against new information to check whether we are facing a threat or an opportunity) but *noticing* patterns is a deliberate act.
- Patterns in sounds suggest meanings on an emotional rather than a semantic level.
- We are drawn to patterns of repetition because they stand out from their surroundings; difference is as important as similarity.
- Students need to think about the significance of rhyme; it often feels satisfying and gives a feeling of flow, order and 'rightness.' If it is disrupted we find it jarring.
- If students learn the basics of scansion they will become better at spotting the metres poets use and possess a language to discuss its effects.

> - Form provides a frame within which writers can work. In shorter texts like poems, form often revolves around metrical patterns, but in longer texts students should be alert for patterns of 'dissonance and consonance.'

One area of pattern not covered in this chapter is grammar. This is such a large and distinct topic that the next chapter is dedicated to it.

Further reading

- Much of the thinking in this chapter was informed by Jeremy Lent's *The Patterning Instinct* which advances the argument that human thought is, to a great extent, based on pattern-seeking and matching.
- For the sections on prosody I drew heavily from Stephen Fry's *The Ode Less Travelled*, Clive James' *Poetry Notebooks*, Thomas Carper and Derek Attridge's *Meter and Meaning* and Mary Oliver's *A Poetry Notebook*.

9 | Grammar

Every human culture has developed a spoken language and, by inference, a system of grammar. No one ever sits us down and teaches us how to speak, we just soak it up from our environment. All children, regardless of their culture, seem to go through very predictable phases of language acquisition: first they learn nouns, then they start to pick up verbs and then begin to combine nouns and verbs with articles, prepositions, pronouns and all the other parts of speech into grammatically coherent and complex language.

In fact, children's ability to intuit previously unheard structures and formulations from minimal grammatical knowledge is remarkable. For instance, when learning English, most children guess that the past tense of the verb 'to go' is 'goed.' But how? No adult ever says this; children independently work out the rule that you add *-ed* to the end of a verb to indicate that it happened in the past. It's only later we learn 'to go' is an irregular verb and 'went' is the correct formulation.

The speed with which children acquire grammar is astonishing. There's so much one needs to learn in order to speak a language fluently that it's been suggested that we must have some sort of instinct for language. Stephen Pinker's book, *The Language Instinct,* is an attempt to document how such an instinct may have evolved and how it operates. More recently, the idea that we have some sort of mental grammar module has been challenged. Jeremy Lent argues in *The Patterning Instinct* that we have an innate capacity to notice and make meaning from patterns and that language is just one such type of pattern to which we've become particularly good at paying attention.

Spontaneous grammar

There are numerous examples of children spontaneously creating language – and grammar – where there is none. When adults immigrate to a new country they often struggle to learn the language of their new home. Within their cultural group they continue to speak their native tongue but when communicating across cultures, diverse immigrant groups often create *pidgin* versions of the host language. Pidgins allow basic concepts to be communicated and simple transactions to be conducted but, because of their lack of grammatical cohesion, struggle to allow the discussion of abstract or complex ideas. But, the second generation, who grow up hearing pidgin, add the missing grammatical structures and create a *creole.*

Pidgins are grammatically simplified versions of language that develop between groups that do not share a language in common. **Creoles** are stable, natural languages that develop from the simplifying and mixing of different languages within a fairly brief period of time: pidgins usually evolve into fully-fledged creole languages. There is documented evidence of around one hundred creole languages emerging since 1500, mostly based on English or French.

A rather dramatic example of the spontaneous development of grammar comes from the experience of deaf children born to hearing parents. Nicaraguan Sign Language developed in the 1970s and 1980s when groups of deaf children were sent to specialist schools. Although adults tried to teach children how to lip-read spoken Spanish, they instead developed their own pidgin sign language by combining their home-grown sign systems. Over time this became creolised into a fully grammatical language as younger children picked up the signs from their peers. This example is especially interesting because not only did the language develop without adult instruction, it developed *despite* it.[1]

Where do the rules of grammar come from? How did these deaf children know enough about grammar to invent their own? The astonishing fact about language is that it evolves. Its rules are not invented, they're *discovered*, by each of us independently as we learn to speak, and by linguists as they attempt to catalogue what ordinary speakers actually do.

Constructing sentences is not like stringing beads on a cord: the order of the words we use must be precisely organised. As Maya Angelou put it, "I know that I must select studiously the nouns, pronouns, verbs, absorbs, etcetera, and by a careful syntactical arrangement make readers laugh, reflect or riot."[2] Grammar is a form of chunking for working memory: it aids recall and interpretation. Sentences are our primary means of exchanging information; grammar is a tool to facilitate that process. According to David Crystal, "Grammar is the way we make sense of words. Without grammar there's only vagueness."[3]

The basic building blocks of grammar are *morphology* and *syntax*.

Morphology

Before it took on a specific linguistic meaning, the word morphology simply meant the form and structure of anything.

Biologists studied the morphology of organisms, geologists were concerned with the morphology of rocks, and, as we've seen Propp was interested in the morphology of folk tales. In language, morphology is the process by which words are assembled from roots, which blossom with prefixes, suffixes and infixes (e.g. 'fan-*bloody*-tastic') to become new words. A morpheme is the smallest unit of meaning and a single word may contain more than one. For instance, 'hats' contains the root *hat* (from the Old English *hæt* meaning 'hood') and the suffix *s*. We hardly notice this but know immediately that 'hat' means something different to 'hats.' We also know that 'hats' means something different to 'hat's.'

One of the oft-voiced opinions about English is that its spelling doesn't follow predictable patterns. This is a little unfair; it's not that spelling is unpredictable, it's that it has become dissociated from pronunciation, as we saw in the previous chapter. Spelling helps reveal patterns in morphemes. For instance, the *s* in cats and dogs is pronounced differently (cat*s* and dog*z*) but the common spelling reveals that they are both plural forms. Or consider the relationship between 'sign,' 'signal' and signature.' In English, the g can't be pronounced in 'sign' but can in the other words. If we were to standardise the spelling of 'sign' to make it more phonetic – 'sine' perhaps – then we would lose the morphological connection with 'signal' and 'signature.' Diachronic change – the process whereby we collectively weigh costs and benefits of the language we use – can sometimes produce frustrating results but, as the case of 'sign' shows, we balance the needs of spelling/sound consistency against the benefits

---

DIACHRONIC CHANGE

Greek: *dia* 'throughout' + *khronos* 'time.'

The historical development of a language.

---

of greater comprehension afforded by seeing clear morphological roots.[4]

Students benefit from learning to recognise that certain types
of words carry different suffixes. Everyone knows that many
adverbs end in *-ly*, but adjectives often end with *-ful, -ious,
-ous, -al, -ial, -ent, -ic* or *-y* (*beautiful, delicious, wonderous,
vocal, special, frequent, tantric, floppy*) and words ending in *-
ment* or *-ion* will probably be nouns (*parliament, vision*). They
should also be pointed to patterns of verb endings: the suffix
-ed indicates the past tense, only verbs with a third person singular noun or pronoun as a subject ever have an added *-s* on
the end and verbs ending in *-ing* are present participles.[5]

Syntax

Whenever we speak, we are constantly linking words together
to create meanings that emerge in new and sometimes unexpected ways. Our ability to combine a finite set of words to
express an almost infinite variety of meanings is what we've
come to call syntax, from the Greek *syntakis* meaning 'orderly
arrangement.'

When children first start putting words together, they're
not always sure of the order they ought to go. Unlike many
languages, word order is crucial in English; when the order
of words changes, so does the meaning. English is a subject-
verb-object language*: The teacher* (subject) *marked* (verb)
the books (object). As such, we know *the dog is biting the
man* means something entirely different to *the man is biting
the dog**, as does *is the dog biting the man?* Here are some
other sentences where changing word order alters meaning:

---

*   According to the journalistic adage, the difference is that *man
      bites dog* is news whereas *dog bites man* is not.

- Only I saw the girl. / I only saw the girl.
- Naturally, I got up. / I got up naturally.
- They are outside. / Are they outside?
- The man with a dog saw me. / The man saw me with a dog.
- Show me the last three pages [of one book]. / Show me the three last pages [of three books].

Some word orders are just wrong: *man the biting dog the is* means nothing. We learn the rules governing word order as children and then rarely think about applying them; we 'just know' which word orders work and which don't, but explaining what we know to anyone learning English as a foreign language is not a straightforward task. How would you explain the rules that govern why each of the following pairs of sentences is either right or wrong?

- I walked to town. / I to town walked.
- That's a fine old house. / That's an old fine house.
- John and I saw her. / I and John saw her.
- She switched it on. / She on switched it.[6]

Whenever we listen to speech or read a text, we run a mental simulation of what is being explained or described. According to Benjamin Bergin, syntax "appears to modulate what part of an evoked simulation someone is invited to focus on, the grain of detail with which the simulation is performed, or what perspective to perform that situation from."[7] We try to make sense of the words we hear and read by trying to visualise them. The order that words appear in makes this easier or more difficult: if we encounter the subject first, we will visualise that subject, then the process described by the verb, and finally the object. The grammar of a sentence replicates the way in which our sensory equipment draws us to notice changes in the environment. If we read,

Juliet kissed Romeo, we picture Juliet, imagine her puckering up and leaning forward, and then we picture her lips making contact with Romeo's. If the sentence is in the passive voice, the process of visualisation is less obvious. If we read, *Romeo was kissed by Juliet*, we imagine looking at Romeo passively waiting for something to happen to him, then we become aware there's some kissing going on, and then, finally, we switch attention to Juliet, the kisser. This is no trouble for such simple sentences, but we're presented with far more difficulty when word order, sentence weight and the passive voice conspire together over longer, more complex sentences.

Noticing grammar

Once students have acquired a basic metalanguage (a language about language) they can begin to think about how sentences work. When children begin putting sentences together to tell stories they find it difficult to hold sequences in their minds. As David Crystal notes, "Storytelling is a multi-directional thing."[8] Not only do we have to focus on what we're currently saying, we have to remember what we've already said and anticipate what we'll say next. Without structure, this places a huge burden on working memory. Students can be shown that English sentences follow the same basic patterns; subjects come before verbs, adjectives generally precede nouns, but adverbs can fit in many different places. We can then begin to draw their attention to the types of sentences writers employ and why they might use them.

If, for instance, a writer uses lots of short, simple sentences the text will take on a staccato rhythm. Lots of full stops slow the reader down and can be useful for creating a sense of tension. Obviously, in the hands of a novice writer this could easily become clunky and repetitive, but in the hands of a master it can be exquisite. Here's an example from chapter 5 of Dostoyevsky's

Crime and Punishment where the murderer Raskolnikov is being interviewed by the police inspector Porfiry:

> "I will not allow myself to be tortured," he whispered, instantly recognising with hatred that he could not help obeying the command and driven to even greater fury by the thought. "Arrest me, search me, but kindly act in due form and don't play with me! Don't dare!"
>
> "Don't worry about the form," Porfiry interrupted with the same sly smile, as it were, gloating with enjoyment over Raskolnikov. "I invited you to see me quite in a friendly way."
>
> "I don't want your friendship and I spit on it! Do you hear? And, here, I take my cap and go. What will you say now if you mean to arrest me?"
>
> He took up his cap and went to the door.
>
> "And won't you see my little surprise?" chuckled Porfiry, again taking him by the arm and stopping him at the door.
>
> He seemed to become more playful and good-humoured which maddened Raskolnikov.
>
> "What surprise?" he asked, standing still and looking at Porfiry in alarm.
>
> "My little surprise, it's sitting there behind the door, he-he-he!" (He pointed to the locked door.) "I locked him in that he should not escape."
>
> "What is it? Where? What?..." Raskolnikov walked to the door and would have opened it, but it was locked.
>
> "It's locked, here is the key!"
>
> And he brought a key out of his pocket.

As the passage continues and Raskolnikov becomes increasingly agitated the sentences become shorter as we wait to find out what Porfiry has behind the locked door. The fact that so much of this extract is in dialogue and broken into separate paragraphs also delays us from discovering whether Porfiry will ferret out Raskolnikov's guilt; with each delay we become evermore focussed on finding out what comes next.

But if you need an example where the pattern is easier to notice, consider this extract from Marcus Sedgewick's novel, *My Swordhand is Singing*:

> An awful self-destructive curiosity pulled Peter closer. Unable to stop himself, he got down on his hands and knees and crawled the final few inches towards the grave. As he approached, something else caught his attention. There was a hole in the soil, at the head of the grave, near the cross. The hole was about the size of a small fist, and perfectly circular, like a rat hole in a river bank.
>
> Peter leant over it.
>
> He looked in.
>
> There was just enough light to see inside the hole.
>
> At the bottom he saw an eye.
>
> It was open, seemingly lifeless, though looking straight at him.
>
> Then it blinked.
>
> Peter screamed and ran as if the devil himself were chasing him.

Longer sentences with fewer full stops create different effects. This short extract from Simon Scarrow's novel

Centurion does a good job of conveying the blurring confusion of a melee:

> The mercenaries began to back away from the rebels, stabbing their spears frantically to try to create a gap between them and their enemies. As soon as some were clear they turned and ran towards Cato's men, immediately endangering their slower comrades as the rebels swarmed into the gaps in the rapidly fragmenting line. A handful were cut off and overwhelmed, attacked from all sides as they desperately swirled around, trying to block the rebels' blows. Inevitably, a blade darted in, and as a man staggered back from the wound he was hacked to the ground in a flurry of sword blows and spear thrusts.

Here, all the description is at the level of action with the verbs and adverbs focussing our attention on the movement. Adjectives would only slow us down as we paused to imagine sharp swords and shiny helmets. This speed is reflected in Scarrow's sentence choices. The longer sentences mean there are fewer full stops for us to pause at, allowing the action to unfold at breakneck speed.

We can also learn to perceive the patterns clauses make within sentences. Normally sentences begin with the main clause – they branch to the right – but sometimes writers elect to withhold the main clause right until the very end of the sentence. This well-known example from Gogol's short story 'The Overcoat' is a corker of a left-branching sentence:

> Even at the hour when the grey St. Petersburg sky had quite dispersed, and all the official world had eaten or dined, each as he could, in accordance with the salary he received and his own fancy; when all were resting from the departmental jar of pens, running to and fro from

their own and other people's indispensable occupations, and from all the work that an uneasy man makes willingly for himself, rather than what is necessary; when officials hasten to dedicate to pleasure the time which is left to them, one bolder than the rest going to the theatre; another, into the street looking under all the bonnets; another wasting his evening in compliments to some pretty girl, the star of a small official circle; another—and this is the common case of all—visiting his comrades on the fourth or third floor, in two small rooms with an anteroom or kitchen, and some pretensions to fashion, such as a lamp or some other trifle which has cost many a sacrifice of dinner or pleasure trip; in a word, at the hour when all officials disperse among the contracted quarters of their friends, to play whist, as they sip their tea from glasses with a kopek's worth of sugar, smoke long pipes, relate at times some bits of gossip which a Russian man can never, under any circumstances, refrain from, and, when there is nothing else to talk of, repeat eternal anecdotes about the commandant to whom they had sent word that the tails of the horses on the Falconet Monument had been cut off, when all strive to divert themselves, Akakiy Akakievitch indulged in no kind of diversion.

What's the effect of this 280-word sentence? Well, just reading it is exhausting. But the structure intensifies both the chaos of St Petersburg and the single-mindedness of the protagonist, Akakiy Akakievitch, in retaining his focus despite being surrounded by potential distractions. And the fact that poor old Akakiy

CLAUSE

Latin: *clausa*, 'conclusion.'

A unit of grammar usually consisting of a subject and predicate.

273

Akakievitch's name appears right at the end of such a colossal sentence feels suffocating and oppressive, giving us an impression of the burdens weighing down on him.

What grammar should we teach?

If the capacity to learn grammar is – at least to some degree – innate, what need is there for formal instruction? The answer, in a nutshell, is writing. It might seem to the casual observer that the way we speak and the way we write are the same, but they're not. Speech is natural. We've been doing it for countless millennia and have evolved a capacity to just pick it up from our environment. Writing is a highly artificial and comparatively recent invention. If you go back to the ancient origins of writing, texts didn't have blank spaces between words; there was no punctuation, no paragraphs: just characters. (Oh, and there were no pages, so you had to unroll your papyrus and, if you wanted to read what it said, you had to start at the beginning and work your way, painstakingly, to the end.) To make the task of reading less laborious, we've systematically improved writing over the centuries with standardised spelling, punctuation, line breaks, page numbers, chapters, indexes, hyperlinks and a host of other devices to improve our ability to make meaning. None of this is acquired naturally.

Crucially, grammar is *not* (or at least, not *just*) a list of rules. In everyday usage, 'grammar' is associated with the 'correct use of the standard language.' But linguists use the term to refer to ways in which words are combined to make sentences, and to label the body of statements they write about the language as they attempt to make explicit the implicit knowledge possessed by all native speakers of English.

Understanding the tension between prescription and description is at the heart of using grammar to make meaning.

Without learning some grammatical metalanguage students struggle to think about their grammatical choices. Knowing the names of things makes it infinitely easier to think or speak about the significance of these choices. Also, teaching becomes much more straightforward if everyone knows the basics. Instead of having to faff about trying to explain how semicolons work, you can simply say, 'they're used to connect independent clauses.' Arguably, knowing the metalanguage of grammar also makes it easier to write creatively. Explicit knowledge of grammar enables students to make decisions about their writing knowingly. And, because grammar is primarily concerned with meaning, metalanguage helps us think more analytically and improves our ability to make sense of other people's use of language, especially in writing.

So, what's holding us back? There are, according to Crystal, four problems which need to be resolved for anyone wanting to teach grammar.[9] These are:

1. Which bits should you teach? There are several thousand points of English grammar to be learned[10] but how should we select which bits should go into the curriculum?
2. There's a lot of abstract thinking required to understand the finer points of grammar. How and when should points like these be addressed?
3. The rules aren't always universally followed because of the effects of language diversity and change. How and when should grammatical variation be handled within a curriculum?
4. There are often differences of opinion among professional grammarians about the best way of describing a particular point of grammar. Should we avoid the awkward bits?

To help us answer these questions, we will combine the wisdom of both the prescriptive and descriptive traditions of grammar.

Prescriptive and descriptive views can be easily parodied, with prescriptivists seen as blind adherents to outdated norms of formal usage and descriptivists as advocating an 'anything goes' position and as condemning all forms of linguistic correction. Rather, we should recognise that we need both accurate descriptions of language that are related to situation, purpose and mode, and prescriptions that take account of context, appropriateness and the expression of meaning. Stephen Pinker, a self-confessed descriptive linguist says, "while I am fascinated by the linguistic exuberance of the vox populi, I'd be the first to argue that having prescriptive rules is desirable, indeed indispensable."[11]

Prescriptive grammar

The prescriptive view of grammar is that it's possible to lay down rules for the correct use of language. There are two problems with the way this view is often implemented. The first is that sometimes the rules do not relate to the actual language use of native speakers. Examples of flawed prescriptive rules include the suggestion that it is wrong to split infinitives (*to blithely wander, to boldly go*); that it's incorrect to end a sentence with a dangling preposition (*I've got some new music to listen to*); that *fewer* applies only to countable nouns whereas *less* must be used for non-countable nouns; that you cannot begin a sentence with a conjunction, and so on. The second problem is that rules that might apply to formal, written language tend not to be appropriate for informal or spoken language.

> ## CONJUNCTION
>
> Latin: *coniugare*, 'to join together.'
>
> A word used to connect clauses or sentences or to coordinate words in the same clause, e.g. *and, but, if*.

But some prescriptions are correct. For instance, the rule that determiners must precede nouns is non-negotiable. If someone were to write *"I've finished reading book my,"* it would be unambiguously wrong; no native speaker would ever say this. The balance required is to work out which prescriptions reflect how language is actually used and which are based on preference and prejudice.

DETERMINER

Latin: *determinare* 'to enclose, bound, set limits to,' from *de* 'off' + *terminare* 'to mark the end or boundary.'

Modifying word that determines the kind of reference a noun or noun group has, e.g. *a, she, every.*

Many prescriptive grammar rules are based on erroneous models of English, following methods of analysing written texts in Greek or Latin. The rules that govern English are so different that imposing rules from classical language is, in Bill Bryson's words, "like trying to play baseball in iceskates."[12] For instance, the injunction against split infinitives arises because the infinitive form of a Latin verb is a single word whereas in English it is two, the subordinator 'to' plus the main verb. Splitting the infinitive in Latin is impossible, doing so in English is not only very common in informal speech,[13] it also leads to interesting possibilities. In the final stanza of 'The Cotter's Saturday Night,' Robbie Burns wrote:

INFINITIVE

Latin: *infinitivus* 'unlimited, indefinite.'

Basic, uninflected form of a verb about which certain people become anxious if split, e.g. *to scoff.*

O Thou! who pour'd the patriotic tide,
That stream'd thro Wallace's undaunted heart,
Who dar'd to, <u>nobly</u>, stem tyrannic pride

He even bracketed his split infinitive with commas to be sure we wouldn't miss it. And, there are instances where not splitting an infinitive would lead to absurdity. Consider this sentence: *Profits are expected to more than double this year.* How would you go about unsplitting that infinitive?

More commonly, avoiding a split infinitive will lead to unhelpful ambiguity, as in this sentence: *The governing body decided immediately to fire the headteacher.* Was the decision immediate or was the firing? It's hard to tell. But, if we were to rewrite the sentence like so: *The governing body decided to immediately fire the headteacher,* then all is clear. We can now infer that the governing body has given the decision due consideration and that the headteacher will be gone as soon as her desk is cleared. There are times when not splitting the infinitive may be preferable, but the most important impetus for the decision to split or not to split should be clarity.

If we are able to knowingly indulge a stylistic preference, then being aware of grammatical conventions is a form of individual liberty.

Descriptive grammar

The descriptive approach to grammar is the product of research into how people actually use language and then attempting to accurately describe these uses. Many people believe they speak in the same way as they write but, in fact, no one does. Descriptivists recognise that formal written language follows different grammatical patterns to informal and spoken language. (See the transcripts on page 172 for an example.) Neither is seen as being right or wrong; all types of language can be shown to follow predictable and logical rules of use.

When it comes to thinking about grammar in the classroom it's not enough to get students to identify the subjunctive mood, distinguish between subordinating and coordinating conjunctions, or use fronted adverbial phrases, they also have to know how all these things make meaning. This requires learning about how and why grammatical choices are made.

Semantics and pragmatics are central to the study of descriptive grammar. Semantics investigates the ways meaning is conveyed in language. As you can imagine, it covers extremely broad territory including vocabulary, discourse, inton-ation, punctuation, typog-

> ## SEMANTICS
>
> Greek: *semantikos* 'significant,' from *sema* ' sign, mark, token; omen.'
>
> Branch of linguistics concerned with study of the meaning of language.

raphy as well as grammar. There isn't space to do this broad field justice here (just as there probably isn't room to do it justice in the curriculum) but the one crucial aspect students need is the ability to ask, *What does this mean? What is its effect?* And this leads to a discussion of the importance of pragmatics. As we saw in chapter 5, pragmatics is the study of the reasons for and effects of our linguistic choices. The aim should always be to ask *why* choices are made and to explore their consequences. Taken together, these elements help children use their grammatical knowledge to make meaning.

Sadly, students have, until recently, tended to get neither prescriptive nor descriptive grammar teaching. In order to demonstrate how descriptive and prescriptive approaches could be bought together, I'll provide examples from three different areas of grammar: determiners and noun phrases, conjunctions and the active and passive voices.

Teaching determiners and noun phrases

It might seem counterintuitive to suggest that teaching determiners should precede nouns, but the possessive determiners (*my, your, his, hers*) help to define nouns. These sorts of determiners, along with *this* and *that,* are concrete in that they tend to refer to things in the here and now. The articles *a* and *the* are more abstract in that they can more easily refer to ideas and objects that are elsewhere (although the use of *the* always suggests shared knowledge).

When teaching word classes, we should avoid imprecise, inaccurate definitions. When children are taught that a noun is 'an object, person, place or thing' confusion is built in. What about nouns that are none of these? What about identity, redness, confusion or tailoring? Are these simply 'things'? If they are, this is unhelpfully elusive. What about words which might, in one context, be nouns, but not in *this* one? What about run? Is it a noun or a verb? *It depends on how it's being used in a sentence.* In this sentence it *is* a noun: *I like to go for a <u>run</u>.* In this one, it is not: *I <u>run</u> for the bus.* Word class is determined by function. One foolproof way to work out whether a word is a noun is to put a determiner in front of it. In the previous case, 'a run' indicates that the word is a noun. As previously noted, a possessive pronoun can be more useful than an article for establishing nounhood: *a music* doesn't really work but *my music* is fine.

When we add a determiner to a noun we get a noun phrase. A phrase contains at least two words and functions as one part of speech. Noun phrases will contain at least one noun and be able to function as the subject or object* of a sentence:

- my father
- two little girls
- another doggy in the window
- a compulsive liar
- some kindness
- that house on the corner
- outer London

* Or prepositional object.

- last month
- every day of my life so far
- singing in the bath
- the surprisingly tall English teacher with curly ginger hair and a cheeky smile

Theoretically, noun phrases can be as long as you like, but as you can see from the last example, they get a bit unwieldy if they're too long. Together the words that form the noun phrase can be picked up and moved around to do different jobs in a sentence:

- <u>Last month</u> I moved to <u>outer London</u>.
- I moved to <u>outer London last month</u>.

- <u>My father</u> is <u>a compulsive liar</u>.
- <u>A compulsive liar</u> told <u>my father</u> that he lived in <u>that house on the corner</u>.

Teaching conjunctions: and & but

Within a sentence, clauses are often connected by the conjunctions *and* and *but*. *And* can be used to link actions or events sequentially, or to show cause and effect. *But* signals that a contrast is being made. The way *but* is used is fairly self-explanatory and tends not to cause much confusion:

He tried <u>but</u> failed.

In this example, the contrast is obvious in the language itself (*try* vs. *fail*); on other occasions, the contrast is less obvious:

It's sad <u>but</u> true.

Why should sadness be contrasted with truth? Why don't we say, "It's sad *and* true?" What in our experience would lead us to conclude that truth is usually happy? 'Sad but true' is an idiomatic expression that, for the most part, we use without much thought; everyone just knows what's being conveyed. Other examples reveal patterns of thought that might otherwise remain concealed:

The house was enormous <u>but</u> very messy.

Here the use of *but* reveals the assumption that enormous houses are likely to be clean and tidy. Noticing clauses joined by *but* is one way of revealing a speaker's or writer's underlying unstated assumptions.

And is by far the most commonly used connective and can be used to accomplish a range of tasks. The following transcript of an 8-year-old boy's spontaneous speech shows *and* being used extensively to hold a narrative together:

... there was this witch doctor and Scooby Doo was – he was standing by the witch doctor and the witch doctor went in and he went – he went chasing him. Scooby Doo went in the cupboard with Shaggy and got some clothes on and they were acting on and then the witch doctor pressed the button and they turned on again then and then Scooby was acting and then they just take him and he keeped on switching it until they all came round and the all clothes fell off him.[14]

And is used to signal a chronologically ordered sequence: *Scooby Doo went in the cupboard with Shaggy and got some clothes on*, but it's also used to suggest a cause and effect relationship: *the witch doctor pressed the button and they turned on again*. In these ordered relationships it is not possible to alter the order of the clauses, but when *and* links two simultaneous actions there is no intrinsic ordering:

The sun shone and a soft breeze blew.

It is also possible for two actions to be conjoined in a simple additive way without any suggestion of temporal or causal relationship:

I ordered a steak and Rosie had a glass of prosecco.

Since *and* expresses so many connective meanings and as it is so frequent in speech it's not surprising that young children often overuse it in their writing, as in this account of a wedding written by a 7-year-old girl:

I wore a long white dress <u>and</u> I wore a pretty veil <u>and</u> I picked some flowers from the garden <u>and</u> I put them on my dress ...[15]

One important function of *and* in a piece of writing like this is to signal to the reader that the sentences are meant to be read together as an integrated whole. Older and more skilful writers do not merely signal that succeeding ideas are linked; they use a number of different connectives, not only to introduce variety but also to make relationships as precise as possible. *And* will sometimes be exactly right, but with time for planning and reflection, writers can make better choices. Chronological sequences can be marked by *next, after that, subsequently*, etc; cause and effect relationships can be expressed by *so, therefore, accordingly, consequently*, etc; simultaneous actions can be joined by *while* or *as*; additive relationships can be indicated by *also, in addition, furthermore* or *moreover*.

Clearly, some of these connectives would seem stilted and inappropriately formal in conversation or informal writing, such as a text message, but they occur frequently in formal expository writing. The reason for their use is that they make the task of interpretation easier for the reader. It's important that the relationship between ideas is signalled as clearly as possible, particularly when the subject matter is demanding or unfamiliar (as in much academic writing).

Before we move on, we should briefly address the 'rule' that a sentence must never begin with *and* or *but*. While it makes sense to suggest that regularly starting sentences like this would soon become tedious, there's absolutely no good reason for banning them outright. Indeed, there may sometimes be good reason for starting sentences like this. As Kingsley Amis said,

> And the idea that *and* must not begin a sentence, or even a paragraph, is an empty superstition. The same goes for *but*. Indeed either word can give unimprovably early warning of the sort of thing that is to follow.[16]

Teaching active and passive sentences

Lots of style guides and prescriptive grammarians have a profound dislike of passive sentences. For instance, George Orwell said, "Never use the passive where you can use the active."[17] But, as Stephen Pinker points out, although this may often be good advice, "No English construction could have survived in the language for a millennium and a half unless it had continued to serve some purpose."[18] So, what *is* that purpose?

In an active sentence the subject of the sentence generally performs the action of the verb:

The firing squad shot the deserter.

Here, the subject – the firing squad – is doing the shooting and the deserter, the object of the sentence, is being shot (and probably dying as a result). If we were to rephrase the sentence in the passive voice, the person or thing affected by the action of the verb becomes the subject of the sentence:

The deserter was shot by the firing squad.

Now, the former active subject (the firing squad) occurs after the verb. It's not only the order of words that's changed, but also the form of the verb itself: the active verb *shot* becomes *was shot* in the passive. What do you think? Which of these sentences do you prefer? For my money, Orwell was wrong on this one. Is there something a little unwieldy about the first sentence which is smoothed out and feels more pleasing in the second? Whichever you prefer is fine: but although both sentences communicate exactly the same information, *the way they tell the story* is different.

Passive sentences allow us to say that something's happened without needing to say who did it. In fact, we can tweak our passive sentence like this:

The deserter was shot.

There's no reason anyone needs to know who did the shooting. This also allows us to avoid taking responsibility. If we say, "Mistakes were made," there's no need to specify who made them.

Omitting the subject in the active sentence is a neat trick, and one that is not normally allowed in English. For example, we have to say, *It is raining*, rather than *Is raining*. What's the 'it' doing in this sentence? It's obvious that it must refer to the weather, after all, what else could conceivably rain? But, what would be the advantage of leaving out the subject? Well, in our previous example it prevents us from drawing attention to whoever it was that did the shooting. We might also want to avoid mentioning the subject because we don't know who or what it is: *The window has been smashed.* The active version of this would be a bit clunky: *Someone (or something) has smashed the window.*

We might also have a reason for wanting to conceal the subject: *It's come to my attention that you have been seen stealing.* If we had to reveal our informant's identity this could lead to unwanted consequences.

The convention in scientific writing is to use the passive voice wherever possible because it lets us say, *The mixture was poured into the beaker*, rather than having to specify the irrelevant detail of who accomplished the feat of pouring. The passive also lets us say, *I've just had my car fixed*, and, *Forty people were killed in an explosion.* We can also avoid unnecessary or annoying repetition. If several actions have been performed by the same people then, if the sentences describing the events are active, the same subject has to be repeated:

> Members of the community association worked very hard preparing for the annual village show. They redecorated the village hall. They sanded and polished the floor. They replaced the lights and they mended all the broken furniture.[19]

A passive version rids of the need for all the *theys*, introduces greater variety and generally just reads as a more sophisticated piece of writing:

> Members of the community association worked very hard preparing for the annual village show. The village hall was redecorated. The floor was sanded and polished. The lights were replaced and all the broken furniture was mended.

Passive sentences have a different word order to active sentences. If we want to refer to two things, one animate, one inanimate, there is a stylistic preference for putting animates before inanimates. For example, *The boy was run over by a lorry*, is more probable than an active version: *A lorry ran over a boy*. This has the effect of keeping the reader's attention on the human victim rather than on the faceless juggernaut.

The ability to change word order allows us to smoothly link sentences together. Within a paragraph, we tend to refer back to an idea that has already been mentioned:

The result was a sample of secondary schools numbering just over a half of those selected for inclusion. Moreover, it was further affected by a high degree of pupil absenteeism, due largely to the fact that the testing took place in the last fortnight of the Lent term.[20]

"The result" is mentioned in the first sentence. The use of the passive "*it was further affected*" allows the result to reappear at the beginning of the second sentence without having to name it again.

As Pinker reminds us, the problem with passives is that they are often not selected with any of these purposes in mind and are instead "symptoms of absent-mindedness in a writer who has forgotten that he should be staging an event for the reader."[21]

Grammar through content and content through grammar

If we accept that elements from the prescriptive and descriptive branches of grammar are important in unlocking the study of English we may now be a little closer to answering Crystal's four questions (see page 275), but the greater part – which features of grammar children should learn and in what order – is still to be addressed.

There is not, as yet, a fully sequenced, empirically validated hierarchical model of teaching grammar but, in the meantime, I can think of no better guide than that offered by Judith Hochman and Natalie Wexler's book, *The Writing Revolution*. The principle that's most crucial to making this approach work is that the content of the curriculum must drive the grammatical instruction. To put it another way, grammar becomes a tool for making meaning out of curriculum content. Rather than giving students arid, decontextualised grammar drills,

Grammar

they are instead asked to use their grammatical knowledge to make meaning.

One of the simplest ideas is to ask students questions about the content they have been studying and get them to respond by adding to a statement ending with the conjunctions 'because,' 'but' or 'so.'[22] For instance, if students have been studying *Macbeth* they could practise expanding the statement, *Macbeth decided to murder King Duncan*:

- Macbeth decided to murder King Duncan <u>because</u> he believed that was the only way the prediction that he would be 'king hereafter' would come true.
- Macbeth decided to murder King Duncan <u>but</u> then changed his mind as his only reason was 'vaulting ambition.'
- Macbeth decided to murder King Duncan <u>so</u> he asked his wife, Lady Macbeth, for help to come up with a plan.

This is a hugely flexible exercise that forces students to sort and select from what they know rather than simply dumping everything they can remember onto the page in an undifferentiated mess. In order to complete this exercise they have to retrieve three items of knowledge: 1) why Macbeth wanted to murder Duncan, 2) why he changed his mind and 3) what actions he took as a result of his decision. The act of writing out answers using these simple conjunctions provides much needed practice at composing analytical sentences.

In order to help students see that the patterns of written language are different to those of speech, they have to become familiar with sentence forms that are rare in spoken language. One useful exercise is to start sentences with different subordinating conjunctions to answer the questions about the content they're studying. The models in Figure 9.1 show how these questions could be scaffolded. Figure 9.2 is a worked example.

288

Macbeth's actions

Although _____, _____

Lady Macbeth's actions

Because _____, _____

Effects on
Lady Macbeth

Effects on
Macbeth

Figure 9.1   Scaffolded sentence level analysis prompts

Lady Macbeth's actions

Because *Lady Macbeth attacks her
husband for being a coward*, he agrees
to go ahead with her plan to murder the
king.

Effects on Macbeth

Figure 9.2   A worked example of sentence level analysis

These exercises should become increasingly demanding as
support is gradually removed:

> How does Shakespeare describe the effects of the wea-
> ther in Act 2 scene 3 of *Macbeth*?
>
> The night has been unruly: where we lay,
> Our chimneys were blown down; and, as they say,
> Lamentings heard i' the air; strange screams of death,
> And prophesying with accents terrible
> Of dire combustion and confused events
> New hatch'd to the woeful time: the obscure bird
> Clamour'd the livelong night: some say, the earth
> Was feverous and did shake.
>
> ***Considering that*** ...

Grammar

Students should also practise using *appositives* –
additional nouns or noun
phrases – to add detail
and variety to an other-
wise simple sentence, such
as in this sentence from *A
Christmas Carol*:

> Once upon a time—<u>of
> all the good days in</u>

APPOSITIVE

Latin: *apponere* 'set near,
set before; apply, give in
addition; appoint, designate.'

Noun or noun phrase that
renames another noun, e.g.
*Cordelia, Lear's faithful
daughter.*

<u>the year</u>, <u>on Christmas Eve</u>—old Scrooge sat busy in his
counting-house.

When teaching content, it might be useful to deliberately and
explicitly introduce a range of useful appositives, like these:

- Macbeth: worthy gentleman, valiant kinsman, dead
  butcher, King of Scotland, bloodthirsty murderer, etc.
- Scrooge: miserable miser, Marley's sole mourner, a tight-
  fisted hand, covetous old sinner, Fred's uncle, etc.

Have a go at adding appositives to these examples:

- Teaching English, <u>the best of all subjects</u>, can be rewarding.
- Dr Jekyll, _____, _____.
- Marking students' work, _____, _____.
- Romantic poetry, _____, _____.

By giving students these sorts of scaffolds, they will also see
the need for bracketing punctuation to show the separation
of the appositive clause from the rest of the sentence.

Another useful sentence-level activity is to combine short,
simple sentences into longer, more complex ones. This not
only helps students to see the various options available to

them when composing sentences, it improves their writing fluency when writing longer passages. How could you combine these sentences?

- Miss Phillips taught 9B four times a week.
- Miss Phillips did not like 9B.
- Miss Phillips spent every break searching for a new job.

By increasing, or decreasing, the number of sentences to be combined the task is made more or less challenging.

Why does Macbeth decide not to kill King Duncan?

- Duncan is Macbeth's kinsman as well as his king.
- As his host, Macbeth has an obligation to protect Duncan.
- Duncan has been a good and wise king.
- Macbeth has no reason to kill Duncan other than his "vaulting ambition."

This kind of grammatical practice doesn't just have to be written. In fact, there's good reason to think that students would benefit from doing much of this work orally, on the basis that speech appears to be particularly 'cognitively sticky' and that we're better at remembering what we say than what we write.

Whenever we point out patterns of grammar, students should be taught in a way that allows them to ask what the structures their attention is being drawn to are and what they accomplish. Like our other conceptual lenses, grammar is another facet of English which students should become attuned to noticing. Whenever they notice grammatical choices in the texts they study they should be able to ask three crucial questions:

Grammar

- *What options were available?*
- *Why was this one chosen?*
- *What impact does it have on the reader?*

Addressing these questions allows students to peer into the minds of other writers, explore their decisions and intentions, and reveal much about the words they choose and the order they choose to arrange them. It should also allow students to notice their own grammatical choices. If they are aware of a 'rule' they can deliberately choose to break or bend it to achieve a particular effect. Creating good grammatical habits means students will have greater mental resources for concentrating on the more interesting aspects of English.

KEY POINTS

- Grammar appears to be an emergent phenomenon which develops organically. It is not an arbitrary set of rules.
- Grammar is made up of morphology (the way words are constructed) and syntax (sentence structure and word order).
- Teaching grammar is made complicated because we have to choose which bits of it to teach and which to avoid.
- Students need a balance of prescriptive and descriptive grammar – both an understanding of what can and can't be done, and an appreciation of how and why ordinary speakers do what they do.
- Students need to be introduced to semantics (meaning) and pragmatics (the reasons for and effects of language choices).

- Grammar is best taught through content: by applying principles of grammar to the texts they are studying, students will increase their knowledge of each and learn to think more analytically.
- By paying attention to grammatical choices, students can consider the effects of these choices.

Further reading

- David Crystal has written dozens of excellent books on grammar but one of his most recent and most useful is *Making Sense*.
- Stephen Pinker's books *The Language Instinct* and *The Sense of Style* are both very useful.
- Judith Hochman and Natalie Wexler's book *The Writing Revolution* is required reading for anyone involved in teaching grammar or writing.

10 Context

When I began teaching, context was pretty much ignored and teachers were encouraged to restrict themselves to the text as the primary – perhaps, the only – source of meaning. I first became aware of the problems caused by a lack of contextual knowledge while teaching *Romeo and Juliet* to a Year 9 class in Weston-super-Mare. We'd arrived at the point of the play where Romeo learns he is to be banished for killing Tybalt and dissolves into desperate hysteria:

> There is no world without Verona walls,
> But purgatory, torture, hell itself.
> Hence-banished is banish'd from the world,
> And world's exile is death: then banished,
> Is death mis-term'd: calling death banishment,
> Thou cutt'st my head off with a golden axe,
> And smilest upon the stroke that murders me.

Hoping they'd be able to demonstrate some empathy with his plight, I asked the class what they made of Romeo's reaction. After some thought, one boy suggested that it was silly to make such a fuss, and that he, were he to be banished from

Weston, would just move in with his nan in Bridgwater. The rest of class nodded thoughtfully.

Although they knew people didn't have phones or tellies 'in Shakespeare's day,' the idea that people lived and thought in utterly alien ways was completely outside their experience. They needed to know something about the political make-up of Renaissance Italy, the dependence Romeo would have had on his family and the fact that every person he had ever known would have lived within the walls of the city-state of Verona. To have an informed opinion they would also need to consider the practicalities of travelling what to us may seem a short distance, but to Elizabethans would have been a lengthy expedition fraught with difficulty and danger, and that communication by post would have been uncertain, as we see in the play. The idea of moving in with a convenient relative is a complete non-starter.

Knowledge in action

According to the American educator, Arthur Applebee,

> Traditions are the knowledge-in-action out of which we construct our realities as we know and perceive them, and that to honour such traditions we must reconstrue our curriculum to focus on knowledge-in-action rather than knowledge-out-of-context.[1]

Applebee argues that students should be taught 'knowledge-in-action' to be able to participate in a living tradition. When we strip literature from its context, we strip it from that which gives it meaning, energy and life. Unless we study literature in context we risk cutting students off from entering into ongoing debates. English has a vibrant, living tradition which stretches back beyond *Beowulf* and forward to an as yet unimagined future. Understanding the contexts of this tradition permits students to feel part of an enduring, valued and relevant tradition that is, "dynamic and changing, acquired through participation, and oriented towards present and future rather than past."[2]

To make meaning, students need both textual and *extra*textual knowledge. Much of this extratextual knowledge (knowledge from outside of the text or texts being studied) is *con*textual. Context literally means 'with text.' So, contextual knowledge is that which accompanies our study of literature. Contextual knowledge is not just historical or literary, it includes knowledge of words and of the wider world. It is the circumstance in which a work has been produced and how these circumstances have shifted over time. But it's more than even this; everything a reader brings to a text is *con*textual: it's what makes our ability to interpret what we read unique.

You can't make connections to what you don't know. Of course, as teachers we are well aware that students can't possibly share in *all* we know, so we share what we think will be most useful. As we saw in chapter 2, this can result in teaching history lessons or fashioning knowledge organisers overstuffed with meaningless facts to memorise. Such approaches might result in students acquiring the knowledge needed to make judicious analogies, but if we're not careful what they learn is likely to remain inert and barely understood.

Forging connections between what we read, what we already know and what we come to learn about the texts we read is the essence of analogising. Providing the knowledge students need at *exactly the point where it will be most useful* can help direct them to particular ways of seeing and knowing. 'Just knowing' stuff is the smallest part of what's needed; what counts is when what we know intersects with what we read and provides us with new meaning and insights.

296

For instance, when I first watched Quentin Tarantino's film, *Reservoir Dogs*, with all its long monologues, blood-soaked pathos, and especially the set-piece stand-off in the final scene where everyone shoots everyone else, my immediate thought was, oh, it's a Senecan revenge tragedy! How was I able to see past all the silly names and ear slicing to see this underlying structure? Well, I took Classical Studies at A level and had read a couple of the Roman dramatist, Seneca's plays. Then, as part of my degree I'd been shown Seneca's influence on *Hamlet*, as well as writing an essay comparing Thomas Kyd's *The Spanish Tragedy* and *Titus Andronicus*. You *could* say I *understood* some essential dramatic principle but in fact, I simply *knew more* than many other people who saw the film and was therefore able to make different intertextual analogies. As this example shows, our knowledge of context can seem to provide us with an instinctively sophisticated interpretation, but students – not knowing what we know – need contextual information to be made explicit.

"There are no wrong answers"

Picture me in full pedagogical flow, picking apart some lines of poetry for the delight and edification of my students as they huddle ever closer in rapt attention. Imagine the lines are these, the final stanza of Thomas Hardy's 'Neutral Tones':

Since then, keen lessons that love deceives,
And wrings with wrong, have shaped to me
Your face, and the God-curst sun, and a tree,
And a pond edged with greyish leaves.

Imagine me pausing, meaningfully, scanning my eyes over the eager faces of the hushed assembly and asking, quietly, "Why do you think Hardy used the phrase 'wrings with wrong'? Why 'wrings'? Why not 'rings,' or 'runs'?"

297

Imagine the faces of my students frowning in concentration and then one tentative hand being raised and a querulous voice asking, "Sir, maybe he couldn't think of anything else? Maybe that was the best he could do?"

The notion that there are no wrong answers in English is unhelpful. Of course, students' ideas should be valued, but this does not mean that ill-informed opinions should be given equal status with considered judgements. It's important to recognise the difference between an opinion and a judgement. As Oakeshott put it, "'Judgement' can be taught only in conjunction with the transmission of information."[3] If a student says 'poetry is boring' they, most probably, are expressing an opinion based on narrow experience. If a critic argues *The Tempest* is racist they are making a judgement (albeit not one which is particularly well-informed). The convention is that a judgement will be both supported by textual evidence and embedded in a coherent argument that considers a range of contextual and literary knowledge. For obvious reasons, students are limited in their ability to do this and tend to rush to wildly asserted misconceptions.

Take, for example, J.B. Priestley's hardy perennial, *An Inspector Calls*. Every time I've finished reading the play with a class, without fail, a number of students will be firmly persuaded that poor, unloved Eva Smith was murdered by the Inspector. I'm not going to bore you with why this interpretation is so wrong-headed, just take it from me that it goes against everything that Priestley was trying to achieve. Even when I've pointed out – precisely and at length – why this view is incorrect, some students remain impossible to convince.

There's a tradition that if students experience a text without having it polluted by their teacher's interpretations they will come to understand it in a more individual, purer way. Even if we, as experts, might prefer reading with no explicitly stated preconceptions it doesn't mean this is the best way for students to study a text. Students will find it easier to understand a text if they are given a conceptual framework in which to place it. If they're not given one, they'll grope around for whatever comes most easily to mind. In the case of *An Inspector Calls*, the default framework is the murder mystery. Most students will have some experience of the whodunnit and that, along with the supernatural elements of the play, will convince them that the Inspector being a murderer is a plausible possibility.

Naturally, we don't want to crush our students' curiosity and nascent analysis, but neither do we want them to get too firm a hold on the wrong end of the stick. This being the case, it might be better to begin the study of *An Inspector Calls* by saying something like, 'Some people may end up believing the Inspector murders Eva Smith but this is wrong. If at any point you find yourself tempted by this view you need to recognise that it's a misconception and look for alternative interpretations.' Rather than taking away students' freedom to analyse and interpret, this is liberating. It allows them to avoid building their ideas on shaky foundations and looking foolish. There really *are* wrong answers in English, and there are most definitely poorly thought out answers.

None of this is to suggest that students' personal responses to texts are unimportant, instead it is to argue that a personal response is enriched and enlarged by knowing something of the context in which a text is produced and received, and that the more educated an opinion is, the greater its value and validity. Helping children develop a sense of connoisseurship liberates rather than constrains their ability to understand the texts they will encounter. In knowing what those before us have said, and appreciating how to apply analysis, students are liberated from the confines of their limited experiences.

So, having said context is, basically, everything that isn't in the text, let us now restrict ourselves to two particular but interrelated contextual lenses: literary theory and the literary canon.

The role of theory

Literary theory provides a bridge to connect text and context. Some of the post-structuralist approaches to literary criticism have done much to devalue ideas of language and literature, but that doesn't have to be the case. Used thoughtfully, taking a theoretical stance can result in exciting new interpretations. Peter Barry expresses the tension between text and theory well:

> Sometimes the sophistication of the theory exposes the limitations of the text, and sometimes the sophistication of the text exposes the limitations of the theory.[4]

Arguably, without theory there would be no call for context at all. Before post-structuralism and cultural materialism, the focus in English was very much on 'close reading.' This approach had its roots in T.S. Eliot's style of literary criticism and was developed as a methodology by I.A. Richards who consciously turned his back on the kind of historical and autobiographical approaches of the past and instead presented students with anonymous, unannotated poems, asking them to provide a critical reading of, to use Leavis' phrase, "the words on the page."[5] This is pretty much the same as the 'unseen' poetry analysis that continues to feature in literature exams today. But even without overtly applying contextual knowledge to our reading, we still – wittingly or otherwise – apply theory. 'Practical criticism' is as theoretical as any other approach to reading literature.

Theorising is an inherent danger in a field where there are no 'correct' interpretations. Theory has value when it avoids dogmatism and where it doesn't attempt to bulldoze texts into submission. Its role should be to frame questions and help us take part in a conversation. Critical theories are, essentially, tools. They can be employed to do certain jobs effectively but they're unlikely to serve you well if used for everything. The old adage that if you only have a hammer every problem is treated as a nail comes to mind. While theory proposes, the reader disposes.

Older students will benefit from knowing something about critical reception and the various different theoretical approaches which seek to extract meaning from texts, particularly a grounding in the basics of Marxist, feminist, psychoanalytic and post-colonial approaches. Playing with theory can make for some entertaining and provocative readings of classic texts which tend to reveal more about the theories than they do about the texts they seek to analyse. As long as students understand the axes each of these approaches has to grind (and don't take any of this too seriously) all should be well.

Essentially, the various perspectives bundled together as 'theory' can be boiled down to five core propositions:

1. The personal is political – reality is constructed from social and political forces.
2. Truth is relative – all investigations are ideologically biased.
3. Language doesn't record reality, it constructs it.
4. Meaning is contingent – the author is 'dead' and texts mean what readers say they mean.
5. Human nature does not exist – we are all products of our race, gender and class.

Each proposition may contain a kernel of truth but taken together, and at face value, they can amount to a counsel of despair. But, despite their superficial truthiness, each is contradicted by our everyday experience.

Context

In response to Bishop Berkeley's theory that all material objects exist only in the mind, Dr Johnson kicked a large stone and said, "I refute it *thus!*"[6] Oakeshott provides a compromise between Johnson's crude materialism and the subjective vagaries of ideologically constructed reality. He suggests our consciousness is the result of what we have experienced and our reactions to these experiences, or occurrences. The world we inhabit is "wholly human" because everything in it is *known* to us in terms of what it *means*, and these meanings have to be learned. You and I might both be participants in the same occurrence, but our different histories will result in different experiences and therefore, different meanings.[7]

We only have Boswell's record of Dr Johnson kicking the rock; had Johnson himself recorded the incident it might have had a very different significance. But, rather than quibble about definitions, let's accept these theoretical positions as *containing* truth, if not entirely true.

The canon

For the early Church, 'canon law' referred to the rules the Church proclaimed that Christians (i.e. everyone) must live by. Over time, the word came to mean a standard of judgement

> ### CANON
>
> Greek: *kanon,* 'straight rod or bar; rule; standard of excellence.'
>
> A collection of books considered worthy of study.

and was used to distinguish officially sanctioned scripture from the 'apocrypha' (works of dubious authenticity). Just as saints are canonised, so are the books of the Bible. It was only in the 18th century that canon came to mean a catalogue of approved authors.

Today, the literary canon refers to those works of literature that have come to be considered the 'best.' But by whom?

Who chose them and why? Arguably, canonical texts select themselves: those works and writers that continue to be read and studied must, so the argument goes, be those most worthy of being read and studied. The novelist A.S. Byatt saw every culture's canon as "an evolving consensus of individual canons. Canonical writers changed the medium, the language they were working in. People who merely describe what is happening now don't last."[8]

But, as Oakeshott observed, "nothing survives in this world which is not cared for by human beings."[9] He saw humanity's collective achievements as an intellectual inheritance that "contains everything to which value may be attributed; it is the ground and context of every judgement of better and worse."[10] A shared canon requires careful tending. It is a fragile thing. Frank Kermode warned that canons "are deconstructible" and "if people think there should not be such things, they may very well find the means to destroy them."[11]

So, although we might reach a collective consensus that some writers are worthier of study than others, we each have to individually accept or reject this choice. We might assert that Shakespeare is 'the best,' but when confronted by a dog-eared copy of *Macbeth* or *Romeo and Juliet,* students are often underwhelmed. As far as they're concerned Shakespeare is alien, old-fashioned, boring and unintelligible. The funny bits aren't funny and everyone ponces around talking endlessly to themselves in rhyme. Why do we bother? Should we not allow students to study something more contemporary, more accessible, more relevant?

C.S. Lewis thought not:

> Every age has its own outlook. It is specially good at seeing certain truths and specially liable to make certain mistakes. We all, therefore, need the books that will correct the characteristic mistakes of our own period. And that means the old books.[12]

Context

It's not so much that Shakespeare, Samuel Johnson or Jane Austen are better than, say, Russell T. Davies, Ta-Nehisi Coates or Margaret Atwood, it's that they offer access to something outside the thin slice of the present.

Students deserve emancipation from "the tyranny of relevance."[13] The study of 'old books' provides an opportunity to travel in time and space, for students to step outside the confines of the present and view themselves from other, unfamiliar perspectives. Education professor Alison Light wrote, "If education keeps alive the human freedom to think differently, then in this sense the seventeenth or the twelfth or the fifth century BC are as 'relevant' as the twentieth."[14]

Critiquing the canon

But, of course, not everyone sees things in quite the same way. Our history colours our experiences, which alters the meaning we make. Nobel Laureate, Toni Morrison wrote that,

> Canon building is empire building. Canon defense is national defense. Canon debate, whatever the terrain, nature, and range (of criticism, of history, of the history of knowledge, of the definition of language, the universality of aesthetic principles, the sociology of art, the humanistic imagination), is the clash of cultures. And all of the interests are vested.[15]

Let's agree that the canon is always selected, sometimes implicitly, sometimes explicitly; all interests are vested and all choices are partial. Literature was certainly part of the British Empire's 'civilising mission' to make its colonial subjects more amenable to rule, and the literary canon is now regularly condemned as 'stale, male and pale.' Instead of teaching the thoughts and works of an elite, should we instead prioritise the voices of the more marginalised? Should we de-emphasise what is traditional in favour of what is politically progressive?

In making this decision, it's vital to insist that the canon is not the preserve of any one class, ethnic group or gender. It is a shared cultural heritage that has something to say to us all. As Alan Bennett says,

> The best moments in reading are when you come across something – a thought, a feeling, a way of looking at things – which you had thought special and particular to you. Now here it is, set down by someone else, a person you have never met, someone even who is long dead. And it is as if a hand has come out and taken yours.[16]

Reading the canon can – *should* – transcend barriers of gender, race, class and hundreds of years. Maya Angelou describes the feeling of a hand extending from the past to take her own in reading the opening lines of Shakespeare's 'Sonnet 29':

> When, in disgrace with fortune and men's eyes,
> I all alone beweep my outcast state
> And trouble a deaf heaven with my bootless cries
> And look upon myself and curse my fate.

She said, "That was me – absolutely me – wishing to be any-thing rather than be black and poor and a girl in the dirt roads of Arkansas."[17]

Claiming that students can only connect with writers if they share an 'identity' is presumptuous. Angelou's connection to Shakespeare was so deep she assumed he was, "a Black American Girl in the South." When her teachers told her the truth her reaction was disbelief: "no white man could know what I feel."[18] But, what if we place our shared humanity before our perceived differences? What if reading the canon builds bridges rather than erecting walls?

Arguing against students' right to be taught the canon might be an act of social injustice. We don't have to like the canon but in choosing not to teach it – or, rather, in refusing to critically engage with it – we disempower students. The Nigerian novelist and literary critic, Chinua Achebe, provides a case in point. As a close reader of the canon he used his extensive knowledge to criticise the hidebound attitudes and casual racism he encountered there. For instance, through a detailed analysis of *Heart of Darkness*, Achebe is able to demonstrate that, "Conrad was a thoroughgoing racist."[19]

Decolonising the curriculum

Without this kind of critical engagement, such incisive interrogation is impossible. Calls for the curriculum to be 'decolonised' are not without merit but are too often unthinking, knee-jerk reactions rather than genuine critical engagement. Simply stripping out white, European, male writers in favour of women and people of colour is likely to undermine the very groups we hope to privilege. Instead, we should take the view that teaching the canon allows us an opportunity to challenge injustice. If 'decolonising the curriculum' is a thoughtful process where the assumptions of the past are challenged, where current values are held up for inspection, and where writers are considered in terms of what they wrote about as well as how they wrote then it will be useful.

Reading Sir Arthur Conan Doyle's Sherlock Holmes stories provides an interesting case study. 'The Five Orange Pips' is a searing indictment of the Klu Klux Klan and their atrocities. 'The Yellow Face' is an exploration of 'mixed marriages' in which an American woman attempts to conceal her marriage to a prominent black lawyer in Georgia from her new English husband, only for him to accept her 'mixed race' child as his own. However, stories like 'The Man with the Twisted Lip' and 'The Adventure of the Three Gables' make use of clumsy racial stereotypes. Was Conon Doyle a racist? By today's standards, probably. Similarly, it's hard to read Dickens or Orwell without becoming aware of uncomfortably misogynistic attitudes. Should we avoid reading the work of such writers? No. Instead we should try to read as carefully and critically as Achebe read Conrad.

If decolonising the curriculum simply means ditching anything from the past that doesn't fit our ideological preferences in favour of what is currently deemed acceptable, we cut students off from being able to impose their own readings on what would otherwise be allowed to pass unchallenged. We urgently need to challenge racism, misogyny, homophobia and all the other varieties of prejudice that continue to plague the world, but we also need to decide whether the best way to challenge these ills is by making a writer's identity more important than her work.

Ideas about what we consider canonical are not static. In 1861, Palgrave's *Golden Treasury of English Verse* purported to contain "none but the best" poetry written in English, but curiously neglected the working-class poet William Blake and included nothing at all by any female poet. *Beowulf* was only rediscovered in 1786 and even after it began to be taught in universities the focus was on the development of the English language rather than its literary value. It only really began to be thought of as belonging to the canon after the work of J.R.R. Tolkien in the 1930s. Today we might include previously marginalised works as Aphra Behn's proto-novel *Oroonoko* and Olaudah Equiano's autobiography. The canon expands to include that which we feel it ought to include.

Whatever texts we choose to teach, we are teaching a canon. If this canon is confined to our personal preferences

Context

or political expediency will it limit or extend? Enrich or impoverish? Gaze outwards or peer within? Cultural analysis is as important as cultural heritage. The question should not be *whether* to teach the canon, but *how* to teach it. If, after studying a canonical text, students can argue coherently why it is flawed and where it fails this should be seen as a success.

Intertextuality

Everything we've read or seen in the past informs what we read in the here and now. Literature is constantly in conversation with itself. This can be explicit, such as when writers take titles from lines in other texts such as Hemingway taking the title of *For Whom the Bell Tolls* from John Donne's 'Meditation XVII' (famous for the phrase "No man is an island") which says, "never send to know for whom the bells tolls; it tolls for thee." Likewise, Chinua Achebe took the title of *Things Fall Apart* from a line in W.B. Yeats' poem 'The Second Coming.' Or it can be implicit; if you've read *Robinson Crusoe* or *Treasure Island* it's impossible for that knowledge not to shade your reading of *The Lord of the Flies* even though Golding makes no explicit reference to either.

The word 'intertextuality,' derived from the Latin *intertexto*, 'to intermingle while weaving,' was coined by the French semiotician Julia Kristeva in the 1960s. Kristeva argued that "any text is constructed of a mosaic of quotations; any text is the absorption and transformation of another."[20] All works of literature have an intertextual relationship – are in conversation – with works that came before. Roland Barthes suggested that "Bits of code, formulae, rhythmic models, fragments of social languages, etc., pass into the text and are redistributed within it" and the result is "unconscious or automatic quotations, given without quotation marks."[21] Certain latent cultural references infuse literature: for instance, star-crossed lovers; a liar's nose growing; a boy never growing up, and have become common currency that no longer require explicit reference or quotation marks.

Teaching intertextuality allows students to appreciate what Harold Bloom called 'the anxiety of influence.' New generations of writers feel the need to self-consciously reject the past in order to make space for new ideas about how to conceive the world, but, "every poet is a being caught up in a dialectical relationship ... with another poet or poets."[22]

Of course, not all intertextual relationships are 'unconscious or automatic.' The literature of the past is full of deliberate allusions to classical and Biblical stories and more recent literature makes constant reference to itself and earlier works. To take some well-known examples, reading Jean Rhys' *Wide Sargasso Sea* without having read *Jane Eyre*, watching Tom Stoppard's play, *Rosencrantz and Guildenstern Are Dead* never having seen *Hamlet*, or making sense of Joyce's *Ulysses* with no knowledge of the *Odyssey* would make for a much shallower set of experiences.

While we're on the subject of Joyce, remember the brief extract of *Finnegans Wake* we looked at on page 51? To make sense of it you'd have to get several Biblical references as well as picking up allusions to the writings of Mark Twain, Jonathan Swift as well as Thomas the Rhymer's 13th-century romance, *Sir Tristrem*.[23] Of course, Joyce is an unusually demanding writer, but reading *Finnegans Wake* is not so different from reading *The Canterbury Tales* or even *Paradise Lost*. Intertextual knowledge is an inescapable and essential aspect of making meaning. Although the texts students are likely to study in school are less demanding, they will nevertheless be in conversation with all that came before them.

Context

> ## KEY POINTS
>
> - The quality of students' interpretations depends on their contextual knowledge; sufficient contextual knowledge is also a prerequisite for empathy.
> - The knowledge students bring to a text (intertextual and extratextual) places limits on the meaning they can make.
> - There is rarely only one interpretation of a literary text, but there are many bad interpretations. Students should be guided away from making ignorant misconceptions.
> - Applying different theoretical filters can open texts up to new and interesting interpretations but they can also risk poisoning a text with irrelevant ideological biases.
> - Students have a right to experience canonical works but we also have a responsibility to help them question and critique the canon.
> - Intertextuality – the study of how writers draw from and effect each other – can be a useful focus when studying texts.

When selecting the canon to make up our curriculum we should be mindful of connections and intersections between texts and with the wider world. It is to this discussion that we now turn.

Further reading

- It's still well worth reading Terry Eagleton's *Literary Theory: An Introduction* (as well as 2003's *After Theory*), and the latest edition of Peter Barry's *Beginning Theory* provides a very readable, up-to-date and thorough overview.

- Harold Bloom's *The Western Canon* is a long (and at times a sad) read but it is a superb defence of canon curation and a monumental piece of literary scholarship.
- The text of Toni Morrison's speech 'Unspeakable Things Unspoken: The Afro-American Presence in American Literature' is short, trenchant and an important counterblast, as is Chinua Achebe's assessment of *Heart of Darkness*.
- For a very readable overview of the literary canon, I'd recommend John Sutherland's book, *A Little History of Literature*.

11 Connecting the curriculum

By considering what knowledge has the most power we can widen the curriculum from the study of texts to broader conceptual understandings. Further, by considering what texts offer the greatest cultural richness we can ensure students are exposed to shared knowledge which they can learn to critique. Careful thought should be given to the texts chosen for study. Too often the curriculum is not carefully sequenced and therefore students do not experience a coherent 'story of English.'

The purpose of a curriculum should be to systematically introduce students to a tradition of knowledge which allows them the greatest choice in the goals they choose to pursue. But all too often, the English curriculum is disconnected. In E.M. Forster's novel *Howards End*, Margaret Schlegel famously urges us to "Only connect!"

> Only connect the prose and the passion, and both will be exalted, and human love will be seen at its height. Live in fragments no longer.

Students' experience of English is fragmentary. They proceed from one text to another with little sense of the rich tapestry of language and literature. If students are to have agency and feel at home in the world, we must ensure they are able to apply their knowledge to connect and shape all that unfolds around them. There are many different stories of English from which to choose: think carefully about the story you want to tell.

But the domain of English is vast and so we must make brutal choices as to what makes it into the curriculum. The US president, Benjamin Franklin once observed that children should be taught a mix of 'what is useful and what is ornamental':

> It would be well if they could be taught *everything* that is useful and *everything* that is ornamental: but art is long and their time is short. It is therefore proposed that they learn those things that are likely to be most useful and most ornamental.[1]

Every curriculum is a selection of what a particular community decided was important, but how are these choices made? Because curriculum time is strictly finite we should carefully consider the *opportunity cost* – the value of the best forgone alternative – of our choices to be sure that what we select achieves what we want.

This chapter will consider principles by which we can assess which aspects of English to select for students to learn.

Art is long and time is short

Every English teacher wants students to experience texts in their entirety but time is short. Might it be better to spend that time reading many short texts and extracts and seeing how each connects? E.D. Hirsch Jr. has argued that literacy depends on shared knowledge which can be acquired by reading brief guides rather than the original texts.[2] In response, we might argue that knowledge and information are not the same thing and that literary knowledge is very much a matter of the visceral experience of living the texts we love and that students should certainly be given the opportunity to read texts in depth.

But, it's perfectly possible to leapfrog from one set text to another omitting everything that connects them. Students might perform well at GCSE whilst knowing only two or three plays or novels, a handful of poems and *nothing* about literature. A Key Stage 4 curriculum may well end up being limited to a detailed study of *Macbeth, A Christmas Carol, An Inspector Calls,* 15 poems and a smattering of 'unseen' non-fiction writing. This is woefully inadequate for developing the depth students need to take part in a tradition of knowledge.

Of course, this is, in part, a flaw in the way English is assessed. Currently, English literature exams *only* assess students' knowledge of and response to set texts, and language exams are little better than a general knowledge quiz. Our focus should be on concepts and ideas rather than procedures and routines for passing an exam. By narrowing our focus to the test, we inadvertently reduce children's ability to do well on that test. Conversely, by broadening our scope to teach what is most cognitively valuable, we maximise children's chances of performing well – on tests and in life.

The knowledge needed to make meaning is like a set of Russian dolls. It's tempting to expend all our effort on the smallest doll (what will be tested in an exam) but that doll only makes sense when we consider the knowledge it's contained within. This larger doll might be the whole exam board syllabus but *that* doll is contained within another – the broader domains of language and literature. Reducing the curriculum to the syllabus of assessment ensures the most disadvantaged are left most adrift.

Although life can only be understood in retrospect, it must be lived forwards. The vogue for planning backwards is intuitively appealing: we can see where students need to get to and it seems possible to draw a line back to wherever they are now. But students experience the curriculum as they proceed through it. If they're always oriented towards a goal, a final destination, it's that much harder to appreciate the value of the here and now. Rather than planning backwards from an end, plan inwards and upwards from the broadest possible beginning. This way, the texts students will later study in depth have a much greater chance of being part of an interconnected whole. As each new author and text is encountered, students build up an increasingly robust, interconnected understanding of the conversation between texts. The more they know, the easier they will find it to integrate each new detail.

Curriculum as a conversation

The curriculum is often conceptualised as a journey – in fact, its Latin root is a 'running course' – and this encourages us to think about leading students from A to B, from one text to the next. But other metaphors might help us view the curriculum differently. Here, we will explore the idea of curriculum as a conversation, and later, as a story, a path through the woods.

In chapter 5, we briefly considered Grice's principles of cooperative conversation: quantity, quality, relation, and manner. Although these principles are used by speakers to ensure effective communication, Applebee suggests that if we view the curriculum as a conversation then the same maxims ought to apply.[3]

- *Quality* – Not only must curriculum materials be clear and accurate, the texts studied must be complex and challenging enough to provoke conversation. We will consider two aspects relating to this principle: powerful and shared knowledge.

- *Quantity* – Clearly a curriculum has to be sufficiently broad to introduce those aspects of the domain deemed essential but it should not be so extensive as to overwhelm the opportunity to challenge assumptions; in this way, the breadth of a curriculum is held in tension with the depth in which topics are explored.
- *Manner* – For students to make meaning they must be given opportunities to argue, debate, challenge, question and critique the knowledge they are taught.
- *Relatedness* – For a curriculum to be meaningful it must be carefully sequenced with each aspect chosen for its connection to every other topic as much as for its individual value. We will explore the ways topics and texts can be arranged in a coherent narrative.

Quality (1): Is it powerful?

One way to determine the quality of a curriculum is to consider the extent to which it contains 'powerful knowledge' and enables students to think new thoughts, ask new questions and explain the world beyond their own limited vantage. Over the preceding chapters we've seen that the epistemic concepts of metaphor, story, argument, pattern, grammar and context offer different ways to make meaning. The argument made here is that these all represent powerful knowledge.

But this can be too abstract to understand easily. To think about how to select cognitively valuable knowledge, we will consider some specific examples. Have a go at ranking these items of knowledge in order of their power to provide reliable explanations and new ways of perceiving the world:

- Thesis statements
- Poetic metre
- The structure and techniques of rhetoric

- Shakespeare
- Narrative structure
- Systematic metaphor
- The rules of grammar
- Using textual evidence

Thesis statements – Learning how to construct a thesis statement is a useful piece of disciplinary knowledge which can do much to elevate and focus students' essay writing. It's certainly useful, but is it powerful? Well, the knowledge that a line of argument should be stated at the outset can be applied beyond English and will be useful in the writing of academic essays in any subject where such things are expected. So, it provides a reasonable foundation from which students can understand the formation of arguments, but in and of itself, it's an empty concept that relies completely on us having something to say about the topic we're writing about. As such it has the same inherent weaknesses as frames like PEE. I'd argue it's less of a constraint and likely to remain useful into higher academic study, but it has little power to change the way anyone thinks about or perceives the world. As a tool, it might help us to refine our thoughts, but it won't provide us with new ones.

Poetic metre – Appreciating metre may be instinctive, understanding it is not. Children enjoy the bouncing rhythm of such classics as Julia Donaldson's *Room on the Broom* or Janet and Allan Ahlberg's *Each Peach Pear Plum* because they recognise how well it all fits together, but they're unlikely to have any idea how it actually works. Everyone can identify the familiar cadence of a limerick, but when children are asked to compose their own they very often struggle to make them scan. Metrical poetry is dreadfully out of fashion. The vogue for free verse has removed the constraints of metre but not necessarily for the better.

317

But it's hard to argue that the knowledge of different metres and the feet which compose them are particularly powerful: it might provide us with greater means for making aesthetic judgements, and the specialised language allows us to express these ideas with precision, but does it change the way we think? The best argument for metre's power is that it gives students a finer sense of why some lines work better than others and provides another means to make meaning.

Rhetoric – Classical rhetorical structure is the basis of transactional writing. Whenever we ask students to write persuasively we're implicitly asking them to use rhetoric. But is the knowledge of ethos, logos and pathos powerful? What about the six-point structure from exordium to peroration? And, beyond idle curiosity, does anybody need to know about the 'flowers of rhetoric' like anaphora, merism, epistrophe or syllepsis? Should we just focus on teaching the underlying ideas and avoiding all the arcane terminology? On the face of it, there's nothing wrong with this approach, but if you're not going to use agreed terminology, what will you use instead? Most English teachers are more than happy to use some Greek or Latin labels (metaphor, simile, alliteration, assonance) so why not others? The thing is, it's very difficult to talk about – let alone teach – what we don't have names for.

Knowing the names of things is essential if you want to talk to somebody else, otherwise they'll struggle to grasp what you're talking about. We use names and labels for reasons of expediency. While I can say, 'You can use a piece of punctuation that looks like a dot floating above a comma to connect two bits of a sentence if both bits make sense on their own and are also closely related,' but it's confusing and time consuming. How much more efficient it would be if I were confident my students shared the knowledge that made it possible to say, 'A semicolon connects two closely related independent clauses.'[4] Not only is this more straightforward, it's less ambiguous and less demanding on attention. Naming chunks facts together as more flexible concepts which can be more easily transferred to new areas of thought. This is as true for rhetoric as it is punctuation. The power of teaching rhetoric comes partly from its ability to provide a frame of reference, and partly from its ability to frame arguments.

Shakespeare – Shakespeare is the only compulsory author specifically named in the English National Curriculum, with students expected to study at least two of his plays. Do Shakespeare's plays teach us essential values? There are important reasons for studying Shakespeare but it would be misguided to think that studying, say, *Macbeth* or *King Lear* provides us with much power to generalise or universalise about human nature; both characters' responses to the action in their respective plays are outré to say the least. Ah, but, you might want to reply, isn't it true that Shakespeare's plays provide universal appeal and that they teach us universal truths about human nature? Well, both these ideas are fiercely contested. We are so familiar with a few of his plays that their original messages have been lost beneath archaeological strata of countless new interpretations. When we watch a play or see a film we're experiencing the artistic vision of the director who chooses what and how to bring ideas to the stage. Shakespeare might be the ultimate victim of cultural appropriation, with everyone feeling able to reinvent him to express whatever it is they see as pressing or important. At the same time, whole swathes of society see Shakespeare as 'posh' and representing the values of the elite. If Shakespeare *did* speak to everyone equally and teach us all how to live then we wouldn't need so many study guides. But even if there were some immortal truth to be gleaned from analysing Hamlet's 'To be or not to be' soliloquy, could it really be true that Shakespeare would be the only or the best place to find this information?

Connecting the curriculum

Students need to study Shakespeare *because* of the way he has been appropriated, reinvented and branded. Understanding modern life, never mind literature, is made immeasurably easier by understanding Shakespeare's place at the heart of the canon. It doesn't matter whether we like his plays or if we can identify with his characters, the fact is 'we' have collectively decided that Shakespeare is a big deal. There's nothing liberating about not studying Shakespeare; the ability to criticise, analyse, reinterpret and deconstruct his output rests on knowing something about it.

Shakespeare – probably all literature – provides an unstable foundation from which to generalise, or make judgements on events in the world. In fact, one of the dangers of Shakespearean knowledge being so widely shared is that it provides a convenient shorthand for filtering the world in ways that are superficially appealing but ultimately unhelpful: two young people recklessly in love? 'Well, that'll be Romeo and Juliet.' A strong woman providing guidance and backbone for a hesitant man? 'Oh, she's a real Lady Macbeth!' It's all too easy to project *anything* on to Shakespeare. As Emma Smith says, "we make Shakespeare mean what we want him to mean."[5] I once saw a production of *Troilus and Cressida* where the actors playing Greeks had English accents and the poor old persecuted Trojans had Irish accents. We've had *Richard III* reimagined as a Nazi, Prospero running a slave plantation, and, in 2017, a Donald Trump lookalike playing Caesar![6] When it's too easy to see whatever it is we want to see, we should look and think a bit more critically.

Narrative structure – Teaching students about Aristotle's theories of plot might seem like little more than a historical curiosity, but his ideas have so permeated the way we think about stories and storytelling that few theorists have been able to escape his ideas. But, of course, narrative theory doesn't stop with Aristotle; the notion that all stories are connected by underpinning structures comes as something of a surprise to students. This is not something they come to school knowing and, once they learn it, they think differently about both the stories they study in English as well as the stories that surround them at home. This is a genuinely powerful piece of knowledge that allows students to make testable predictions about *all* the stories they come into contact with, and provides them with structures with which they can experiment when writing their own stories. If they know they will be reading a tragedy, that should come with certain expectations about what will happen. If these expectations are not met then that provides them with scope to consider how and why a writer may have chosen to bend or break the rules, as well as a basis to make judgements on whether these decisions are successful.

Systematic metaphor – The realisation that metaphors are systematic – that war is a common way to think of arguments or medicine, or that seeing and holding are common metaphors for understanding – provides us with a conceptual framework to describe everyday ways of thinking and speaking and reveals much about how we came to think as we do. But what power does it possess for the study of English in school? The theory is possibly too remote from the kinds of work done in English lessons in secondary school to justify spending much time on this, but it can be revelatory to show students that our everyday language and thought relies on hidden layers of meaning and that metaphor can be taken so for granted that it becomes invisible to us. By working to make it visible we can find wonder in the mundane.

The rules of grammar – As we saw earlier, the idea that grammar is a list of arbitrary instructions that are unconnected to meaning is an unhelpful hangover of outworn beliefs about how English works. But, being able to compare our writing with the writing of others and see that they conform to descriptions on which meaning depends is extremely powerful. It leads to questions: Why do adjectives come before nouns? Why are some verbs irregular? What would happen if a change were made? Would the meaning of an utterance still be clear if a change to syntax is made? Seeing grammar as a spontaneous process, one that arises naturally but once it's emerged is slow to change, is a fascinating way to view the way we speak. As with rhetoric, knowing the names of things – metalanguage – enables students to reflect on how they and others use grammar, as well as providing them with constraints which they can then experiment with breaking.

Lots of people who should know better take perverse pride in their lack of grammatical knowledge. How, one might argue, can a concept be powerful if I don't need to know about it in order to be able to speak and write? Answering that question is only possible when in possession of powerful grammatical knowledge: grammatical rules are, once learned, applied instinctively and unthinkingly. No one needs to explicitly know the rules in order to use them but it's very difficult to think about these rules without being aware of what they are.

Using textual evidence – The use of evidence – a key part of the construction of arguments – can, like many aspects of English knowledge, appear deceptively straightforward. Children pick up how to use 'evidence' when they first learn to justify their actions with the conjunction 'because.' But a reason (which is what we get when we explain *why* something is) is not quite the same thing as evidence. Reasons can be plausible or otherwise and go some way to explaining motivation but *evidence* is gathered through empirical testing: *this* happens because of *that*. We have to notice what's going on to guess the cause of effects in the world out there, just as we learn to notice the effects caused by words in a text. However much extratextual knowledge we possess, our chief way of making meaning is to look at the structures of language in front of us. Students find it relatively easy to answer the question 'what does this make you think or feel?' but much harder to think about *how* that thought or feeling was produced. By selecting evidence from the texts we read, we learn to justify and explain our responses. Arguably this ability to explain and justify is useful in the wider world, but that misses the point: knowing the conventions of how to use textual evidence (how to punctuate quotations, how to embed evidence in our own writing, how to avoid plagiarism, etc.) is disciplinary knowledge which allows students to respond with more subtlety and insight.

Quality (2): Is it shared?

We can also examine the quality of our curriculum through the lens of shared knowledge. Does the knowledge we aim to teach permit entry into wider conversations? And if it does, what might be lost? The challenge is described by Hirsch:

> *Because of an inherent and inescapable inertia in the knowledge that is shared among hundreds of millions of people, the Core Knowledge plan was necessarily traditional.* ... It appeared to perpetuate the dominance of the already dominant elements of American life, while the aim of many intellectuals in the 1990s was to reduce that dominance and privilege, and valorize neglected cultures and women. ... *The aim of giving everybody entrée to the knowledge of power ran smack up against the aim of depriviling those who are currently privileged.*[7]

> [my emphasis]

This is a difficult tension to resolve. On the face of it, building a curriculum around the thoughts and deeds of historically marginalised groups looks like a really good idea.

Who wouldn't want children to know about the achievements of women and people of colour? There are two problems here. The first is, as we saw in the previous chapter, refusing to teach literature written by 'dead white men' won't help anyone to understand why people of colour and women have been historically marginalised. When we express our righteous indignation that some knowledge is valued over other knowledge, and decide to teach this other knowledge in the name of liberty and social justice, what we're actually doing is denying children choice. The second problem is that teaching an English curriculum focussed on the writing of marginalised groups would, by definition, not be shared knowledge. As Hirsch puts it, "If we tried to teach children a fully non-traditional knowledge set, they could not master the existing language of power and success."[8] This kind of curriculum denies students access to the 'knowledge of the powerful.'

Deciding that children do not need to know things that someone somewhere might consider elitist or offensive condemns them to the margins of society. Our dilemma is to navigate the tight confines of the school curriculum to find ways to teach the knowledge "shared among hundreds of millions of people" as well as to teach knowledge that deprivileges "those who are currently privileged."

Choosing texts

Whatever sequence we settle on, the flesh of our curriculum will be the texts we choose to teach. When selecting a text to study, English teacher Andy Tharby suggests we ask a series of questions about the texts we are considering teaching:[9]

- lexical challenge – how demanding are the vocabulary and syntax?
- the appropriateness of its content for the age group we're teaching

- the extent to which it has had 'conversations' backwards and forwards with other texts, that is to say, how influential it has been
- its quality – whether it introduces a broad range of literary conventions and offers sufficient stylistic merit to repay careful study
- to what extent it fulfils a role or niche within a broad and coherent curriculum
- and lastly, personal preference – there's little point teaching texts we feel are inferior to other, possible choices that could fulfil the same purpose.

As Applebee points out, when teachers turn to 'mediocre' texts, "Instruction is likely to deteriorate into vocabulary development and reading practice, because there is little else to do with the text."[10] By wrestling with these questions we are more likely to select texts that fulfil the principle of quality.

Quantity: breadth versus depth

How then should we connect? What are the best bets to prevent students from 'living in fragments'? The answer is not breadth *or* depth but *both*. Breadth of knowledge provides intellectual Velcro: new pieces of the puzzle stick more easily. If we take the time to introduce students to the conceptual understandings that underpin English each time we introduce more breadth, the more quickly and easily they will grasp those aspects studied in depth. The solution is to carefully select a few texts to study in depth, a much wider range of texts to just read with no time given over to analysis, and a vast range of extracts connecting these chosen texts together.

Depth requires breadth. Without sufficient breadth, topics studied in depth become confusing, arbitrary and meaningless. If texts are seen as exemplars of literature, as vehicles for teaching literary concepts as much as objects of study in their own right, we are more likely to see them as parts of a much broader conversation.

What if the study of *Macbeth* involved less time analysing the play and more time reading around it? You could include some extracts from Marlowe's *Doctor Faustus*, selections from Holinshed's *Chronicles* on the murders of Duncan and Banquo (surprisingly similar to events in the play) as well as some critical response, including some of Dr Johnson's 'Miscellaneous observations of the Tragedy of Macbeth.' You should definitely dip into other lit crit. (*Macbeth: Critical Essays* edited by S. Schoenbaum is an excellent source of critical essays and contains, amongst other treats, L.C. Knight's classic 'How many children had Lady Macbeth?'). You could also add something lighter like James Thurber's short story, 'Macbeth Murder Mystery.' Woven together with this, constantly compare Shakespeare's verse with that of other poets. Read as many poems as you can, at least one per lesson (and don't be afraid of reading the same poems over and over; they should be as familiar as songs) to get students used to the cadences of different metres.

Less time writing about and more time reading might be the way to prioritise breadth over depth. According to a small-scale study conducted by Jo Westbrook and colleagues, 'just reading' can make a significant difference to students' standardised reading comprehension scores. Twenty English teachers were recruited to take part in the study with their normal curriculum replaced by reading two novels back to back over twelve weeks. The students were given a standardised reading assessment at the beginning of the trial and again twelve weeks later. Students made an average of 8.5 months' worth of progress, but amazingly, the rate of progress was *doubled* for the most disadvantaged students.[11] What seemed to make the difference was listening to and engaging in cognitively demanding narratives.

Although you may fear that depth is sacrificed, it's more than compensated for by the breadth of literary knowledge students will acquire. By reading that which we find most beautiful, stirring and profound – for its own sake, not (just) because of its cultural capital, not (just) because it expands our knowledge of the world and certainly not (just) because it's in the exam – students might learn to appreciate that, as Frank Furedi puts it, "reading – especially serious reading – is itself a culturally beneficial activity."[12] When students return to exam texts in the last few months of a course they will remember and understand far more than if they've drunk from the same stagnant well of content filtered through exam technique over and again.

Manner: critique and conversation

For curriculum to be a conversation it must ensure a core of traditional knowledge is supplemented with carefully selected non-traditional knowledge. We should aim to teach the knowledge with the most cultural significance and *then learn to critique it*. After all, we can't really criticise something we don't understand. No one should be taught to unthinkingly agree that the canon represents the pinnacle of artistic achievement or that Shakespeare is the finest-ever writer, but if we don't learn about these culturally important aspects of literature, we won't know enough to understand the effects of colonialism and that the legacy of the Bard is as much to do with cultural imperialism as it is to do with literary merit.

The point of all this is to help children develop a more educated palate. When they are given a curriculum that offers them a broad sweep of culturally significant knowledge, they are empowered to say what they prefer from a position of knowing. Educated opinions have far more currency than ignorant ones. The greater the breadth of children's knowledge, the greater their sense of connoisseurship, the more able they are to think critically, and the wider the range of options open to them.

The curriculum is an opportunity to induct students into 'the conversation of humankind' which Oakeshott tells us is "impossible without a diversity of voices."[13] By possessing shared, culturally rich knowledge students gain the ability to share ideas with a community of minds, living and dead. And by knowing what others know, students have a language to ask questions and make objections; they are orientated towards a tradition beyond the thin slice of the present and encouraged to use it to locate themselves, here and now. As Michael Young puts it, the curriculum we teach should serve "to remind us that it is access to a 'relation to knowledge' not facts ... that is the purpose of education."[14] This 'relation to knowledge' is very much akin to Applebee's notion of 'knowledge-in-action.'

Relatedness: hierarchical and cumulative sequencing

Hierarchical subjects such as maths are like a Jenga tower: students have to have foundational knowledge firmly in place before they can move on to more advanced concepts. If students don't understand place value, for instance, they are effectively shut off from the rest of mathematics. Much of the substantive knowledge in English is cumulative; it builds outwards rather than upwards. It's obviously not the case that students must first master Chaucer before they encounter Shakespeare, nor would it be true to say that the study of poetry ought to precede the study of drama. The further outwards their knowledge spreads, the more likely students are to see connections between the texts they study, but their study does not depend on making any *particular* perception.

Some aspects of English may be more hierarchical. For instance, inference and analysis depend on solid reading comprehension; in turn, reading comprehension is impossible without fluent decoding, and fluent decoding requires the effortless recall of the phoneme / grapheme correspondences that make up English orthography. If students cannot decode fluently, their ability to make progress will be severely curtailed. Grammatical knowledge may also be hierarchical in nature. We know from the study of children's acquisition of language that nouns are learned before verbs and that this insight might be useful in building students' knowledge of language. An important question to consider is which other aspects of English are hierarchical, and what to do about teaching them. Is there a hierarchy to understanding metaphor or story? Should certain types of argument precede others? Does our knowledge of patterns in language build upwards or outwards? Currently, there are no empirical answers to these questions.

Concepts and ideas are more likely to be meaningful if they build on what has gone before and lay the foundations for what will follow. For more hierarchical areas of the curriculum, like grammar, sequencing may be simpler: knowledge should be sequenced from first principles upwards so that students master parts of speech before starting to think about sentence clauses and connecting paragraphs. For cumulative aspects of the curriculum like literary knowledge, a chronological sequence provides a useful way to demonstrate the spread of ideas and influence.

The story of English

Think of an English curriculum you have planned or taught. Can you remember what topic Year 8 covered in term 1? Do you know why they covered it in term 1 and not, say, term

3? If it had been taught in term 3 would anything have been different?

We are often unclear about the sequence of the curriculum we teach. It can be hard to remember what was taught from term to term precisely because there is no sequence; the order is poorly thought through or not thought through at all. It wouldn't make much difference if a topic was swapped between terms – or even years – because there's no guiding rationale behind the sequence. If you can shift a topic between terms without it ruining your curriculum sequence your curriculum is probably not coherent. So, how do we stop the curriculum being just 'one damn thing after another'?

The curriculum is often seen as a journey from A to B to the exam. The problem with following a path is that we miss most of what's either side. If we take story as our conceptual metaphor for the curriculum we might be more likely to end up with something coherent. Our advantage as English teachers is that much of our time is already spent teaching stories. This is straightforward: if we plan to teach *Macbeth* we'd be well advised to start at Act 1 scene 1 and continue to the end of Act 5. Similarly, chapter 1 is the best possible place to begin studying *Great Expectations*. The difficulty is in designing a coherent sequence between *Macbeth* and *Great Expectations*. Would you start with one because it was written earlier or because you think it's easier to understand? Thinking in terms of individual texts makes it hard to tell a coherent story, but if we think in terms of the story we want our whole curriculum to tell, sequencing becomes easier.

What is the 'story of English'?

One story is the development of the language from that spoken by the Anglo-Saxon invaders exemplified in *Beowulf* and in poems of the *Exeter Book* and in the prose of Bede's *A History of the English Church and People*. From there we could consider the influence of French after the Norman invasion and compare the work of Geoffrey Chaucer with that of the Gawain Poet to see the tensions between Old English and Middle English. We might also consider the evolution of English as witnessed by the Paston letters and in various anonymous ballads like 'Barbara Allan' and 'Sir Patrick Spens.' We could contrast courtly language in Thomas Malory's *La Morte d'Arthur* with the everyday speech of *The Book of Margery Kempe*. From there we could jump to the Renaissance moving from *Everyman* to More's *Utopia* to the emergence of the theatre of Marlowe and Shakespeare before studying the assembling of the King James Bible. After that we would want to look at Dr Johnson's dictionary and the move to exclude the English of unfashionable dialects to arrive at the modern foundations of how we speak and write today. While this would certainly tell a coherent story, it's unlikely to meet with approval because it's too distant from the familiar landmarks of the English curriculum.

Maybe instead we could tell the story of the development of literature. We could begin with Greek myths and Homer's *Odyssey* before jumping forward to, once again, *Beowulf*, but as well as noting the Old English in which it was written we could read it in translation and appreciate its poetry and the story it tells. We could tell some mini stories like the development of rhetoric from Aristotle to Cicero to some of the most famous speeches of the 20th and 21st centuries. We could look at the genre of Romance from its early origins in Arthurian legend, through some of Chaucer's *Canterbury Tales* to the poetry of Keats and Tennyson. We could tell the story of the sonnet from its beginnings in Renaissance Italy, to its mastery by Shakespeare and then into its creative flowering in recent decades.

What, for instance, is the story of the novel? One answer is that it begins with Daniel Defoe but another is that it starts with Caxton and the first English printing presses. The story of the novel is also the story of mass literacy. You could listen to *Beowulf* chanted by a skald; *The Canterbury Tales* was written to be recited; you could watch Shakespeare's plays at the theatre, but to experience a novel you had to be literate. We can trace the novel's roots from Cervantes' *Don Quixote*, Bunyan's *Pilgrim's Progress* and Aphra Behn's *Oroonoko*, but it is with *Robinson Crusoe* and then Jonathan Swift, Henry Fielding, Samuel Richardson and Lawrence Sterne that we get the first true novels in English. Arguably, it isn't until Jane Austen that the possibility of the novel to reveal characters' inner lives was fully realised, which moves in to the territory of Leavis' 'great tradition.' Telling this story in an intellectually honest way presents some challenges, but with the careful selection of novels like *Treasure Island* or *Oliver Twist* we can find a suitable focus against which to tell our back story.

Perhaps instead we could sequence our curriculum thematically, with golden threads woven throughout our plans. How might this look? It might work to tell the stories told in this book, of metaphor, story, argument, pattern, grammar and context. Maybe we could tell the stories of the different structural forms: the story of epic, of tragedy, of comedy and so on. Whatever choice we make, as long as we follow clear, sequenced narratives, students will be supported in making sense of the past to inform their present.

KEY POINTS

- Studying a greater breadth of the domain of English enables in-depth study to be more easily understood and integrated.
- 'Planning backwards' can narrow the scope of what's studied to what's tested. Ironically this is likely to have a negative effect on students' test performances.
- By considering what knowledge has the most power we can widen the curriculum from the study of texts to broader conceptual understandings.
- By considering what texts offer the greatest cultural richness we can ensure students are exposed to shared knowledge which they can learn to critique.
- Careful thought should be given to the texts chosen for study.
- Too often the curriculum is not carefully sequenced and therefore students do not experience a coherent story of English.
- There are many different stories of English from which to choose: think carefully about the story you want to tell.

In the final chapter we will examine a series of worked examples bringing all of these different ideas together in a curriculum model you can adapt for your own use.

Further reading

- Michael Young's essay 'The Curriculum and the Entitlement to Knowledge' provides a fascinating account of knowledge and the curriculum and helps explain more about the idea of 'powerful knowledge.' It is available as a PDF online.

Connecting the curriculum

- Similarly, E.D. Hirsch's book *Why Knowledge Matters* is probably his most useful introduction to the concept of 'cultural literacy.'
- Whilst a bit dated in parts and written specifically for an American audience, Arthur N. Applebee's *The Curriculum as Conversation* offers some useful ideas about the importance of meaning in the English curriculum.

12 Into action

At long last we get to the meat of it all. What follows is one possible way to organise an English curriculum. Although there are many ways to get the curriculum wrong, there's no one right way to get it right. As long as you've considered how to introduce powerful concepts, made sure students will experience cultural richness and considered the coherent sequencing of concepts, things should not go too far astray.

The map is not the territory

Best-laid plans often go awry and, to paraphrase Voltaire, 'the best is the enemy of good.'[1] You will never arrive at a finished, perfect curriculum, but that shouldn't be the point. A curriculum is necessarily iterative; a Forth Bridge in a constant state of being repaired and repainted.

The three-year plan which follows is the product of eight years of thought and tinkering. I've worked with a number of different schools and teachers, all of whom have taken on different aspects in many different ways. It's conceived as a coherent sequence designed to help 11–14-year-olds make meaning in English, and although a lot of deliberation has gone into its construction it is very far from perfect.

Into action

As the Polish-American philosopher Alfred Korzybski said, "A map is not the territory it represents, but, if correct, it has a similar structure to the territory, which accounts for its usefulness."[2] A curriculum plan is a map; the territory is the experience of each individual student in every classroom. A map provides general guidance but it can never anticipate every topographical peculiarity you will encounter. Lessons provide essential feedback on the accuracy of the map. Some of this can be funnelled back to create evermore accurate maps, but most will only be relevant to the particular combination of teachers and students embarked on actual expeditions. That said, it's a wise expedition leader who consults as many charts and atlases as are available before setting off.

As you will see, the general sequencing is chronological. The idea is that as texts and periods of literature are introduced they build on previously encountered writers and texts to encourage students to see literature and language as a conversation in which they can begin to participate. Each area of study is interrogated through the different epistemological outlooks discussed in previous chapters. I've suggested an outline of what could be covered within each area and more detailed resources are available online (learningspy.co.uk/making-meaning-resources/).

Year 7: The origins of English

Content	Ancient origins	Links to legends	The art of rhetoric	Romance
	- Extracts from *Heroes of Greece and Troy*,	- The Epic of Gilgamesh	- Shakespeare – *Julius Caesar*	- *Sir Gawain and the Green Knight* (Armitage)
	- *Homer's Odyssey*, Simon Armitage	- *Beowulf* – Heaney	- Speeches	- Chaucer, *The Knights Tale*
	- Emily Wilson's *Odyssey*	- Extracts from Tolkien, Le Guin, etc.	- Cicero & Aristotle	- Spenser, *The Faerie Queene*
				- Keats, *La Belle Dame*
				- Tennyson, *The Lady of Shalott*
Metaphor	Homeric epithets	Kennings	Flowers of rhetoric	Symbolism
Story	Heroes; myth; the epic		5-act structure	The romance; quests
Argument	Is Odysseus admirable?	What makes a good king?	Ethos, logos, pathos; arrangement; Act 3 scene 2	Using evidence
Pattern	Phonemes	Alliteration & caesura	Metrical feet: iambic pentameter	Rhyme, alliteration; metre
Grammar	Determiners; clauses	Nouns & noun phrases; types of sentence; appositives	Verbs & verb phrases; conjunctions	Adjectives and adjective phrases; active and passive sentences
Context	Literary timeline; Aristotle's poetics	Old English; Christianity	Origins of rhetoric; Elizabethan anxieties	Middle English; courtly love

Into action

This first year of study at secondary school might seem daunting. How, you might wonder, can it be reasonable to teach all these classic texts to 11-year-olds? Well, to quote Jerome Bruner, "any subject can be taught effectively in some intellectually honest form to any child at any stage of development."[3] The 'trick' is to find the appropriately 'intellectually honest form' in which to teach the *Odyssey*. I've suggested Simon Armitage's radio play for storytelling (it is delightfully earthy and accessible) and extracts from Emily Wilson's very readable recent translation to get a sense of the verse. I would also take the opportunity to use Roger Lancelyn Green's marvellous *Heroes of Greece and Troy* to tell some of the story of the Iliad but Stephen Fry's *Mythos* would work just as well. This is also an ideal opportunity to introduce some of Aristotle's ideas about plot.

With *Beowulf* there are many versions of the poem in modern English but none beats the beauty and accessibility of Seamus Heaney's so that would be my choice for telling the story, but it could be supplemented by prose versions if deemed necessary. I suggest including a summary at least of the ancient *Epic of Gilgamesh* in order to connect the idea of epic through the ages as well as leaping forward to Tolkien's *Lord of the Rings* to show how *Beowulf* influences modern writing. There's also an excellent opportunity to study the Anglo-Saxon metaphor-making machine, the kenning, and also to show the first steps on the development of modern English.

A detailed plan for the 'art of rhetoric' unit is available online (appendix 1) but for now the key focus is on Shakespeare's play *Julius Caesar*. Chronologically speaking, this is a bit of a cheat, but as the play is both set in Cicero's Rome and contains one particularly fine example of rhetoric it seems too good an opportunity to pass up. At the same time, this is a good time to introduce the nuts and bolts of rhetoric via

Aristotle, Cicero and a range of excellent speeches from history and literature. Sam Leith's book *You Talkin' To Me?* is a superb resource as are Mark Forsyth's *The Elements of Eloquence* and Jay Heinrich's *Thank You for Arguing*.

The unit on Romance provides a miniature chronology from the medieval roots of the genre to its Romantic reimagining in later centuries. I suggest dipping into *Gawain and the Green Knight* using Simon Armitage's excellent verse translation, and Nevill Coghill's fine verse translation of *The Canterbury Tales*. I do think students should experience some extracts in Chaucer's original verse but Year 7 is probably too soon for more than a taste. The Keats ballad 'La Belle Dame sans Merci' and Tennyson's 'The Lady of Shalott' are both excellent 'modern' poems to teach alongside the older texts. *The Faerie Queene* is just there for flavour but Book III with Britomart, the female knight modelled on Queen Elizabeth, can be interesting to explore.

Year 8: The development of form

	The sonnet form	Religion & superstition	Comedy	The story of the novel
Content	- Early lyric poetry - Petrarch to Shakespeare to Donne to Wordsworth to Duffy and Armitage	- Tyndale and the King James Bible - Extracts from *Paradise Lost*, *Pilgrim's Progress*, *Doctor Faustus*	- Aristophanes - *Much Ado & As You Like It* - Restoration comedy (Sheridan, Behn) - Oscar Wilde	- Extracts from *Robinson Crusoe*, *Gulliver's Travels* - Austen, *Pride & Prejudice* - Dickens, *Great Expectations*, *Oliver Twist* - Stevenson, *Treasure Island*
Metaphor	Love metaphors	Biblical imagery; allegory	Analysing metaphors	Extended metaphors
Story	Can sonnets tell stories, or are they arguments?	Tragedy; links to epic	The structure of comedy	Narrative voice
Argument	The Shakespearean sonnet	Is the Bible literature? Satan's rhetoric	Dialogue	How does the novel try to persuade us?
Pattern	The sonnet form; rhyme	Tyndale's style; Marlowe's 'mighty line'	Epigrams	Serialisation – chapters
Grammar	Adverbs & adverbials; sentence combining	Prepositions & prepositional phrases; topic sentences	Planning and drafting essays; writing purposes	Paragraphing; discourse markers
Context	History of the sonnet	The influence of KJV Bible on English	How comedy has evolved	Caxton & literacy

Year 8 is a series of 'mini-stories.' The story of the sonnet kicks off the year and could include a few examples of the lyric poems that preceded the sonnet ('On Monsieur's Departure' reputed to be by Elizabeth I is a fascinating example) before looking at some examples of Petrarch's oeuvre. I think students should at least see some sonnets by Wyatt, Sidney and Spenser before spending some time on Shakespeare. My favourites are all in this book: 29, 116 and 130, but there are many others that students would benefit from seeing (Sonnet 18 is possibly the most celebrated). Donne and Milton both wrote excellent sonnets, but as mentioned earlier, the sonnet disappears until reinvigorated by Wordsworth. It's definitely worth comparing the Romantics' take on the form before moving on to Hardy and then some more modern varieties to show how the conventions can be played with to make new meanings. An anthology of sonnets is available online in appendix 2.

Unit 2 may sound a bit dull. It really isn't. William Tyndale is *the* most overlooked figure in English literary history and has arguably had at least as great an influence on our language and literature as Shakespeare. Some sections of the King James Version of the Bible on which to focus might include the wooing of Rebecca, the life of Joseph, the adventures of Sampson, the saga of David, Daniel, The Nativity, Paul at Ephesus and Paul's sea voyage. It can be profitable to discuss the difference between the virtuous woman (Proverbs 31 and 10) and her opposite (Proverbs 7). You should look at a couple of psalms (any from 18, 22, 45, 50, 65, 88, 91, 107, 109, 137 or 148 would work well) and, for completeness sake, Revelation 1 and 22 are a surprising treat. Additionally, I really recommend Melvyn Bragg's *The Book of Books* for an excellent overview of the long and influential history of the KJV. Even though the King James Version of the Bible wasn't published until after Shakespeare's death, he almost certainly encountered

Tyndale's translation and you can feel its echo in his verse. *Paradise Lost* can be a daunting read, but it's packed with great moments. I'd recommend using John Carey's *The Essential Paradise Lost* as a guide. *Pilgrim's Progress* is not a great favourite of mine but in its favour it's full of hard to miss allegory – in fact it's a perfect text to use when introducing this element of metaphor. There's an almost limitless number of texts you can move onto to show Tyndale's influence, but Donne's religious sonnets might work well as a bridge from the previous unit.

The story of comedy makes for enjoyable teaching. The great thing about drama is that you can read and perform a lot of plays (as long as you resist the temptation to analyse everything!). I don't think you have to read the full text of any of Aristophanes' plays but you should at least take a look. *The Birds* is a great start with some recognisable references (for instance, cloud cuckoo land). I've suggested both *As You Like It* and *Much Ado About Nothing* but *A Midsummer Night's Dream* would do just as well (and, it links back to the *Knight's Tale* from Year 7). Whichever you choose, I'd suggest at least covering extracts from the others. For me, *As You Like It* is probably the best of Shakespeare's comedies and Rosalind one of his finest characters. The move in tone from Elizabethan comedy to Restoration farce should be noted (Christopher Booker's *The Seven Basic Plots* is invaluable). Sheridan's *The Rivals* and *School for Scandal* can both be a lot of fun, but I suggest caution with Behn's plays as they can be a bit 'mature' (*The Rover* turns attempted rape into an hilarious joke!). Oscar Wilde was a superb dramatist and students tend to really enjoy the sheer silliness of *The Importance of Being Earnest* or *Lady Windermere's Fan*. Where you go from there is up to you, but I think it works really well to show the structure of comedy resulting in a happy ending in at least one 'serious' novel.

We discussed the story of the novel on pages 331–2 but the big problem you have with novels is their length so you can probably only get through one – two at a push. Needless to say, whichever you choose should be supplemented by extracts from the others. I wouldn't recommend reading *Robinson Crusoe* in its entirety (it's very dull at times) but definitely read a few chapters and give a good summary as it's the jumping-off point. A top tip is to include a few sections from *Tristram Shandy* – the blank page for the readers to draw their own pictures, diagrams of the plot so far, asterisks to represent censored or forgotten passages – just because they're so wonderfully improbable. My personal preference would be for *Great Expectations* because I think it's a fabulous story with great characters and some wonderful set pieces. Wemmick's castle and his relationship with 'the aged P' is hilarious (at least, to me). The advantage of *Treasure Island* is that it's relatively short so you can get through far more extracts and maybe another shorter novel of your choosing.

Year 9: Into the world

	The gothic tradition	War poetry	Dystopia	Freedom	Women in Literature
Content	- Gothic anthology (*The Castle of Otranto, Vathek, The Monk, The Italian, Northanger Abbey*) - *Dracula, Frankenstein* - Brontë, *Wuthering Heights* - Shelley & Byron - Du Maurier, *Rebecca*	Tennyson Hardy Owen Sassoon Armitage	- Extracts from *Utopia* and a dystopia anthology - Huxley, *Brave New World* - Orwell, *Animal Farm, 1984*	- Olaudah Equiano - Civil rights – biographies & speeches - Extracts from Baldwin, Angelou, Morrison & Coates - Achebe, *Things Fall Apart*	A feminist 'retelling' of the story of English - Sappho - Aphra Behn, *Oroonoko* - Mary Wollstonecraft - The Brontës - Charlotte Perkins Gilman, *The Yellow Wallpaper*
Metaphor	Systematic metaphors	Irony	Symbolism	Metonymy	Comparing metaphors
Story	Characterisation	Thought	Theme	Identity	Intertextuality
Argument	Dialectic	War as argument	How should we live?	Arguments for justice	Arguments for equality
Pattern	Periodic sentences	Noticing poetic patterns	Noticing patterns in novels	Noticing patterns in novels	Noticing patterns in novels
Grammar	Summarising; explaining; discussing; describing	Thesis statements; introductions & conclusions	Drafting & revision	Using discourse markers; linking paragraphs	Multi-paragraph compositions
Context	Romanticism; Gothic conventions	'The Great War'	Civil war to Cold War	Slavery & colonialism; the canon	Feminism

Year 9 is another year of mini-stories, this time kicking off with a delve into the gothic. I'd spend some time with a short anthology of extracts from important gothic texts (see appendix 3 online) and would supplement with some suitably dark Romantic poetry such as 'The Raven' by Edgar Allan Poe, Byron's 'Darkness,' Coleridge's 'Christabel,' Keats' 'The Eve of St Agnes' or 'Isabella' and maybe extracts from Rossetti's 'Goblin Market.' As with the unit on the novel in Year 8, you can probably only choose one text to read in its entirety; Dracula and Frankenstein are always popular but are both heavy going at times and may work better as extracts. My preference is for *Wuthering Heights* because its concerns are startlingly modern. Heathcliff and Cathy are both exquisitely awful and the narrative structure provides layers of ambiguity.

I chose war poetry as a focus because, well, there's some great stuff and it's easily neglected. This moves the story of English squarely into the 20th century although it's worth stepping back a little to include 'The Charge of the Light Brigade' because it's such a masterfully constructed piece of poetry. Hardy's Boer War poems, 'Drummer Hodge,' 'The Man He Killed' and 'Channel Firing,' are also worth reading. Wilfred Owen is always more popular than Siegfried Sassoon but I'd suggest swapping between them and maybe even shuffling in some Robert Graves. Of course, you should read the obvious ones like 'Dulce et Decorum Est' and 'Anthem for Doomed Youth' but some of the lesser-known ones are also excellent. (See appendix 4 online for an anthology.) And then some modern poems. Simon Armitage's 'Remains' stands out as does Duffy's 'War Photographer.'

Dystopia is such a popular genre for so many younger readers that it makes sense to see where it's come from. I once heard Margaret Atwood say that most modern dystopian novels are not in fact dystopian at all because they end happily. The first principle is that you can't really grasp dystopia until you've understood utopia so an overview of Thomas More's treatise is a sensible start. My suggestion is that you should try to read both Orwell novels in their entirety. The only way you're going to make this happen is by 'just reading' them. My advice is to forego extensive analysis for the benefit (and pleasure) of reading more. You could swap out *Animal Farm* for *Brave New World* instead if you prefer, but there's something powerful about being able to compare a writer to himself. I've also put together a dystopian reader for your delight and convenience. (See appendix 5 online.)

It's at this point in the curriculum that students should be encouraged to critique the certainties they've been presented with. I recommend centring the 'freedom' unit around Achebe's *Things Fall Apart*, and, while you're welcome to choose anything else you think suitable, you'll be hard pressed to beat it. It links so well to what's gone before (particularly the work done on the Bible) and you get to blast off with *that* Yeats poem! Again, the key here, as elsewhere, is breadth. The wider students' reading the better and so there's another reader available to those that want it. (See appendix 6 online.)

And finally, here we are at the end of Year 9. This final unit aims to re-tell the story of English from a feminist perspective. As you can see there are five units here instead of the four covered in Years 7 and 8 and so time will be necessarily compressed. This being the case, Charlotte Perkins Gilman's short story *The Yellow Wallpaper* is the perfect focus. Reading is again supplemented by an anthology of superb writing by women.

Assuring the curriculum

Whether or not you think my suggestions for the English curriculum have merit, you will, of course, need to make many decisions based on the practical matters of budgets, stock cupboards and the expertise of your colleagues. That being the case, you will, inevitably, end up making many curricular decisions at a local level.

The following questions can be used as discussion prompts to consider the extent to which your decisions encourage students to become increasingly effective participants in the conversation of English.

1. Does this choice add to students' knowledge of what others in society consider to be valuable?
2. Does this choice enable students to take part in discussions or debates that they would otherwise be excluded from?
3. Does this choice enable students to critique what others have decided is important or true?
4. Does it allow students to think beyond the confines of their experiences?
5. Does it open up new ways of thinking about the world?
6. Does it provide the means for students to critically evaluate what they have already been taught?
7. Does it make it easier to speak to others about abstract concepts?
8. Is it rooted in *how* to perform a task, or in *why* the task should be performed?
9. How do I know this choice is better than an alternative?
10. Would this be good enough for our own children?

KEY POINTS

- A curriculum is never finished and should always be added to, improved, edited and shaped with the experience of teaching.
- The curriculum is the lived experience of students in classrooms; a plan can inform this experience but never replace it.
- Chronology makes for a ready-made narrative structure; individual topics can be turned into mini-stories.
- In order to read more texts, it is probably inevitable that there will be less analysis. This is a worthwhile trade off.
- A curriculum can aim to explicitly cover the various modes of meaning discussed in this book or introduced in a more ad hoc manner; however, grammar almost certainly benefits from careful hierarchical sequencing.
- How will you ensure your curriculum is designed to help children make meaning?

This then is my vision for making meaning in English. You will find some of it seems to work and some of it may seem unworkable; some of it you may like, some you will not. Please feel free to take what appeals and ignore anything that doesn't. My hope is that you will find it, if nothing else, a useful worked example for your own ideas. I offer it to you in the knowledge that it will be copied, adapted, improved, rewritten, misused, misattributed, spurned and ignored. You are welcome to do with it whatever you will, but if you decide to teach any of it, I'd love to hear about your successes and struggles.

Online appendices

The appendices can be found online at: learningspy.co.uk/ making-meaning-resources

Notes

Introduction

1 Arthur Applebee, *Curriculum as Conversation*, p. 30.
2 Michael Polanyi and Harry Prosch, *Meaning*, p. 66.
3 Michael Oakeshott, "The voice of poetry in the conversation of mankind," p. 490.

1 What is English *for*?

1 According to a Royal Society of Literature report, most writers earned below £10,000 from their writing in 2018.
2 George Sampson, *English for the English*, p. 4.
3 David Perkins, *Making Learning Whole*, p. 42.
4 George Sampson, *English for the English*, p. 16.
5 David Holbrook, *English for Maturity*, p. 19.
6 The subject association The English and Media Centre has as the first of its 'aims and guiding principles,' "We seek to develop our radicalism for new times and new generations of teachers." Available at: www.englishandmedia.co.uk/about
7 Matthew Arnold, *Culture and Anarchy*, p. 9.
8 Matthew Arnold, *Reports on Elementary Schools, 1852–1882*, p. 19.
9 ibid, p. 87.

10 ibid, p. 157.
11 Quoted in *English for the English*, pp. 18–20.
12 *Newbolt Report*, p. 131.
13 ibid, p. 129.
14 F.R. Leavis, *New Bearings in English Poetry*, p. 9.
15 George Steiner, *Language and Silence*, p. 15.
16 Noam Chomsky, *Chomsky on Democracy & Education*, p. 71.
17 *Bullock Report*, p. 528.
18 *Newbolt Report*, p. 51.
19 David Crystal, "English grammar in the UK: a political history," p. 5.
20 David Holbrook, *English for Meaning*, p. 215.
21 ibid, p. 212.
22 ibid, p. 13.
23 James Callaghan, "A rational debate based on the facts." Available at: www.educationengland.org.uk/documents/speeches/1976 ruskin.html
24 *Kingman Report*, p. iv.
25 *Cox Report*, 2.2, p. 57.
26 ibid, 2.21–2.25, p. 60.
27 Ofsted, *English 2000–05*, p. 11.
28 Ofsted, *Excellence in English*, p. 27.
29 ibid, p. 36.
30 Ofsted, *Moving English Forward*, p. 23.
31 ibid, p. 28.
32 Ofsted, *Engaging and inspiring learners in English, especially at Key Stage 3: Priestnall School*, p. 2.
33 See, "What I learned on my visit to Ofsted." Available at: https://learningspy.co.uk/blogging/learned-visit-ofsted/
34 Ofsted, *Inspection of Colne Valley High School*, 18–19 September 2019.
35 Ofsted, *Inspection of Parkside Middle School*, 11–12 September 2019.
36 English programmes of study: Key Stage 3 National curriculum in England, p. 2.
37 Matthew Arnold, *Culture and Anarchy*, p. 5.
38 Adapted from Michael Young and Johan Muller, *Curriculum and the Specialization of Knowledge*, p. 92.

Notes

2 Problems in English

1 *Newbolt Report*, 79, pp. 74–5.
2 Michael Oakeshott, *The Voice of Liberal Learning*, p. 49.
3 ibid, p. 70.
4 Michael Polanyi, *The Tacit Dimension*, p. 4.
5 Tim Shanahan, "Why following the simple view may not be such a good idea." Available at: https://shanahanonliteracy.com/blog/why-following-the-simple-view-may-not-be-such-a-good-idea
6 Robert Marzano, "The art and science of teaching / teaching inference." Available at: www.ascd.org/publications/educational-leadership/apr10/vol67/num07/Teaching-Inference.aspx
7 David Flint and Rob Bircher, *Edexcel GCSE Geography B: Evolving Planet Student Book*, p. 21.
8 Arthur Applebee et al., *The Language of Literature*, p. 577.
9 Ernest Hemingway, *Death in the Afternoon*, p. 192.
10 Richard P. Feynman, "Cargo cult science: some remarks on science, pseudoscience, and learning how to not fool yourself."
11 Christine Counsell, "Better conversations with subject leaders," pp. 107–8.
12 Daisy Christodoulou, *Making Good Progress?*
13 Samuel Johnson, *The Rambler* No. 2, Saturday 24 March, 1749–1750.

3 An epistemology of English

1 Michael Polanyi and Harry Prosch, *Meaning*, p. x.
2 Edward Freeman, *The Times*, 8 June 1887, quotes in Collins, *The Study of English Literature*, p. 27.
3 John Churton Collins, *The Study of English Literature*, p. 41.
4 Percy Shelley, *A Defence of Poetry*. Available at: www.poetryfoundation.org/articles/69388/a-defence-of-poetry
5 Michael Polanyi, *The Tacit Dimension*, p. 4.
6 Elizabeth Newton, "Overconfidence in the communication of intent: heard and unheard melodies."
7 William Strunk Jr. and E.B. White, *The Elements of Style*, pp. xv–xvi.
8 Michael Young, "The curriculum and the entitlement to knowledge.'

9 The 'unthinkable' and the 'not yet thought' are concepts discussed by Basil Bernstein, *Pedagogy, Symbolic Control and Identity: Theory, Research, Critique*, pp. 29–30.
10 Michael Young and Johan Muller, *Curriculum and the Specialization of Knowledge*, p. 133.
11 Michael Young, *Bringing Knowledge Back In*, p. 23.
12 Michael Polanyi and Harry Prosch, *Meaning*, p. 98.

4 Noticing and analogising

1 Michael Oakeshott, *The Voice of Liberal Learning*, p. 23.
2 William James, "The principles of psychology." Available at: http://psychclassics.yorku.ca/James/Principles/prin11.htm
3 For a complete account see Iain McGilchrist's *The Master and his Emissary*.
4 Iain McGilchrist, *Ways of Attending*, p. 14.
5 Michael Polanyi and Harry Prosch, *Meaning*, p. x.
6 ibid, p. 34.
7 John Keats, letter to George and Thomas Keats, 21 December 1817.
8 R.S. Thomas, *Residues*, p. 69.
9 Ralph Waldo Emerson, "The American Scholar." Available at: http://digitalemerson.wsulibs.wsu.edu/exhibits/show/text/the-american-scholar
10 Andrew Bennett and Nicholas Royle, *This Thing Called Literature*, p. 16.
11 ibid, p. 17.
12 I.A. Richards, *The Philosophy of Rhetoric*, p. 30.
13 The idea that analogies and metaphors are at the heart of all thought is explained in fascinating detail in Douglas Hofstadter and Emmanuel Sander's *Surfaces and Essences*.
14 Terry Eagleton, *How to Read Literature*, pp. 8–15.
15 Richard Feynman, *The Pleasure of Finding Things Out*, p. x.
16 H.W. Janson, *History of Art*, p. 11.

5 Metaphor

1 José Ortega y Gasset, *The Dehumanisation of Art*, p. xx.
2 Aristotle, *Poetics*, Book 9.3 p. 34. Actually, Aristotle defines metaphor as "the application of a noun which properly applies to something else."

Notes

3 José Ortega y Gasset, *The Dehumanisation of Art*, p. 33.
4 Aristotle, *Rhetoric*, Book 3.2. In my copy it's translated as "style, clearness, charm, and distinction" (p. 161) but this is rather inadequate.
5 Friedrich Nietzsche, "On Truth and Lie in an Extra-Moral Sense," pp. 46–7.
6 Ralph Waldo Emerson, *The Essential Writings of Ralph Waldo Emerson*, p. 296.
7 Michael Oakeshott, "The voice of poetry in the conversation of mankind," p. 528.
8 I.A. Richards, *The Philosophy of Rhetoric*, p. 94.
9 Michael Polanyi and Harry Prosch, *Meaning*, p. 79.
10 I.A. Richards, *The Philosophy of Rhetoric*, p. 117.
11 Not everyone is enthusiastic about enthusiasm. Dr Johnson defined it in his dictionary as "a vain confidence of divine favour or communication."
12 George Lakoff and Mark Johnson, *Metaphors We Live By*, p. 3.
13 Robert Siegler, *Emerging Minds*, p. 85.
14 Robert Eaglestone, *Literature*, p. 42.
15 Zoltán Kövecses, *Metaphor*, p. 49.
16 Michael Oakeshott, "The voice of poetry in the conversation of mankind," p. 517.
17 ibid, p. 529.
18 Dom Moraes, *My Son's Father*, p. 191.
19 Zoltán Kövecses, *Metaphor*, pp. 156–7.
20 Mark Forsyth, *The Elements of Eloquence*, p. 152.
21 William Empson, *Seven Types of Ambiguity*, p. 32.
22 Michael Oakeshott, "The voice of poetry in the conversation of mankind," p. 541.

6 Story

1 E.M. Forster, *Aspects of the Novel*, p. x.
2 Mark Turner, *The Literary Mind*, pp. 4–5.
3 Daniel Willingham, *Why Don't Students Like School?*, p. 67.
4 T.S. Eliot, "The Metaphysical Poets." Available at: www.usask.ca/english/prufrock/meta.htm
5 This example comes from Daniel Kahneman's *Thinking, Fast and Slow*, p. 50.
6 Frank Kermode, *The Sense of an Ending*, p. 45.

7 There are a number of variants of this anecdote but it is, sadly, completely unsubstantiated: https://quoteinvestigator.com/2013/01/28/baby-shoes/

8 Joan Didion, *The White Album*, p. 11.

9 Natalie Haynes, *OedipusEnders*, BBC Radio 4, Broadcast on 28 August 2010.

10 Aristotle, *Poetics*, Book 8.4, pp. 28–9.

11 Philip Pullman, *Daemon Voices*, p. 77.

12 Rob Pope, *The English Studies Book*, p. 219

13 Aristotle, *Poetics*, Book 6.4, p. 19.

14 A.C. Bradley, *Shakespearean Tragedy*, p. 18.

15 Northrop Frye, *Anatomy of Criticism*, p. 212.

16 Terry Eagleton, *Sweet Violence*, p. 3.

17 Aristotle, *Poetics*, Book 2.2, p. 5.

18 Christopher Booker, *The Seven Basic Plots*, pp. 116–17.

19 Of course, the genres of Shakespeare's plays were attributed after his death by John Heminges and Henry Condell. Knowing this can help students understand why assigning genres is a bit messy. For a very different reading of *Romeo and Juliet* as inevitably tragic, see Emma Smith's *This is Shakespeare*, pp. 67–81.

20 T.S. Eliot, "Tradition and the individual talent." Available at: www.bartleby.com/200/sw4.html

21 Available online at: https://ia601601.us.archive.org/24/items/in.ernet.dli.2015.215175/2015.215175.Explorations.pdf

22 Sebastian Faulks, *Faulks on Fiction*, p. 11.

23 Freud used *Hamlet* as his case study for the Oedipal Complex, but Harold Bloom points out, correctly I think, that it would be better to see Freud as suffering with a Hamlet Complex. (*The Western Canon*, p. 350.)

24 Mikhail Bakhtin, "Epic and novel: toward a methodology for the study of the novel," p. 50.

25 E.M. Forster, *Aspects of the Novel*, p. 69.

26 ibid, p. 73.

27 Sebastian Faulks, *Faulks on Fiction*, p. 14.

28 Joseph Campbell, *The Hero with a Thousand Faces*, p. 23.

29 John Yorke, *Into the Woods*, p. x.

30 ibid, p. 139.

Notes

31 Both transcripts were taken from this online resource: http://resource.download.wjec.co.uk.s3.amazonaws.com/vtc/2015–16/15-16_50/wjec/unit4/Wales%20Unit%204%20Section%20A%20Digital%20Resources.pdf

32 G. Wilson Knight, *The Imperial Theme*, p. x.

7 Argument

1 *Monty Python*, "Argument sketch." Available at: www.dailymotion.com/video/x2hwqn9

2 Stephen Fry, *The Ode Less Travelled*, p. x.

3 Made you look!

4 There's some debate about whether this arrangement should be attributed to Cicero or the anonymous writer of the medieval text of rhetoric, *Ad Herennium*.

5 Cicero, *On Oratory and Orators*, p. 177.

6 Quintilian, *Institutio Oratoria*, IV.1.5.

7 John Milton, "Whether day or night is the more excellent," *Prolusions*, 1674.

8 Cicero, *On Oratory and Orators*, p. 176.

9 Quintilian, *Institutio Oratoria*, IV.2.31.

10 Laura Lederer, *Modern Slavery*, p. 9.

11 Accessed from: www.speeches-usa.com/Transcripts/richard_nixon-checkers.html

12 Accessed from: www.softschools.com/examples/literary_terms/refutation_examples/338/

13 Accessed from: www.pbs.org/wgbh/aia/part4/4h2927.html

14 Aristotle, *Rhetoric*, p. 208.

15 Cicero, *On Oratory and Orators*, p. 153.

16 F.R. Leavis, cited in R.P. Bilan, *The Literary Criticism of F.R. Leavis*, p. 65.

17 Mikhail Bakhtin, *Problems of Dostoevsky's Poetics*, p. 281 (see E. Waisolek, Bakhtin, Mikhail. Problems of Dostoevsky's Poetics (Book Review)).

18 Mikhail Bakhtin, *The Dialogic Imagination*, p. 303.

19 Harold Bloom, *The Western Canon*, p. 38.

20 Michael Oakeshott, "The voice of poetry in the conversation of mankind," p. 198.

21 Michael Oakeshott, *The Voice of Liberal Learning*, p. 39.
22 Saul Bellow, "The Thinking Man's Wasteland."
23 Joseph Brodsky, *Conversations*, p. 99.
24 Gerald Graff and Cathy Birkenstein, *They Say / I Say*.
25 Michael Oakeshott, "The voice of poetry in the conversation of mankind," pp. 509–10.
26 T.S. Eliot, "Tradition and the individual talent."
27 Dick Mack, "Writing with Precision, Clarity, and Economy," p. 31.
28 ibid, p. 34.
29 Ernest Gowers and Rebecca Gowers, *Plain Words*, p. 5.
30 Filip Buekens and Maarten Boudry, "The dark side of the loon. Explaining the temptations of obscurantism," p. 1.
31 Harry Frankfurt, *On Bullshit*, p. 14.
32 This sentence was written by Judith Butler and won 1998's Bad Writing Contest. See: www.denisdutton.com/bad_writing.htm
33 AQA, A level English Literature B (7717/1A) Paper 1A: Literary Genres: Aspects of Tragedy. Available at: https://filestore.aqa.org.uk/resources/english/AQA-77171A-SMS.PDF
34 David Bartholomae, "Writing assignments: where writing begins," p. 311.
35 Taken from the AQA A level assessment objectives. Available at: www.aqa.org.uk/subjects/english/as-and-a-level/english-literature-a-7711–7712/scheme-of-assessment/assessment-objectives
36 Stephen Pinker, *The Sense of Style*, pp. 50–1.

8 Pattern

1 Patricia Kuhl, "Early language acquisition: cracking the speech code."
2 D. Crystal, *The Cambridge Encyclopedia of Language* (3rd ed.).
3 See Perlman et al., "Iconicity can ground the creation of vocal symbols."
4 Margaret Magnus, *Gods in the Word*, p. 7.
5 Sameer Rahim, "Interview with Seamus Heaney," *The Telegraph*. Available at: www.telegraph.co.uk/culture/books/5132022/Interview-with-Seamus-Heaney.html
6 If you're interested, originalpronunciation.com is a trove of information on all things OP.

Notes

7 J.V. Cunningham, "Tradition and poetic structure: essays in literary history and criticism." Available at: https://archive.org/stream/traditionpoeticsoocunn/traditionpoeticsoocunn_djvu.txt

8 He actually said, "For my pleasure I'd as soon write free verse as play tennis with the nets down." *The Collected Prose of Robert Frost*, p. 168.

9 I.A. Richards, *Principles of Literary Criticism*, p. 145.

10 Clive James, *Poetry Notebook 2006–2014*, p. 43.

11 Both these examples come from Norman Douglas' rather wonderful (and scandalous) collection, *Some Limericks*. These are two of the cleaner ones! He says in the introduction, "I may be abused on the ground that the pieces are coarse, obscene, and so forth. Why, so they are; and whoever suffers from that trying form of degeneracy which is horrified by coarseness had better close the book at once."

12 Stephen Fry, *The Ode Less Travelled*, p. 282.

13 Peter Elbow, "The shifting relationships between speech and writing," p. 15.

9 Grammar

1 Ann Senghas, *Intergenerational Influence and Ontogenetic Development in the Emergence of Spatial Grammar in Nicaraguan Sign Language*, p. 517.

2 Jeffrey Elliott (ed.), *Conversations with Maya Angelou*, p. xx.

3 David Crystal, *A Little Book of Language*, p. 37.

4 Mark Seidenberg, *Language at the Speed of Sound*, pp. 131–5.

5 NB: Nouns ending in *-ing* are gerunds.

6 These examples from both of these lists are taken from David Crystal's *The Cambridge Encyclopedia of Language*, p. 214.

7 Benjamin Bergen, *Louder Than Words*, p. 118.

8 David Crystal, *Making Sense*, p. 68.

9 David Crystal, "English grammar in the UK: a political history," pp. 27–8.

10 *A Comprehensive Grammar of the English Language* has over 3,500 entries.

11 Stephen Pinker, *The Sense of Style*, p. 192.

12 Bill Bryson, *Mother Tongue*, p. 6.

13 According to corpus studies of spoken language the adverbs 'always' and 'completely' are used more often to split an infinitive than not. (Elly van Gelderen, *Grammaticalization as Economy*, pp. 245–6.)

14 R. Fawcett and M. Perkins, *Child Language Transcripts*, volume II, p. 22 (see Cheryl M. Scott, "RP Fawcett and MR Perkins").

15 David Crystal, *Making Sense*, p. 115.

16 Kingsley Amis, *The King's English*, p. 45 (see Ingrid Tieken-Boon van Ostade, *English Usage Guides*).

17 George Orwell, *Politics and the English Language*.

18 Stephen Pinker, *The Sense of Style*, p. 55.

19 *Cox Report*, p. 71.

20 *Bullock Report*, p. 18.

21 Stephen Pinker, *The Sense of Style*, p. 56.

22 This exercise is adapted from *The Writing Revolution*, pp. 40–4.

10 Context

1 Arthur Applebee, *Curriculum as Conversation*, p. x.

2 ibid, p. 20.

3 Michael Oakeshott, *The Voice of Liberal Learning*, p. 60.

4 Peter Barry, *Beginning Theory*, p. xiv.

5 F.R. Leavis, *Education and the University*, p. x.

6 James Boswell, *The Life of Samuel Johnson*, p. 333.

7 Michael Oakeshott, *The Voice of Liberal Learning*, pp. 9–10.

8 A.S. Byatt interviewed by Tim Lawrence and Peter Guttridge on "Reloading the ancient canon." *The Independent*, 21 November 1994.

9 Michael Oakeshott, *The Voice of Liberal Learning*, p. 42.

10 ibid, p. 43.

11 Frank Kermode, *Forms of Attention*, p. 79.

12 C.S. Lewis, from the introduction to his translation of *On the Incarnation*.

13 Ian Warwick and Ray Speakman, *Redefining English for the More Able*, pp. 29–30.

14 Alison Light, "Two cheers of liberal education," p. 41.

15 Toni Morrison, "Unspeakable things unspoken: the Afro-American presence in American literature," p. 12.

Notes

16 Alan Bennett, *The History Boys*, p. 56.
17 Jeffrey Elliott (ed.), *Conversations with Maya Angelou*, p. 207.
18 Excerpted from an interview with Vikas Shah, "Why we write." Available at: https://thoughteconomics.com/why-we-write/
19 Chinua Achebe, "An image of Africa: racism in Conrad's *Heart of Darkness*," p. 6.
20 Julia Kristeva, "Word, dialogue and the novel."
21 Roland Barthes, "Theory of the text," p. 39.
22 Harold Bloom, *The Anxiety of Influence*, p. 91.
23 See the online annotated version *Finnegans Wake* at: www.finwake.com/1024chapter1/fw01.htm

11 Connecting the curriculum

1 Esmond Wright, *Benjamin Franklin: His Life as He Wrote it*, p. 120.
2 E.D. Hirsch Jr. et al., "Responses to Robert Scholes." Available at: www.aft.org/periodical/american-educator/spring-2006/building-knowledge
3 Arthur Applebee, *Curriculum as Conversation*, pp. 52–64.
4 It's actually more complex (and more interesting) than that. See Cecelia Watson's book, *Semicolon*.
5 Emma Smith, *This is Shakespeare*, p. 66.
6 James Shapiro tells the full story of this remarkable production in *Shakespeare in a Divided America*, pp. 8–18.
7 E.D. Hirsch, *Why Knowledge Matters*, p. 160.
8 ibid, p. 160.
9 Andy Tharby, *Making Every English Lesson Count*, pp. 12–14.
10 Arthur Applebee, *Curriculum as Conversation*, p. 55.
11 Jo Westbrook et al., "'Just Reading.'"
12 Frank Furedi, *The Power of Reading: from Socrates to Twitter*, p. 209.
13 Michael Oakeshott, "The voice of poetry in the conversation of mankind," p. 490.
14 Michael Young, "The curriculum and the entitlement to knowledge," p. 6.

12 Into action

1 Voltaire quoted an unnamed Italian poet in his Dictionnaire Philosophique in 1770: "Il meglio è l'inimico del bene." It later appeared in his poem 'La Béguele,' as "le mieux est l'ennemi du bien."
2 Alfred Korzybski, "Science and sanity: an introduction to non-Aristotelian systems and general semantics."
3 Jerome S. Bruner, *The Process of Education*, p. 33.

Bibliography

Achebe, Chinua (1977) "An Image of Africa: Racism in Conrad's *Heart of Darkness.*" *Massachusetts Review*, 18. Available at: https:// polonistyka.amu.edu.pl/__data/assets/pdf_file/0007/259954/ Chinua-Achebe,-An-Image-of-Africa.-Racism-in-Conrads-Heart-of-Darkness.pdf

Applebee, Arthur N. (1996) *Curriculum as Conversation: Transforming Traditions of Teaching and Learning.* University of Chicago Press: Chicago.

Applebee, A.N., A.B. Bermudez, S. Blau, R. Caplan, P. Elbow and S. Hynds (2002) *The Language of Literature.* McDougal Littell: Evanston.

Aristotle, trans. Malcolm Heath (1996) *Poetics.* Penguin Books: London.

Aristotle (2012) *The Art of Rhetoric.* HarperCollins: London.

Arnold, Matthew, ed. P.J. Keating (2015) *Culture and Anarchy and Other Selected Prose.* Penguin Classics: London.

Arnold, Matthew, ed. Francis Sandford (1889) *Reports on Elementary Schools 1852–1882.* Macmillan: London.

Bakhtin, Mikhail (2000) "Epic and Novel: Toward a Methodology for the Study of the Novel." In *Modern Genre Theory.* Ed. David Duff. Longman: New York.

Bakhtin, M.M. (2010) *The Dialogic Imagination: Four Essays* (Vol. 1). University of Texas Press: Austin.

Barry, Peter (2017) *Beginning Theory: An Introduction to Literary and Cultural Theory, Fourth Edition.* Manchester University Press: Manchester.

Barthes, Roland (1981) "Theory of the Text." In *Untying the Text: A Post-Structuralist Reader*. Ed. Robert Young. Routledge & Kegan Paul: London and New York.

Bartholomae, D. (2005) "Writing Assignments: Where Writing Begins." In *Writing on the Margins*. Palgrave Macmillan: New York.

Bellow, Saul, ed. Benjamin Taylor (2016) *There is Simply Too Much to Talk About: Collected Non-Fiction*. Penguin Books: New York.

Bennett, Andrew and Nicholas Royle (2019) *This Thing Called Literature: Read, Thinking Writing*. Routledge: Abingdon and New York.

Bergen, Benjamin, K. (2012) *Louder Than Words: The New Science of How the Mind Makes Meaning*. Basic Books: Philadelphia.

Bernstein, Basil (2000) *Pedagogy, Symbolic Control and Identity: Theory, Research, Critique, Second Edition*. Rowman and Littlefield: Oxford.

Bilan, R.P. (1979) *The Literary Criticism of F.R. Leavis*. Cambridge University Press: Cambridge.

Bloom, Harold (1973) *The Anxiety of Influence: A Theory of Poetry*. Oxford University Press: Oxford.

Bloom, Harold (1994) *The Western Canon: The Books and School of the Ages*. Harcourt, Brace & Company: New York.

Booker, Christopher (2004) *The Seven Basic Plots: Why We Tell Stories*. Bloomsbury: London.

Boswell, James, ed. David Womersley (2008) *The Life of Samuel Johnson*. Penguin Classics: London.

Bradley, A.C. (2012) *Shakespearean Tragedy: Lectures on Hamlet*. Emereo Publishing: Brisbane.

Bragg, Melvyn (2011) *The Book of Books: The Radical Impact of the King James Bible 1611–2011*. Sceptre: London.

Brodsky, Joseph, ed. Cynthia L. Haven (2002) *Conversations*. University Press of Mississippi: Jackson.

Bruner, J.S. (1960) *The Process of Education: A Searching Discussion of School Education Opening New Paths to Learning and Teaching*. Vintage Books: New York.

Brysbaert, Marc (2019) "How Many Words Do We Read Per Minute? A Review and Meta-analysis of Reading Rate." Preprint. Available at: https://psyarxiv.com/xynwg/

Bryson, Bill (1990) *Mother Tongue: The Story of English Language*. Penguin: London.

Bibliography

Buekens, Filip and Maarten Boudry (2014) "The Dark Side of the Loon. Explaining the Temptations of Obscurantism." *Theoria*. 81. 10.1111/theo.12047.

Bullock Report, The (1975) *A Language for Life*. Her Majesty's Stationery Office: London. Available at: www.educationengland. org.uk/documents/bullock/bullock1975.html

Campbell, Joseph (2008) *The Hero with a Thousand Faces, Third Edition*. New World Library: Novato.

Carper, Thomas and Derek Attridge (2003) *Meter and Meaning: An Introduction to Rhythm in Poetry*. Routledge: London.

Chomsky, N. (2003) *Chomsky on Democracy & Education*. Psychology Press: New York.

Christodoulou, D. (2017) *Making Good Progress? The Future of Assessment for Learning*. Oxford University Press: Oxford.

Cicero, Marcus Tullius, ed. and trans. J.S. Watson (1970) *On Oratory and Orators*. Southern Illinois University Press: Carbondale.

Cicero, Marcus Tullius, selected, ed. and trans. James M. May (2016) *How to Win An Argument: An Ancient Guide to the Art of Persuasion*. Princeton University Press: Princeton.

Collins, John Churton (1891) *The Study of English Literature: A Plea for its Recognition and Organization at the Universities*. Macmillan: London.

Counsell, Christine (2020) "Better Conversations with Subject Leaders." In *The ResearchED Guide to the Curriculum*. Ed. Claire Sealy. John Catt Educational: Melton.

Cox, Bryan (1991) *Cox on Cox: An English Curriculum for the 1990s*. Hodder & Stoughton: London.

Cox Report, The (1989) *English for Ages 5 to 16*. Her Majesty's Stationery Office: London. Available at: www.educationengland. org.uk/documents/cox1989/cox89.html

Crystal, David (2010) *The Cambridge Encyclopedia of Language, Third Edition*. Cambridge University Press: Cambridge.

Crystal, David (2011) *A Little Book of Language*. Yale University Press: New Haven.

Crystal, David (2017) "English Grammar in the UK: A Political History." Available at: http://www.davidcrystal.com/Files/Books AndArticles/-5247.doc

Crystal, David (2017) *Making Sense: The Glamorous Story of English Grammar*. Profile Books: London.

Cunningham, J.V. (2011) "Tradition and Poetic Structure: Essays in Literary History and Criticism." Available at: https://archive.org/stream/traditionpoeticsoocunn/traditionpoeticsoocunn_djvu.txt

Department for Education (2015) "Reading: Supporting Higher Standards in Schools." Available at: www.gov.uk/government/publications/reading-supporting-higher-standards-in-schools

Didion, Joan (2017) *The White Album: Essays.* Fourth Estate: London.

Eaglestone, Robert (2017) *Doing English: A Guide for Literature Students, Fourth Edition.* Routledge: London.

Eaglestone, Robert (2019) *Literature: Why it Matters?* Polity Press: Cambridge.

Eagleton, Terry (2003) *Sweet Violence: The Idea of the Tragic.* Blackwell Publishing: Oxford.

Eagleton, Terry (2008) *Literary Theory: An Introduction, Anniversary Edition.* Blackwell Publishing: Oxford.

Eagleton, Terry (2014) *How to Read Literature.* Yale University Press: New Haven.

Elbow, Peter (1985) "The Shifting Relationships between Speech and Writing." *College Composition and Communication,* 36, 3 (October 1985), pp. 283–303. Published by: National Council of Teachers of English.

Eliot, T.S. (1919) "Tradition and the Individual Talent." Available at: www.poetryfoundation.org/articles/69400/tradition-and-the-individual-talent

Eliot, T.S. "The Metaphysical Poets." Available at: www.usask.ca/english/prufrock/meta.htm

Elliott, Jeffrey ed. (1989) *Conversations with Maya Angelou.* University Press of Mississippi: Jackson.

Emerson, Ralph Waldo (2000) *The Essential Writings of Ralph Waldo Emerson.* Random House Digital, Inc.

Empson, William (1953) *Seven Types of Ambiguity. William Empson.* Chatto & Windus: London.

Everett, Daniel (2018) *How Language Began: The Story of Humanity's Greatest Invention.* Profile Books: London.

Faulks, Sebastian (2011) *Faulks on Fiction: Great British Characters and the Secret of the Novel.* BBC Books: London.

Feynman, R.P. (1974) "Cargo Cult Science: Some Remarks on Science, Pseudoscience, and Learning How to Not Fool Yourself." The

Bibliography

1974 Caltech Commencement Address. *The Best Short Works of Richard P. Feynman-The Pleasure of Finding Things Out*, pp. 205–16.

Flint, David and Rob Bircher (2013) *Edexcel GCSE Geography B: Evolving Planet Student Book*. Edexcel.

Forster, E.M. (2012) *Aspects of the Novel*. Hodder and Stoughton: London.

Forsyth, Mark (2013) *The Elements of Eloquence: How to Turn the Perfect English Phrase*. Icon Books: London.

Frankfurt, H.G. (2009) *On Bullshit*. Princeton University Press: Princeton.

Fry, Stephen (2007) *The Ode Less Travelled: Unlocking the Poet Within*. Hutchinson: London.

Frye, N. (1971) *Anatomy of Criticism: Four Essays*. 1957. Princeton University Press: Princeton.

Furedi, Frank (2015) *The Power of Reading: From Socrates to Twitter*. Bloomsbury: London.

Geary, James (2012) *I Is An Other: The Secret Life of Metaphor and How it Shapes the Way We See the World*. HarperCollins: New York.

Gowers, Ernest and Rebecca Gowers (2014) *Plain Words: A Guide to the Use of English*. Penguin: London.

Graff, Gerald and Cathy Birkenstein (2018) *They Say / I Say: The Moves that Matter in Academic Writing, Fourth Edition*. W.W. Norton: New York.

Hemingway, Ernest (2000) *Death in the Afternoon*. Vintage: London.

Hirsch, E.D. (2019) *Why Knowledge Matters: Rescuing Our Children From Failed Educational Theories*. Harvard Education Press: Cambridge, MA.

Hochman, Judith and Natalie Wexler (2017) *The Writing Revolution: A Guide to Advancing Thinking Through Writing In All Subjects and Grades*. John Wiley & Sons: San Francisco.

Hofstadter, Douglas and Emmanuel Sander (2013) *Surfaces and Essences: Analogy as the Fuel and Fire of Thinking*. Basic Books: New York.

Holbrook, David (1979) *English for Meaning*. NFER Publishing Company: Windsor.

Holbrook, David (2010) *English for Maturity: English in the Secondary School, Second Edition*. Cambridge University Press: Cambridge.

James, Clive (2014) *Poetry Notebook 2006–2014*. Picador: London.

James, William (1890) "The Principles of Psychology." Available at: http://psychclassics.yorku.ca/James/Principles/prin11.htm

Janson, H.W. (1962) *History of Art*. Harry N. Abrams: New York.

Kahneman, Daniel (2011) *Thinking, Fast and Slow*. Macmillan.

Kaufman, Walter ed. and trans. *The Portable Nietzsche*. Penguin: London.

Kennedy, George A. (2013) *Quintilian: A Roman Educator and his Quest for the Perfect Orator, Revised Edition*. Sophron.

Kermode, Frank (2000) *The Sense of an Ending: Studies in the Theory of Fiction*. Oxford University Press: Oxford.

Kermode, Frank (2011) *Forms of Attention: Botticelli and Hamlet*. University of Chicago Press: Chicago.

Kingman Report, The (1988) *Report of the Committee of Inquiry into the Teaching of English Language*. Her Majesty's Stationery Office: London. Available at: www.educationengland.org.uk/documents/kingman/kingman1988.html

Knight, G. Wilson (2002) *The Imperial Theme*. Taylor & Francis: Abingdon and New York.

Knowles, Murray and Rosamund Moon (2006) *Introducing Metaphor*. Routledge: Abingdon.

Korzybski, Alfred (1954) "Science and Sanity: An Introduction to Non-Aristotelian Systems and General Semantics." International Non-Aristotelian Library Publishing Company.

Kövecses, Zoltán (2010) *Metaphor: A Practical Introduction, Second Edition*. Oxford University Press: Oxford.

Kristeva, Julia (1986) "Word, Dialogue and the Novel." In *The Kristeva Reader*. Ed. T. Moi. Blackwell: Oxford.

Kuhl, Patricia (2004) "Early Language Acquisition: Cracking the Speech Code." *Nature Reviews Neuroscience*, 5, pp. 831–43.

Lakoff, George and Mark Johnson (2003) *Metaphors We Live By*. The University of Chicago Press: Chicago.

Land, George and Beth Jarman (1993) *Breaking Point and Beyond*. Harper Business: San Francisco.

Leavis, F.R. (1932) *New Bearings in English Poetry: A Study of the Contemporary Situation*. Chatto & Windus: London.

Leavis, F.R. (1936) *Revaluation: Tradition and Development in English Poetry* Chatto & Windus: London.

Bibliography

Leavis, F.R. (1948) *Education and the University: A Sketch for an 'English School.'* G.W. Stewart: New York.

Leavis, F.R. (1975) *The Living Principle: English as a Discipline of Thought.* Chatto & Windus: London.

Leavis, F.R. (2008) *The Great Tradition.* Faber and Faber: London.

Lederer, Laura J. (2017) *Modern Slavery: A Documentary and Reference Guide.* Greenwood: Santa Barbara.

Leith, Sam (2012) *You Lookin' At Me? Rhetoric from Aristotle to Obama.* Profile Books: London.

Light, Alison (1989) "Two Cheers of Liberal Education." In *Dialogue and Difference: English into the Nineties.* Eds Peter Brooker and Peter Humm. Routledge: London.

Mack, Dick (1986) "Writing with Precision, Clarity, and Economy." *Bulletin of the Ecological Society of America,* 67, 1 (March, 1986), pp. 31–5. Ecological Society of America. Available at: https://static1.squarespace.com/static/576016c8f699bb9740 cc489a/t/5c90394a1905f4fdfad02644/1552955724022/Mack+ 1986+%28writing+tips%29.pdf

Magnus, Margaret (2010) *Gods in the Word: Archetypes in the Consonants.* Lightening Source: Milton Keynes.

Marzano, Robert (2010) "The Art and Science of Teaching/Teaching Inference." *Reimagining School,* 67, 7, pp. 80–1. Available at: www. ascd.org/publications/educational-leadership/apr10/vol67/ num07/Teaching-Inference.aspx

McGilchrist, Iain (2012) *The Master and His Emissary: The Divided Brain and the Making of the Western World.* Yale University Press: New Haven.

McGilchrist, Iain (2019) *Ways of Attending: How Our Divided Brain Constructs the World.* Routledge: London.

Midgley, Mary (2006) *Science and Poetry.* Routledge Classics: Abingdon.

Milton, John (1957/1674) "Whether Day or Night is the More Excellent." In *Prolusions,* 1674. *Complete Poems and Major Prose.* Ed. Merritt Y. Hughes. Prentice Hall: New Jersey.

Moraes, Dom (1968) *My Son's Father.* Secker & Warburg: London.

Morrison, Toni (2000) "Unspeakable Things Unspoken: The Afro-American Presence in American Literature (1990)." *A Turbulent Voyage: Readings in African American Studies,* 246.

Newbolt Report, The (1921) *The Teaching of English in England.* Her Majesty's Stationery Office: London. Available at: www.educationengland.org.uk/documents/newbolt/newbolt1921.html

Newkirk, Thomas (2014) *Minds Made for Stories: How We Really Read and Write Informational and Persuasive Texts.* Heinemann: Portsmouth.

Newton, L. (1990) "Overconfidence in the Communication of Intent: Heard and Unheard Melodies." Unpublished doctoral dissertation, Stanford University, Stanford, CA.

Nietzsche, Freidrich (1954) "On Truth and Lies in an Extra-Moral Sense." *The Portable Nietzsche,* 42, pp. 46–7.

Oakeshott, Michael (1962) "The Voice of Poetry in the Conversation of Mankind." In *Rationalism in Politics and Other Essays.* Methuen: London.

Oakeshott, Michael, ed. Timothy Fuller (1986) *The Voice of Liberal Learning.* Yale University Press: New Haven.

Ofsted (2005) *English 2000–05.*

Ofsted (2009) *English at the Crossroads.*

Ofsted (2011) *Excellence in English.*

Ofsted (2012) *Moving English Forward.*

Ofsted (2014) *Engaging and Inspiring Learners in English, Especially at Key Stage 3: Priestnall School.*

Oliver, Mary (1994) *A Poetry Handbook: A Prose Guide to Understanding and Writing Poetry.* Mariner Books: Boston, MA.

Ortega y Gasset, José (2019) *The Dehumanisation of Art and Other Essays on Art, Culture and Literature.* Princeton University Press: Princeton.

Orwell, George, *Essays.* Penguin: London.

Orwell, George (1948) *Politics and the English Language.* Penguin Books: London.

Paterson, Don (2018) *The Poem: Lyric, Sign, Metre.* Faber and Faber: London.

Perkins, David (2009) *Making Learning Whole: How Seven Principles of Teaching can Transform Education.* Jossey-Bass: San Francisco.

Perlman, Marcus, Rick Dale and Gary Lupyan (2015) "Iconicity Can Ground the Creation of Vocal Symbols." Royal Society Open Science.

Bibliography

Pinker, Stephen (2014) *The Sense of Style: The Thinking Person's Guide to Writing in the 21st Century.* Allen Lane: London.

Pinker, Steven (2015) *The Language Instinct: How the Mind Creates Language.* Penguin: London.

Polanyi, Michael (1966) *The Tacit Dimension.* Routledge: Abingdon.

Polanyi, Michael and Harry Prosch (1975) *Meaning.* University of Chicago Press: Chicago.

Pope, Rob (2002) *The English Studies Book: An Introduction to Language, Literature and Culture, Second Edition.* Routledge: London.

Pullman, Philip (2017) *Daemon Voices: On Stories and Storytelling.* Vintage: New York.

Quintilian, trans. H.E. Butler (1921) *The Instituto Oratoria of Quintilian.* Harvard University Press: Cambridge, MA.

Rahim, Sameer (2009) "Interview with Seamus Heaney." *The Telegraph.* Available at: www.telegraph.co.uk/culture/books/5132022/Interview-with-Seamus-Heaney.html

Richards, I.A. (1936) *The Philosophy of Rhetoric.* Oxford University Press: Oxford.

Richards, I.A. (2017) *Practical Criticism: A study of Literary Judgement.* Routledge: London.

Richards, I.A. (2003) *Principles of Literary Criticism.* Routledge: London.

Richardson, Mark ed. (2007) *The Collected Prose of Robert Frost.* Harvard University Press: Cambridge, MA.

Royal Society of Literature (2019) "A Room of One's Own: What Writers Need to Work Today." Available at: https://wp.alcs.co.uk/app/uploads/2019/07/RSL-A-Room-of-My-Own-Report-19-June-2019.pdf

Sampson, George (1921) *English for the English: A Chapter on National Education.* Cambridge University Press: Cambridge.

Schoenbaum, S. ed. (1991) *Macbeth: Critical Essays.* Routledge: London.

Scholes, Robert, James Phelan and Robert Kellogg (2006) *The Nature of Narrative, 40th Anniversary Edition.* Oxford University Press: Oxford.

Scott, Cheryl M. (1982) "RP Fawcett and MR Perkins, Child language transcripts 6–12, volumes 1–4. Pontypridd: Department of Behavioural and Communication Studies, Polytechnic of Wales, 1980. Pp. xiv+ 261, 274, 308, 317." *Journal of Child Language,* 9, 3, pp. 704–8.

Seidenberg, Mark (2017) *Language at the Speed of Sound: How We Read, Why So Many Can't, and What Can be Done About It.* Basic Books: New York.

Senghas, Ann. (2003) *Intergenerational Influence and Ontogenetic Development in the Emergence of Spatial Grammar in Nicaraguan Sign Language.* Department of Psychology, Barnard College of Columbia University. Elsevier, Inc.

Shanahan, Tim (2020) "Why Following the Simple View May Not Be Such a Good Idea." *Shanahan on Literacy.* Available at: https://shanahanonliteracy.com/blog/why-following-the-simple-view-may-not-be-such-a-good-idea

Shapiro, James (2020) *Shakespeare in a Divided America.* Faber and Faber: London.

Shelley, Percy (n.d.) *A Defence of Poetry.* Available at: www.poetryfoundation.org/articles/69388/a-defence-of-poetry

Siegler, Robert (1998) *Emerging Minds: The Process of Change in Children's Thinking.* Oxford University Press: Oxford.

Smith, Emma (2019) *This is Shakespeare: How to Read the World's Greatest Playwright.* Penguin: London.

Standish, Alex and Alka Sehgal Cuthbert eds (2017) *What Should Schools Teach? Disciplines, Subjects and the Pursuit of Truth.* Institute of Education Press: London.

Steiner, George (2010) *Language and Silence: Essays 1958–1966.* Faber and Faber: London.

Storr, Will (2019) *The Science of Storytelling.* William Collins: London.

Strunk, William and E.B. White (2000) *The Elements of Style, Fourth Edition.* Allyn & Bacon: Needham Heights.

Tharby, Andy (2017) *Making Every English Lesson Count.* Crown House Publishing: Camarthen.

Thomas, R.S. (2002) *Residues.* Bloodaxe Books: Hexham.

Turner, Mark (1998) *The Literary Mind: The Origins of Thought and Language.* Oxford University Press: Oxford.

van Gelderen, Elly (2004) *Grammaticalization as Economy.* John Benjamins Publishing: Amsterdam.

van Ostade, Ingrid Tieken Boon (2017) "The King's English by Kingsley Amis: A Publisher's Project." *English Usage Guides.* Oxford University Press: Oxford.

Bibliography

Warwick, Ian and Ray Speakman (2018) *Redefining English for the More Able: A Practical Guide.* Routledge: London.

Wasiolek, E. (1987) "Bakhtin, Mikhail. Problems of Dostoevsky's Poetics (Book Review)." *Comparative Literature, 39,* p. 187.

Watson, Cecilia (2010) *Semicolon.* Fourth Estate: London.

Weldon, Fay (1993) *Letters to Alice: On First Reading Jane Austen.* Sceptre: London.

Westbrook, J., J. Sutherland, J. Oakhill and S. Sullivan (2019) "'Just Reading': The Impact of a Faster Pace of Reading Narratives on the Comprehension of Poorer Adolescent Readers in English Classrooms." *Literacy,* 53, 2, pp. 60–8.

Willingham, Daniel (2009) *Why Don't Students Like School?* Jossey-Bass: San Francisco.

Wilson, Emily (2018) "Translator's Note." *The Odyssey.* Norton: New York.

Wilson, John Dover (1959) *What Happens in Hamlet?* Cambridge University Press: Cambridge.

Wright, Esmond ed. (1989) *Benjamin Franklin: His Life as He Wrote It.* Harvard University Press: Cambridge, MA.

Yorke, John (2013) *Into the Woods: How Stories Work and Why We Tell Them.* Penguin: London.

Young, Michael (2008) *Bringing Knowledge Back In: From Social Constructivism to Social Realism in the Sociology of Education.* Routledge: London.

Young, Michael (2014) "The Curriculum and the Entitlement to Knowledge." Edited text of a talk given at Magdalene College, Cambridge, 25 March. Available at: www.cambridgeassessment. org.uk/Images/166279-the-curriculum-and-the-entitlement-to-knowledge-prof-michael-young.pdf

Young, Michael and Johan Muller (2016) *Curriculum and the Specialization of Knowledge: Studies in the Sociology of Education.* Routledge: London.

Index

Note: Page locators in *italic* refer to figures and in **bold** refer to tables.

Index

Index

Index

Index

nominalisation 211–13
noticing 92–7, 102–104; grammar
  269–73; metaphor 118–19; metre
  238–9; in practice 100–101;
  rhyme 229–31; sound 220–4
noun phrases 279–81
nouns 267, 277; appositive 289–
  90; head 52–3
novels 249, 343; heroes of 166;
  story of 331–2
Nutt, Joe 71

'O Captain, My Captain' 260
Oakeshott, Michael 8, 43, 91–2,
  109, 110, 120, 202, 205–206, 298,
  302, 303, 328
object 267, 268, 280, 284
'Ode on a Grecian Urn' 74–5
'Ode to a Nightingale' 240
Odyssey 149, 150–1, 161, 241, 247,
  309, 331, **337**, 338
Oedipus the King 154
Ofsted 26–33
Oliver, Mary 262
Oliver Twist 65, 168, 332, **340**
Oroonoko 307, 332, **344**
Ortega y Gasset, José 106, 107
orthography 49
Orwell, George 284–5, 346;
  Animal Farm 63, 135, 257, **344**,
  346; *Nineteen Eighty-Four* 97,
  168, **344**
Othello 112, 113, 235
'The Overcoat' 272–3
Owen, Wilfred: 'Anthem for
  Doomed Youth' 345; 'Dulce et
  Decorum Est' 241, 345
'Ozymandias' 237

Paradise Lost 180, 190–2, 240,
  340, 342
paragraphs 56, 59, 81
A Passage to India 100–101
passive voice 269, 284–5, 285–7
pathos 189
pattern 87, 88, 216–62; alliteration
  218, 227–9, 260; anaphora

226–7; end stopped rhyme
  229–31, 232–5; enjambment
  and caesura 242–3; eye
  rhyme 237–8; form 248–57;
  form in fiction 256–7; iambic
  pentameter 239–42, 244–5, 251,
  259; internal rhyme 235–6;
  meaning in sound 224–6; metre
  238–48; noticing rhyme 229–31;
  noticing sound 220–4; rhyme
  schemes 231–2; slant rhyme
  236–7; sonnets 251–6; stress
  244–5; teaching 258–61
PEE (point, evidence, explain) 56,
  81, 82, 317
peroration 193, 198, 200
personification 122–4, 141
Persuasion 65
Petrarch 251
Petrarchan sonnets 251–3, 341
phonemes 220–4, 225; consonants
  221–2, 223, 224, 258; glides 222,
  223; liquids 222, 223; plosives
  222, 223, 224, 225, 228; *schwa*
  172, 221; sibilants 222, 227,
  228; unvoiced 222; voiced 222;
  vowels 221, 237–8, 258
phronesis 73
pidgins 264–5
Pilgrim's Progress 134–5, 332,
  340, 342
'Pink Dominoes' 236
Pinker, Stephen 213, 263–4, 284,
  287, 293
Plath, Sylvia, 'Daddy' 258
Plato, *Dialogues* 201, 224
plosives 222, 223, 224, 225, 228
plot 152; comedy 156–60;
  structures 160–2; tragic 154–6;
  unity 152–4
Poe, Edgar Allen, 'The
  Raven' 235–6
'Poem' 241
Poetics 73, 184
poetry: epic 149, 150–1, 165, 171,
  229, 247, 332, 338; limericks
  249–50; Romantic 65, 74–5, 255,

Index

Index